# AFGHANISTAN
*in*
# TRANSITION

*Beyond 2014?*

# AFGHANISTAN *in* TRANSITION

## *Beyond 2014?*

Shanthie Mariet D'Souza (ed)

**Afghanistan in Transition: Beyond 2014?** / *Shanthie Mariet D'Souza (Ed.)*

ISBN 978-81-8274-674-9

First Published in 2012



*Supported By*

Institute of South Asian Studies (ISAS)
468A Bukit Timah Road
Singapore 259770
Tel: 65 - 6516 6179
Fax: 65 - 6776 7505
Email: isassec@nus.edu.sg
Website: www.isas.nus.edu.sg



*Published by*

PENTAGON PRESS
206, Peacock Lane, Shahpur Jat,
New Delhi-110049
Phones: 011-64706243, 26491568
Telefax: 011-26490600
email: rajan@pentagonpress.in
website: www.pentagonpress.in

Printed at Syndicate Binders, A-20, Hosiery Complex, Phase II, Noida-201305

# Contents

## *SECTION III*
## AID, GENDER, DEVELOPMENT, ECONOMIC OPPORTUNITIES, TRADE, INVESTMENT,CONNECTIVITY & STRATEGIC COMMUNICATION



## *SECTION IV*
## REGIONAL AND INTERNATIONAL COMMUNITY'S PERSPECTIVES ON TRANSITION

# Foreword

Developments in Afghanistan have important bearing on international and regional security. The planned drawdown of forces by the United States (U.S.) and its allies by 2014, as announced at the Lisbon NATO summit, has created anxieties inside Afghanistan and in the region. To address these concerns and gauge the level of preparedness of the Afghans for an effective transition, a workshop on "Afghanistan in Transition: Beyond 2014?" was organised by the Institute of South Asian Studies (ISAS) in January 2012.

The Institute of South Asian Studies is dedicated to the study of contemporary South Asia. It generates knowledge and insights about South Asia and disseminates them in a manner that is useful to policy-makers, the business community, academia and civil society.

This is the first time that a workshop on Afghanistan providing a forum for Afghan scholars and policy-makers to freely express their views had been organised in this part of the world. More importantly, it was an attempt to understand the issues, challenges and opportunities in the transition to Afghan-led and Afghan-owned process. Various narratives by speakers from diverse background, each with good academic and policy experience and unique perspectives derived from their deep knowledge of ground realities, helped the non Afghan participants gain rare insights of the perceptions and the needs on the ground.

Coming at the heels of the just concluded Istanbul and Bonn conference, this workshop was a timely and useful academic and policy exercise. Ahead of other upcoming international conferences—Chicago, Kabul and Tokyo, this workshop delved on key issues—security, political, reconciliation, governance, trade, and investment, including regional and international dimensions, with particular emphasis on recommendations for way forward. In looking at various scenario's in the near term (2012-14) and long term (Beyond 2014), the participants provided policy recommendations and suggested alternate courses of action.

Participants and paper contributions from other countries such as Pakistan, India, China and the U.S. have provided a wider regional perspective of the transition process. The workshop, I believe, fulfilled its key objective of providing a platform for scholars, as well as policy-makers to meet and discuss issues and events that are relevant to restoring 'peace and stability' in a vital part of Asia.

This edited volume is a compilation of the papers presented at the workshop. It also has chapters and views from other scholars working on the regional perspectives of the transition process. Amidst preparations of transferring authority to the Afghans by 2014, there are wide ranging concerns on the existing capacity of the Afghan institutions to take matter into their own hands. Concerns have been expressed about the capacity of the Afghan security forces to withstand the onslaught of the insurgency and governing institutions have been viewed as weak or ineffective. While such problems are symptomatic of a 'transitional state', it would be naïve not to look at the tremendous progress the Afghans have made in certain critical areas. Unfortunately, most of these achievements have not been reported in the international media or academic writings. To that end, the present volume provides scholars a much needed forum to highlight the achievements made and also address the challenges that pose a critical threat to such progress.

As the international community gropes for answers on the 'future of Afghanistan' and a possibility of effective transition by 2014, this book would add to the current policy debate in addressing critical gaps that require attention in the near term and long term. With the objective of wider dissemination, this book is intended to give scholars, policy-makers, practitioners working on issues of long term stabilisation both a macro and micro perspective. As the debate on the transition and drawdown gathers momentum, this would be a value addition to the present academic and policy discourse in understanding the complexities, challenges and prospects of bringing in the much needed peace and stability in Afghanistan and the region.

I would like to congratulate the ISAS team that organised this workshop, particularly Dr Shanthie D'Souza who was the moving spirit behind this event. By editing this book which contains the papers presented at the workshop as well as other essays, she has added another dimension to the discussions on Afghanistan.

ISAS
Singapore

**Ambassador Gopinath Pillai**
Chairman

# Acknowledgements

This book is a value addition to the ongoing debate on transition (*inteqal*), particularly because it brings together diverse Afghan thinking on several inter-linked and complex issues that need immediate attention to actualize effective *inteqal*. This volume consists of papers presented at the workshop titled 'Afghanistan in Transition: Beyond 2014?' organised by the Institute of South Asian Studies (ISAS), National University of Singapore (NUS) on 9-10 January 2012 in Singapore. The workshop was envisioned as an academic and policy exercise to hear the Afghan voices, understand their needs and disseminate their views on the *inteqal* process to a larger audience in Asia and beyond. Additional paper contributions from the region and the US add to the understanding of the complex internal-external dynamics of the Afghan imbroglio.

I am indebted to the authors of the chapters for their valuable and rich contribution to this volume. I am also grateful to those paper contributors who could not make it to the workshop and yet contributed to this effort. This book would not have been possible in such a short period without their cooperation, enthusiasm and support.

My heartfelt gratitude to Ambassador Gopinath Pillai, Chairman ISAS, for his guidance and encouragement in this endeavour. I am deeply grateful to Professor Tan Tai Yong, Director ISAS, for entrusting me the responsibility to conceptualise, design and deliver this project. A special word of thanks to Mr. Johnson Paul, Senior Associate Director, for the support and help in actualizing this initiative. Thanks are also in order to the administrative and support team of the workshop—Jacqueline, Gloria, Anusha, Kama, Sithara, Felicia, Kirby and Yusuf.

And as always, a personal gratitude to my family and friends for their constant support in this endeavour.

June 2012 **Shanthie Mariet D'Souza**

# About the Editor/Contributors

**Professor Ali A. Jalali,** a presidential contender and former interior minister of Afghanistan (Jan. 2003-Sept.2005), is currently serving as both a distinguished professor at the Near East South Asia Center for Strategic Studies (NESA) and as a researcher at the Institute for National Strategic Studies (INSS). As interior minister, he created a trained force of 50,000 Afghan National Police (ANP) and 12,000 Border Police to work effectively in counter-narcotics, counter-terrorism, and criminal investigation. Minister Jalali implemented a nation-wide program under the Afghanistan Stabilisation Program (ASP) to extend the central government's authority to all the 34 provinces and 365 districts throughout the country. Minister Jalali has been involved in politics and media for most of his life. He previously served the Voice of America for over 20 years, covering Afghanistan, South and Central Asia, and the Middle East, including assignments as Director of the Afghan Radio Network Project and chief of the Pashto and Persian services. He has written extensively about the military of Afghanistan for scholarly journals and the mass media, in addition to reporting on Afghanistan and Central Asia for VOA for almost two decades.

Minister Jalali is the author of several books, including a three-volume military history of Afghanistan. His most recent book, *The Other Side of the Mountain* (2002), co-authored with Lester Grau, is an analytical review of the Mujahedin war again the Soviet forces in Afghanistan from 1979 to 1989. His recent publications on transition in Afghanistan have contributed to sharpening the policy debate as well as to the pedantic deliberations. Minister. Jalali has native fluency in English, Pashto, Dari, Persian (Farsi) and Tajik, is fluent in Russian, fluently translates from French and has functional knowledge of Arabic, Turkish and Urdu. His areas of interest include reconstruction/stabilisation and peacekeeping operations in Afghanistan and regional issues affecting Afghanistan, Central and South Asia.

**H.E. Mohammad Masoom Stanekzai** is minister adviser on Home Security to the President of the Islamic Republic of Afghanistan and Secretary General for the High Peace Council of Afghanistan, an organisation that leads national peace and reconciliation efforts. Minister Stanekzai has served as the vice chair of the

Afghanistan's Demobilisation and Reintegration Commission, responsible for the disbandment of illegal armed groups since 2005. Between 2002 and 2004, he served as the Minister of Telecommunication of the Afghan Transitional Government. During this time, he developed and implemented a major reform and restructuring program that helped the sector to flourish as one of the successful models of post-conflict reconstruction in the country. Prior to that, Minister Stanekzai was director of the Agency for Rehabilitation and Energy Conservation in Afghanistan.

Minister Stanekzai has over 25 years of experience in management, design and implementation of program/projects in different sectors including telecom, humanitarian aid, community development, security sector reform and governance. He has worked with the Afghanistan Independent Human Rights Commission, NGOs, the U.N., and private sectors in Afghanistan, Pakistan and Iran. His most recent accomplishments include completing the development of a regulatory framework and organisational setup for the operation of private security companies in Afghanistan as well as the strategic framework for the Afghanistan Peace and Reintegration Programme. He also led the vetting process of candidates for the 2009 election as well as appointment of senior government officials in relations to their linkages with illegal armed groups.

**Arian Sharifi** holds a BA in Political Science from Wesleyan University, and a Master in Public Affairs (MPA) with specialisation in International Relations from Princeton University's Woodrow Wilson School of Public and International Affairs. He was the winner of the prestigious White Fellowship Award for Excellence in Government in 2007. Mr. Sharifi is currently a partner at Afghanistan Financial Services, and works as a Research Analyst for the Combating Terrorism Center (CTC) at West Point, as well as an adjunct instructor of Public Policy at the American University of Afghanistan. In his work with the CTC, Sharifi served as the primary Dari, Pashtu and Urdu analyst, responsible for helping other CTC researchers collate and interpret publications produced by the Haqqani Network, as well as hundreds of personal letters between the Network's top leadership during the Afghan-Soviet war. Similarly, as Operations Research Analyst at the Centre for Political Violence and Terrorism Research in Singapore, Mr Sharifi conducted research on some of the major terrorist groups in South-Central Asia. Mr. Sharifi worked as Director of Communications and Public Relations Advisor at the Afghan government's Ministry of Finance between 2006 and 2008, managing the Ministry's external relations with the donor community, the National Assembly and other GIRoA agencies. He also led the organisation's public and media affairs, appearing on national and international media outlets in interviews, panel discussions, debates and commentaries on a daily basis. In addition, Sharifi established the ministry's first anti-corruption unit, which was awarded over $1.5 million by the United Nations Development Program (UNDP).

**Ahmad Wali Masoud** is currently the President of the Masoud Foundation. From 1992 to 2006, Masoud has held various posts at the Embassy of Afghanistan in London. From 1992-93, Masoud was the Second Secretary holding briefly the position of First Secretary before becoming the Minister of Counselor and the Charged Affaires in 1993, a position he held until 2002. From 2002 to 2006, he was the Ambassador, Extraordinary and Plenipotentiary of Afghanistan in London. Mr Masoud has an extensive professional background in the media. He was the editor of the Ariana News Bulletin, an Afghan Publication for freedom, from 1990 to 1992. During the heyday of the Soviet Union, Masoud was a representative of the Resistance of Afghanistan, in the United Kingdom, propagating for the liberation of Afghanistan from Russian occupation (1989-92). Concurrently, he worked at the Times Newspaper, in the editing department of foreign news. In 2008, Masoud launched the *Mandegar Daily*, a popular newspaper in Afghanistan known for its critical views of the Afghan government. From 1993 through to 2001, Masoud was a member of the Official Government Delegations representing Afghanistan at international conferences.

He obtained his secondary education in Peshawar. He completed his higher education in the United Kingdom obtaining a Diploma in Development Administration and one in Strategic Studies from the South Devon College of Art and Technology, Torquay, and Polytechnic of Central London respectively.

**Shahmahmood Miakhel** is the Country Director for United States Institute of Peace (USIP) in Afghanistan since 2009. Prior to joining USIP, he worked as a governance adviser/deputy head of governance unit for the United Nation Assistance Mission (UNAMA) in Afghanistan (2005-09) and served as Senior Adviser/Deputy Minister of Interior of Afghanistan (2003-05). Miakhel has also worked as a reporter for Pashto and Dari Services of Voice of America (1985-90) and as the deputy director of SOS/Belgium, an international organisation assisting Afghan refugees in Pakistan. Miakhel worked for UNDP/UNOPS in Afghanistan as Senior Liaison Officer to establish District Rehabilitation Shuras (DRS) in Eastern and South-Eastern provinces of Afghanistan. He also consulted on the Williams-Afghan Media Project at Williams College to preserve war footage of Afghanistan in the 1980s. A native of Afghanistan, Miakhel was elected to the Emergency Loya Jirga in 2002, the Peace Jirga between Afghanistan and Pakistan in August 2007 and Consultative Peace Jirga in June 2010. He has published three books in Pashto: *Emergency Loya Jirga and the Election Process in the Eastern Provinces of Afghanistan*, *Challenges and Achievements in the Ministry of Interior*, a personal account from 2003-05, and *In the Light of Truth*, a personal account of the *Mujahideen* uprising in the Kunar Province and refugee life in Pakistan. Miakhel has an executive MBA from Preston University in Pakistan, and completed a fellowship program on Democracy, Development and Rule of Law at Stanford University in 2006.

**Najeeb Ur Rahman Manalai** is a human rights advocate, currently working as National Human Rights Officer at the Human Rights Unit of United Nations Assistance Mission in Afghanistan (UNAMA). The focus of his work has been promoting an inclusive peace process and mainstreaming human rights values and principles in all efforts aimed at peace and reconciliation as well as the overall development process in Afghanistan. He has contributed to upholding UN's partnership with Afghan national human rights institutions and the civil society. In addition, he has conducted policy relevant studies and contributed to formulation of recommendations for the Afghan government, donor agencies and other partners on issues relevant to security, justice, peace and reconciliation and human rights. Prior to this, he held research positions at various prestigious organisations in Afghanistan. He has written many analytical pieces on current Afghan issues published in national and international media. Manalai is fluent in English, Dari, Pashto and Urdu.

**Rangina Hamidi** is the Founder and President of Kandahar Treasure, the first women's private enterprise in Kandahar, Afghanistan. She provides life-changing economic opportunities for approximately 350 Afghan women, giving them a platform at Kandahar's unique embroidery work. As one of Kandahar's leading voices for Afghan women, she has guided the development of groundbreaking networks for women, establishing pioneering weekly women's meetings, social programs and activities for women in Kandahar. These forums led to a historic moment for the local women when on the International Women's Day in 2009 they marched for peace at the famous Kherqa Shrine. Rangina's aim is to work for bringing permanent and lasting change to Kandahar's long history of violence. It is her mission to empower women economically so as to build their influence to contribute to the peace process. Her work in Kandahar began when she returned to Afghanistan in 2003. She had escaped Afghanistan in 1981, at the age of four, during the Soviet occupation. She moved first to Pakistan and then in 1988, settled in the United States with her family, receiving her education at the University of Virginia. Upon her return to Kandahar, she served as the manager of the Women's Income Generation Project with Afghans for Civil Society, a grassroots organisation dedicated to the social development of southern Afghanistan. Ms Hamidi was recognised internationally for work when she was selected as one of the 18 finalists for the CNN 2007 Hero Award, and chosen as the "Personality of the Week" by Radio Free Europe in January 2008. She has been heard on numerous radio programs including NPR, the BBC and Voice of America, and has been quoted in international publications including, *The Times Asia* magazine, *The Globe* and *Mail*, *Der Speigel*, *Business Week*, *The Guardian* and *The Telegraph*. Hamidi was selected for prominent professional and academic training programs, including Project Artemis of the Thunderbird University and the business development organisation Bpeace both of which assisted in the launch of Kandahar Treasure.

**Muhammad Sabir Siddiqi** is the director of Development and Public Awareness (DPA) and served as a senior advisor to the anti-corruption agency in Afghanistan. From 2003 to 2009, he worked with different national and international organisations in Afghanistan, such as USAID, United Nations and IDLG, as political advisor and governance specialist. He has attended several important national and international events, including the London International conference on Afghanistan in 2010, Anticorruption Conference in Paris—2010 and AFPAK civil society forum—Islamabad 2011. He has written several articles on political thought, decentralisation, and anticorruption and his articles are published in international and national publications in Iran and Afghanistan. He studied *Sharia* and Law at the International Islamic University in Islamabad, Pakistan. He was awarded the Fulbright Scholarship in 2006 and studied Public Administration at the University of Oregon, U.S.A. Siddiqi is multi-lingual, speaking four languages English, Dari, Pashto and Arabic languages.

**Haroun Mir** is the Director and Co-founder of Afghanistan Center for Research and Policy Studies (ACRPS). He has more than ten years of work experience in consultancy, management, research and analysis. He has carried out consultancy missions for Afghan Members of Parliament on key policy issues. He has written strategy papers on economic and regional cooperation and conference backgrounders for prestigious organisations like the World Bank and the Carnegie Endowment for Peace. Mir has conducted analyses and research for the Asia Foundation, National Democratic Institute (NDI), International Republican Institute (IRI), Center for International Private Enterprise (CIPE), the U.S. Institute for Peace (USIP), Embassies (Canada, US, Sweden, Norway Japan, Germany, India), International organisations (EU, IMF, UNDP) and media outlets (mostly international). He also carries out economic analysis for the local and international media. Mr Mir served as an active Afghan government official for six years in Kabul. He has also regularly appeared in national and international media- Tolo TV, Ariana, TV1 (Afghan), NBC, CNN, Fox News, ARD, TF1, TF2, Al Jazeera. He is a published author on Central and South Asian affairs.

**Professor Rasul Bakhsh Rais** has a PhD in Political Science from the University of California, Santa Barbara. Before joining the Lahore University of Management Sciences (LUMS), he served as Professor/Director, Area Study Centre and Associate Professor in the Department of International Relations, Quaid-i-Azam University, Islamabad for nearly 22 years. He was a Professor of Pakistan Studies at Columbia University, New York, for 3 years from 1991 to 1994. He was awarded the Fulbright fellowship at Wake Forest University 1997-98; Social Science Research Fellowship at Harvard 1989-90; Rockefeller Foundation fellowship in International Relations at the University of California, Berkeley 1985-85. Professor Rais has been published widely in professional journals on political and security issues pertaining to South Asia, Indian Ocean and Afghanistan. His current research interests are "Modernism, State and Challenge of Radical Islam in Pakistan." At LUMS, Professor Rais teaches courses on the Theories of Democratic Transition, American government and Politics, and Comparative Politics. His most recent addition to his teaching portfolio is a course on the Theory and Practice of Non-violence: Gandhi, King Jr, Ghaffar Khan and Nelson Mandela. Professor Rais is the author of *Recovering the Frontier State: War, Ethnicity and State in Afghanistan* (Lanham: Lexington Book, and Oxford University Press, 2008), *War without Winners: Afghanistan's Uncertain Transition after the Cold War* (Oxford University Press, 1996), *Indian Ocean and the Superpowers: Economic, Political and Strategic Perspectives* (Croom Helm, London, 1986) and editor of *State, Society and Democratic Change in Pakistan* (Oxford University Press, 1997).

**Daniel Norfolk** is currently conducting research on regional approaches to conflict at the Graduate Institute of International and Development Studies, Geneva. He has served at the High Commissions of Britain and Canada in New Delhi, and analysed relations between South Asian states for the International Development Research Centre (IDRC) and the International Institute for Strategic Studies (IISS). As a Research Fellow with IDRC, he focused on Indian foreign policy, security and development. He has provided assistance for the organisation and facilitation of the Track-II 'Ottawa Dialogue' in Copenhagen, focusing on India-Pakistan-Afghanistan relations. He will be joining the Centre on Conflict, Development, and Peace-building at the Graduate Institute in Geneva this August.

**Professor Marvin G. Weinbaum** is professor emeritus of political science at University of Illinois at Urbana-Champaign. He has also served as an analyst for Pakistan and Afghanistan at the U.S. Department of State's Bureau of Intelligence and Research from 1999 to 2003. He is currently a scholar-in-residence at the Middle East Institute in Washington DC. At Illinois, Dr Weinbaum served for fifteen years as the director of the Program in South Asian and Middle Eastern Studies. After retiring at Illinois, he has held adjunct professorships at Georgetown and George Washington universities. Dr Weinbaum's research, teaching, and consultancies have focused on the issues of national security, state building, democratisation, and political economy. He has written/edited six books and more than a 100 book chapters and journal articles, mostly about Pakistan, Afghanistan, and Iran, but also on Egypt and Turkey. Dr Weinbaum received his doctorate from Columbia University in 1965.

**Dr. Shanthie Mariet D'Souza** is Research Fellow at the Institute of South Asian Studies (ISAS), National University of Singapore. The present volume is part of her ongoing research on the Transition and Prospects for Long term stabilisation of Afghanistan. Her research interest and expertise includes Regional Dynamics of the Afghan insurgency; Afghan Insurgency and the Counter Insurgency campaign; United States Counter terrorism policy in South Asia; Non State Armed Groups; Terrorism and Strategies in Counter terrorism; India's foreign and security policy, Great Power Politics; Conflict Management and Regional Cooperation in South Asia. Dr. D'Souza has been a Fulbright Scholar at South Asia Studies, The Paul H Nitze School of Advanced International Studies (SAIS), Johns Hopkins University, Washington DC (2005-06). She has been Associate Fellow, Institute for Defence Studies & Analyses, New Delhi; Research Associate at Database & Documentation Centre of the Institute for Conflict Management, Guwahati, Assam and Editorial Assistant at the United Service Institution of India, New Delhi. Shanthie has conducted field studies in the United States, Pakistan, Afghanistan, Jammu & Kashmir and India's North East. She has frequently travelled to various provinces of Afghanistan for her field research. Among her most recent published work is a co-edited book, Saving Afghanistan (2009) and papers on Talking to the Taliban, Unity of Effort in Afghanistan, NATO in Afghanistan, US-Pakistan Counter-Terrorism Cooperation, Indo-US Counter Terrorism Cooperation, Global War on Terrorism, Mumbai terror attacks and India-Pakistan relations, Jihad beyond Jammu & Kashmir, India-Afghan relations, China-Afghan relations, Iran-Afghan relations, Regional Perspectives of the Af-Pak Strategy, Countering the Naxalites, Autonomy movements in India's North East, Media and Gender in Counter terrorism.

# 1

# Introduction

*Shanthie Mariet D'Souza*

Afghanistan is once again at the crossroads in its search for peace and stability. As 2014, the date for drawdown of international forces draws near, the international community is confounded by the complexities of an effective transition (*inteqal*) as by the modalities for ensuring it. A decade after the military intervention that dislodged the Taliban-Al-Qaeda combine, peace and stability has eluded Afghanistan. There is still no consensus in Western capitals on what constitutes the 'end-state' in Afghanistan. As the Western public increasingly tire of supporting a long drawn war, the global economic slowdown, the Euro crisis and the pressures of electoral campaign politics, have all complicated the quest for the long-term stabilisation of Afghanistan. Premature announcements of exit and dwindling financial assistance have added to the Afghan anxieties of being 'abandoned' once again. It is, thus, not surprising that the Afghans view the *inteqal* process as a last opportunity for the international community to set the course right in Afghanistan.

With efforts towards transition of power in Afghanistan gaining ground, there have been concerted efforts to build on the local capacities and institutions. However, there are accompanying concerns on the existing capacity of the Afghan institutions to garner strength and ability, to prevent the reversal of gains made during the last decade and also on the willingness of the present day Afghan administration to provide an inclusive, transparent and corruption free administration. Amidst these bleak assessments, there have been indications of progress in certain critical areas, most of which has gone largely unreported in the international media. It is thus imperative to take cognizance of such achievements as also the challenges in building local capacities and institutions in key sectors—security, political, economic and governance, for these would form the basis of future progress.

Most of the chapters in this book consist of papers presented during a workshop organised by the Institute of South Asian Studies (ISAS), National University of Singapore (NUS) in January 2012. This book brings together varied Afghan perspectives and voices to set the agenda, address critical gaps in the ongoing *inteqal* process, 2012-14 and suggest alternate course of action by setting a forward looking agenda, beyond 2014. The strength of this volume stems from the rich contributions by experts and practitioners from the field comprising of serving and former ministers, potential presidential contenders, political luminaries, academia, members of think tanks, international organisations (IO) and non-governmental organisations (NGO), thus, providing in-depth analysis of the perceptions, needs and preparedness on the ground.

By delving into range of complex but inter-related issues of security and political sector reform, peace building and peace processes—reconciliation, reintegration, rule of law, economic opportunities, investment, trade and connectivity, civilian surge, aid-delivery, coordination and effectiveness, alternative livelihood, strategic communication, gender, NGOs, both from a micro and macro perspective, this volume highlights important components of transition that need immediate and sustained attention.

The book has elicited policy recommendations to cope with the emerging challenges and suggest alternate course of action through scenario building exercises for the near and long term. To understand the ramifications of the internal-external dimensions of transition, chapters on regional perspectives and also the U.S. perspective have also been included to provide important insights into the role of external players in the way out of the present imbroglio.

Written in first person and narrative style, some chapters provide little understood and less reported grass root perspectives. Most of the chapters have significant overlap given the complex inter linkages of issues on long term stabilisation. This introductory chapter also includes views and summary presentations of some of the speakers who have not provided papers. Others who could not make it to the workshop for various reasons, have contributed papers to this volume. The presentations and papers have contributed to making this book a unique, comprehensive and much needed exercise in understanding the Afghan mind on issues critical to stabilising their country.

## Book Outline

The book is organised into four sections. ***Section One*** contains two papers on *Setting the Agenda: An Afghan Perspective*, providing the background of Afghan thinking on the prospects and challenges for an effective transition.

Most of the discourse on 'transition' in Afghanistan has occurred in the West with little discussion inside Afghanistan on the preparedness for the *inteqal* process. The net result is the lack of understanding of the perceptions and needs on the ground. While most of the assessments by the present U.S. administration and the Afghan government have been optimistic, academia, media and civil society organizations (CSO) have expressed concerns at the rush towards transition, largely perceived as an 'exit' or 'abandonment' by the Afghans. In the present day assessments regarding the possibility of effective transition by 2014, analysts posit that the withdrawal of western forces would lead to a collapse of the entire security system.[1] Others point out that transition will either fail or be determined by Afghanistan's internal dynamics and the role of regional states, regardless of what the U.S., Europe, and other aid donors do.[2]

Amidst such mixed assessments, the talks and attempts of making the transition an Afghan-led and owned process appears to be a mere lip service. The quantum of the assistance and arbitrary timetables seem to have been dictated by the donor countries' national agendas and public support rather than realistic assessments of the needs on the ground. This volume, on the contrary, is based of the premise that it is important to have the Afghans on a common platform to put forward the needs, address critical gaps and provide alternate suggestions. That the Afghans voices need to be heard to enable them take the 'lead' and set realistic benchmarks and timelines is the emphasis of this endeavour.

While many NATO countries, under considerable domestic pressure, have announced early withdrawal, the U.S. Secretary of Defence Leon Panetta exacerbated the situation in early 2012 by stating that the transition process could be completed by 2013.[3] Contrary to the 2010 Lisbon Declaration which stated that the "transition will be conditions-based, not calendar-driven, and will not equate to withdrawal of ISAF-troop,[4] at the Chicago Summit in May 2012, U.S. President Obama and the NATO leaders agreed to end their role in the Afghan war, saying it is time for the Afghan people to take responsibility for their own security and for the U.S.-led international troops to go home. "We're now unified behind a plan to responsibly wind down the war in Afghanistan," President Obama said during a news conference after the meeting. He called the decision a "major step" toward the end of the war. [5]The Summit decision called for the beginning of full transition in all parts of Afghanistan by mid-2013 and the Afghan forces taking the lead for security nation-wide. The ISAF will gradually drawdown its forces to complete its mission by 31 December 2014.[6]

These early announcements of exit have complicated the transition process. Afghans point out that any premature withdrawal of the international forces from the country should be based on improved conditions on the ground and in a phased out manner to prevent the reversal of gains on the ground.

### *An Afghan Perspective of Transition: Setting the Agenda*

In setting the agenda and defining *The Challenges and Prospects of Transition in Afghanistan*, Professor Ali A. Jalali highlights the grey areas of the transition process. In the next two and half years, Afghanistan is expected to undergo a complex process of transition in security, political and economic spheres. The country is scheduled to take over full security responsibility by 2014 as the bulk of the NATO troops drawdown. The dynamism of these intertwined shifts will shape the end-state with a long-term impact.

Prof. Jalali points out that the security transition in Afghanistan comes against a backdrop of many years of poorly resourced and ill-coordinated reconstruction efforts. It has led to continued insecurity and violence that has peaked in 2011, the worst since the removal of the Taliban from power in 2001.[7] The ever-increasing complexity of strategic and operational environment stymied the development of any unified, long-term vision for the nation and its people. All parties have approached the emerging issues in divergent, uncoordinated ways, with operations on every front being fragmented reactions to events rather than strategic undertakings designed to support long-term goals.

According to Prof. Jalali, a turning point in the conflict was marked by a new U.S-led counterinsurgency (COIN) strategy supported by a military surge in 2009-2010 that blunted the insurgents' momentum in key areas and helped significant build up of Afghanistan National Security Forces (ANSF). These gains are real but remain reversible. Jalali argues that the strategic context where the transition takes place is complex and multi-dimensional. The interplay between the Afghan government, the armed opposition forces (AOF), the International Security Forces (ISAF) and other domestic and foreign actors who are aligned directly or indirectly with the three major players will shape the future of Afghanistan as a state and as a geographic area with the potential to prevent or facilitate trans-national terrorist attacks. No amount of military power, foreign or domestic, and the extent of its involvement in Afghanistan will gain much unless the Afghan government improves its capacity to control its territory, win the trust of the people and prevent infiltration and subversion from abroad. Prof. Jalali, thus, forewarns that a full security transition in 2014 is not a guarantee for peace and stability in Afghanistan, nor does a peace deal with the Taliban by itself promise sustainable peace in the region.

Sustainable peace in Afghanistan can be achieved only through the establishment of an "end state", Jalali argues, that is acceptable to the Afghan people while it does not undermine the legitimate security interests of other actors in the region and beyond. This necessitates addressing legitimate national, regional and international concerns emanating from the Afghanistan situation. Given the local and regional political and security dynamics, the transition process is going to be multi-dimensional, complex, and non-linear.

## Peace Talks, Reconciliation and Reintegration

The ambiguity of the peace processes—reconciliation, reintegration, talks and negotiations with the insurgents have further complicated the search for the 'political solution' to end the 'long war' in Afghanistan. As individual countries are involved in unilateral and parallel efforts of negotiations, setting up office and contacts outside Afghanistan, has further reinforced the notion that the West is willing to cut a deal with the insurgents and leave. Such secretive and uncoordinated attempts have also raised concerns among the women, human rights groups and ethnic minorities, with whispers of civil war gathering momentum. Amidst such anxieties and ambiguities, little attention has been paid to the indigenous peace building efforts like the High Peace Council (HPC) and the Afghan Peace and Reintegration Programme (APRP).

The chapter on *Reconciliation and Reintegration in Afghanistan: Challenges and Milestones Facing Peace Talks, Transition and Stability in the Region* by Minister Mohammad Masoom Stanekzai brings to light the fact that the country is entering into its most crucial phase in its search for peace and stability. Although considerable progress has been made on several fronts, including infrastructure development, governance, health, education, political environment and the security sector, the achievements made are delicate and hence, reversible, if not managed well. With abundant support from outside the Afghan borders behind them, insurgents are increasingly shifting tactics focusing on high profile targets, thereby rejecting any notion that they are losing the war. The large incidence of high profile attacks recorded in the country in 2011 had an enormous impact on the public perception regarding stability.

In Stanekzai's opinion, transition is a joint objective of the Afghans and the international community. This can only be realised when real and sustained progress is made in a number of areas including security, peace and reconciliation, strategic partnerships, long-term engagement, and regional cooperation. Given the geo-political realities of the region and the multi-dimensional nature of the conflict in Afghanistan, there is a need for adopting a collective, integrated and proactive rather than reactive approach informed by the best practices and lessons from the past. He offers insights on the key measures and priorities for the APRP that can act as enablers for achieving a successful transition. Based on his first hand experience in dealing with peace process, he puts forward various scenarios of what Afghanistan would look like both in the near term and long term when supported by an effective peace, reconciliation and reintegration process.

***Section Two*** of the book comprises three papers on issues of *Security, Political Processes & Governance.*

The current security situation in Afghanistan continues to be fragile. Analysts argue that the troop surge has achieved notable security gains on the ground but these gains remain reversible. Each month since May 2011 had fewer enemy-initiated attacks than the corresponding month one year earlier. This is the longest sustained downward trend in enemy-initiated attacks recorded by ISAF.[8] While the security situation is said to have improved in south-western Afghanistan, the main concerns remain in the eastern Afghanistan, primarily Paktika, Paktia, and Khost provinces (the P2K region), bordering Pakistan's

Federally Administered Tribal Areas (FATA), and area of operations of the Haqqani Network.

## Security Sector Reform (SSR) and Preparedness of ANSF

There are mixed opinions about the increasing capability and preparedness among the ANSFs. Analysts have cited their impressive performance during the high profile attacks which disproved their 'rag tag' image. At the same time, concerns exist on their capability of gathering adequate intelligence on the planning and execution of well coordinated multiple sieges, a tactic that is gaining predominance. Example is cited of the multi-city Taliban attack on 15 April 2012, when Taliban suicide attackers carried out attack on Kabul, and three other eastern provinces—Nangarhar, Logar and Paktia. The fact that the insurgents could slip into the protected capital evading several security check points with a huge stockpile of weapons and penetrate the most secure inner circle of Kabul's ring of steel is a matter of deep worry. NATO commended the Afghan security forces for effectively defending the city and ultimately quelling the attack. But Afghan forces did receive some back-up from helicopters and NATO Special Forces. Observers point out that the NATO's praise for the ANSF is understandable, for it is on such success that the exit strategy is predicated.[9]

At the 2010 Lisbon Summit, NATO agreed on a plan to transfer security responsibility to the Afghans. The first tranche of provinces, districts, and municipalities, which has 25 percent of Afghanistan's population, was handed over to the Afghans in July 2011. The second tranche was announced in November 2011, making Afghans take the lead on security for more than 50 percent of the country's population.[10] As per the decisions arrived at the May 2012 Chicago Summit, full transition in all parts of Afghanistan will begin by mid-2013.[11] The contours of post-2014 security assistance to Afghanistan will be mentoring, training, and funding the ANSF. However, will the ANSFs—product of a rushed, under-resourced and frequently revamped recruitment and training procedure—be able to deliver, remains a critical question.

While analysts perceive some success in terms of raising a capable and independent ANA, serious concerns have been expressed in the capabilities of the Afghan National Police (ANP) and the convoluted attempts in establishing rule of law. Analysts point out that while the ANA is seen as a success vis-a-vis the ANP, the chronic deficiencies and problems of funding, equipment, training, desertion, equipment, ethnic balancing and infiltration cannot be overlooked. Further, there are serious concerns of creating a "hyper-militarised" state.[12] The feasibility of building a large army without addressing larger issues of civil-military relations have been questioned. On the other hand, there are concerns that reducing the numbers of ANSF for funding reasons ignores the needs on the ground.[13]

The rapid pace at which recruitment for both the ANA and the ANP has been made is said to have compromised the quality of the personnel recruited.

Analysts suggest that the ANSF are already "unmanageable" and hence, the term 'expansion' is nothing but a paradox".[14] In effect, there is very little to indicate that the ANA will be able to act autonomously over a large swathes of the country side in the next two or three years. Especially remote in the coming years is the possibility of transferring responsibility for the protection of the provinces bordering Pakistan to the Afghan army.[15] Similarly, the ANP are perceived to be ineffective, corrupt and ill disciplined.[16] The persisting weakness among the ANP is bound to affect the ANSF performance in the long term. The ANP is expected to perform law enforcement, border protection and counter-narcotics functions. Stop gap measures of recruiting the tribal militias under the Afghan Local Police (ALP)[17] would run contrary to efforts of long term institution building and reforms in the security sector.

Prof Jalali in his chapter forewarns of the gap between the assumed level of threat and the capacity of the ANSF to meet them by 2014, is expected to be wide and real. Despite a major effort by the NATO Training Mission in Afghanistan (NTM-A) in recent years, the development of the institutional capacity of the ANSF will take years. In outlining major challenges facing the development of the ANSF, Prof. Jalali emphasises on quality, including its professional and institutional capability and its capacity to function in an unstable and conflict-ridden environment. Furthermore, its effectiveness also depends on simultaneous development of other government institutions.

In the light of such apprehensions, Arian Sharifi's chapter *Security in Afghanistan Beyond 2014: Preparedness of ANSF*, looks at four scenarios in the post-2014 Afghanistan. (1) Soon after the withdrawal of the international forces from Afghanistan, the government in Kabul collapses and the Taliban takes over; (2) With the security vacuum created by the withdrawal of the international forces, former *jihadi* groups start struggling for power, the central government collapses, and a civil war follows; (3) The central government survives for two-three years (as with the Soviet withdrawal in 1989), but insurgent attacks increase, and eventually the central government collapses; and (4) The ANSF is able to help preserve the current regime in Afghanistan for the medium term (around ten years), despite the rising levels of insurgent attacks.

Sharifi argues that the latter scenario to be the most plausible. Even after 2014, a considerable number of international troops, mostly American, will remain in Afghanistan, providing strategic support to the ANSF. Additionally, the coalition countries, particularly the U.S., will continue providing financial assistance to Afghanistan for the foreseeable future. This will aid the ANSF, which is growing fast both numerically as well as in quality to be a "good enough force to be capable of defending and preserving the regime." Sharifi, however, qualifies this scenario and the survival of the present regime beyond medium term with a host of interlinked issues—political and administrative reforms, economic development, and the resolution of outstanding issues between Afghanistan and its neighbours.

## Political Sector Reform and Institution Building

While most of the debate on transition has veered towards security component, meaningful discussion of the political transition, particularly when the year of handover of responsibility coincides with the 2014 presidential elections in Afghanistan, seems to be missing. Analysts point out that "Placing sole responsibility for Afghanistan's future stability on the ANSFs without making progress in creating a stronger political consensus among Afghanistan's diverse factions-both armed and unarmed-is a high-risk gamble".[18]

Over the past decade, the highly centralised executive form of political system has been constantly challenged. The constant bickering between the President and Parliament, deteriorating security, poor governance and near absence of rule of law, has sparked debates inside and outside Afghanistan for the need for wide ranging political sector reforms. The magnitude of the problem and simmering discontent has led the Afghan observers to forewarn, "If in 2001 the West was afraid that the absence of a strong centralised government in Kabul would prompt Afghanistan's dissolution, by 2011 the West has come to fear that a dysfunctional centralised government could cause this same outcome."[19]

Concerns that the lack of institution building and reforms in the political sector will hamper the transition process were voiced by various speakers during the workshop. Fawzia Koofi, a potential presidential contender and Member of Parliament (MP) from Badkshan, in the presentation titled, *Challenges of Institution Building in Afghanistan* delved on the problems of reconstruction and institution building in nascent democracies. For her, the main issue facing post-conflict societies is the construction a politically stable and democratic state that has both the institutions and legitimacy to remain viable in the long run.

The Bonn Agreement of December 2001 brought the over two decades of civil conflict in Afghanistan to an end. This Agreement laid the framework for building a functioning and democratic government. In the subsequent decade, significant progress was made in some areas. However, Koofi asserted that the process stands threatened by the failure of central government institutions to deliver the basic services. Weak institutions have led to a deterioration of security and have undermined the process of state-building. Moreover, the creation of institutions is being pushed by the international donors who are keen to adhere to a timetable, without ensuring that these institutions have the financial, human, and physical resources to function effectively. Instead of building on long term institutions, reliance on individuals i.e. key power brokers and the associated patronage systems has proved to be problematic. Centralisation of power with the president has curtailed the power of other institutions like the parliament.

Koofi argued that the state-building process results in a fundamental re-structuring of many facets of a society and changes the way that state relates to the rest of the world. Among several concerns that either shape the state-building process or that arise directly from it, establishing peace and security is of paramount importance in a country like Afghanistan. However, without the rule of law, and equitable socio-economic development that address the needs of citizens from all parts of the country, it is impossible to deal with other aspects of state-building, she argued. She pointed at the lack of adequate role for women representatives in the parliament. Although 28 percent of the Members of Parliament (MPs) are women, their role in peace and reconciliation as well as transition process is quite limited.

The absence of rule of law has been highlighted as a critical issue affecting the legitimacy of the government in Kabul. Koofi argued that stabilising Afghanistan following NATO's departure will not be possible unless the international community establishes a realistic strategy for the government to respect the rule of law. Parliament and the Supreme Court are two important institutions that would help develop Afghanistan's nascent democracy. Moreover, there is a need to accommodate and enable the traditionally marginalised groups participation in the government and decision making process. "The NATO transition of security forces in Afghanistan could be effective if we put the right people in power—especially our new hi-tech generation. The youth have learned enough and now know how to serve our people and the country", she stated.

That resolution of the insurgency would be the key to stability in Afghanistan was not lost on Fawzia Koofi. She argued "Securing our borders is the only way to stop the Taliban from attacking our cities. The Taliban must stop getting military supplies from other side of the border, namely, Pakistan. Bonn and other International conferences have not addressed this issue. We cannot have a stable Afghanistan without stopping nefarious trade, transactions, and trade along our borders."

## Peace building, Constitutional and Electoral Reform

The strong centralised form of Presidential system has been constantly challenged not only internally but also by the continuing Taliban violence and intimidation. In 2011, systematic targeting and elimination of power brokers, government officials and police chiefs, added new set of complexities by creating a 'crisis of confidence'. These targeted high profile killings raised the specter of civil war in the north and in the south, it led to erosion of President Karzai's support base among the Pushtuns. The insurgents have been able to effectively use the deficiencies of the present political system, lack of governance, ineffective administration, corruption and ills of the present government to their advantage. They have even set up shadow governments in areas where the writ of the Afghan government is limited or non-existent.

The challenges associated with the institution building, stem from inadequate understanding of the nature of the Afghan state and the political processes. Ahmad Wali Masoud, in the chapter on *Political Reform and Peace Building in Afghanistan* emphasises on the need to address the challenges of political instability and reform based on historical and socio-cultural understanding of the Afghan state. The second Bonn conference in December 2011 did not address the need for political reform, he argues. The 2004 constitution, which is sourced mostly from the 1964 constitution when Afghanistan was a monarchy, has established one of the most highly centralised governments in the world. A gradual political reform toward a less centralised government is a necessary step. Amending the 2004 constitution to establish different forms of government based on decentralisation, while preserving the unity of Afghanistan, remains the only viable option, according to Massoud. This would help build consensus among Afghans and lay the foundations of a durable peace as the international forces leave Afghanistan in 2014. If Afghanistan is to achieve some degree of stability after 2014, a concerted effort must be exerted toward political reform through checks and balances. The imbalance between the central authority and local power centres needs to be corrected, he asserts.

In addition, to the existing challenges in the political sector, the complexity of holding elections in the year of handover of authority is daunting. Analysts point out that "The Afghan presidential election slated for 2014 is an uninspiring prospect given the sky-high levels of corruption, nepotism, and patronage that beleaguers the Afghan political system. To make things worse, Karzai has suggested holding the elections in 2013 to avoid an overlap with the planned end of NATO's combat mission. And there is still no functional plan in place for a smooth transfer of political power to a post-Karzai government."[20] In the absence of large scale political sector and electoral reform, the danger of repeat of previous instances of electoral malpractices at a crucial time of transition is cause for widespread concern.

Dr. Sima Samar, Chairperson of the Afghanistan Independent Human Rights Commission (AIHRC), who could not make it to the workshop due to a crisis in the AIHRC, highlights the need for electoral as well as constitutional reforms in Afghanistan. Two rounds of elections in Afghanistan have depicted the ineffectiveness of the current electoral system. The Afghan constitution has inherent limitations in dealing with disputes arising from power relations between the three branches of the government and jurisdictions of institutions over governing elections. According to her, the current electoral system has produced an ineffective parliament and would further weaken democracy in the country. Therefore, a "change in the current Single Non Transferable Vote (SNTV) system and electoral law is an urgent need to have future elections free of fraud and irregularity." Likewise, adding new provisions of law to make up for the limitations in the current constitution will protect the Afghans against protracted disputes over question of jurisdiction, electoral calendars and issues related to power relations of the government. For her, the choice is a proportionate electoral system or a mixed system.

## Governance Deficit

Problems in the political sector have been exacerbated by a corresponding governance deficit. Shahmahmood Miakhel in his chapter on *Myths and Impact of Bad Governance on Stability in Afghanistan* draws upon events that he has witnessed and reported on during the last 35 years. His paper outlines the main historical and current drivers of insurgency in Afghanistan, as well as the importance of governance for effective transition. His emphasis is on the need to dispel a few myths regarding Afghans and Afghanistan, for the continued propagation of such myths is bound to make a negative impact on political reform, governance and stability in Afghanistan. Miakhel underscores the need for good governance, without which stability would be impossible, irrespective of the support from external sources. "Good governance cannot happen without good leadership, and good leadership must derive from fair and free election in Afghanistan", he says. In order to prevent the cycle of instability from continuing, there is a pressing need to focus on the political transition in 2014. A smooth transition of power has the potential to create new momentum for better governance and accountability.

***Section Three*** of the book consists of three papers on *Civilian Surge, Aid, Development, Gender, Economic Opportunities, Trade, Transit, Investment and Strategic Communication.*

Most of the discourse on transition has focused on the numerical strength of the troops that would be adequate to maintain the country's security. Little attention has been paid to the civilian capacity building, economic opportunities, trade, transit and investment that would change the narrative of Afghanistan from being an aid dependent 'rentier state' to a self sustaining economy, thereby bringing in long term stability.

Far from a narrow security centric approach that laboured in futility to ensure order in this war torn country, the narrative is apparently shifting to regional confidence building, development, governance, and most lately, trade, transit and investment, aiming to use the country's resource and transit potential to build its economic viability, sustainability and self reliance. To a large extent, the genesis of this thinking is based on the inadequacies of the security-dominated approach of the last decade. Without tangible progress on the ground, gains in security continue to be 'fragile' and 'reversible'.

## Civilian Surge, Aid Effectiveness, War economy and Alternative Livelihood

A decade-long policy of the international community doing things independently has created an aid dependent populace. The intrinsic nature of aid-giving and execution of development projects through contracts and sub contracting, has done little to build on local capacities or ownership. Afghanistan's problem essentially lies in the lack of "unity of effort" (UoE) on the part of the international community in developing a well-coordinated and long-term strategy to strengthen the local institutions and 'bring the state back' into the development process. In rebuilding conflict-ridden states like Afghanistan, aid delivery through 'alternate delivery mechanisms' like the IO's and INGO's or direct delivery through embassies, and community-based groups play a crucial role in providing immediate humanitarian relief and assistance. However, for long-term stabilisation, it is important to route aid through the state institutions. This is critical to shore up and enhance the government's capacity and credibility.

In the chapter on *Afghanistan in the Course of Transition: Challenges and Opportunities for Civilian Surge, Aid Coordination, War Economy and Alternative Livelihood*, Najeeb Manalai highlights that the transition of lead security responsibility from the international military forces to Afghan security forces, as an inevitable process. However, many Afghans are unsure of the direction of the *inteqal* process and are skeptical of the weak performance of the Afghan government and security apparatus. Concerns about tackling the evolving security challenges, the fall of the Afghan government and losing the current gains towards democracy and stability emerge as serious worries. Manalai argues, the complexity of many aspects of the transition issue has created unrest among Afghans. He assesses some of the essential challenges—relevant to security, economic stability, war economy and coordination of international aid —in the short and long term from an Afghan perspective.

## Gender, Development and Non-Governmental Organisations

The role of women in rebuilding conflict ravaged Afghanistan has been largely under reported. Women are long term stake holders in bringing peace and stability to the conflict ridden country. According to a survey conducted by Asia Foundation, 'most Afghans want their girls educated, they want women to be able to go to the marketplace freely, they want them to be in public freely, they don't agree with what the Taliban had done in the 1990s'.[21] However, in the present discourse on transition the gender narrative has taken a back seat. There are concerns that achievements made in the last decade with regard to women's rights could be lost. For example, Valerie Hudson writing in Foreign Policy cites senior U.S. officials who state "Gender issues are going to have to take a back seat to other priorities."[22]

Rangina Hamidi's chapter *Aid, Development, Women, Non-Governmental Organisations: Grass Root Perspective* provides a narrative of women in Kandahar and questions the effectiveness of foreign aid in effecting change at the grass root level. Written in narrative style, Rangina recounts the story of Anargula, a mother of six with a handicapped husband to raise pertinent questions on the nature of international intervention. With the presence of more than 40 nations, their troops and development funds, why has so little changed for hundreds of families in Afghanistan who struggle to meet their daily needs?

Rangina identifies three main reasons for the ineffectiveness of international aid in Afghanistan: (i) short sightedness of the outcomes; (ii) lack of coordination between development agencies and governments; and (iii) aid being led and delivered by warlords and corrupt government officials.

The Afghan government has stated that meeting its goals requires $120 billion in aid over the period through 2025. Rangina asserts that this level of aid, however, is almost certainly too high to be credible, and many of the promises of reform in governance and to remove the economic barriers to growth and development are extremely unlikely to be kept. Regardless of what donor countries have said in the past or say at the future conferences, it is nearly certain that the Afghan government cannot obtain the level of aid it requested at the Bonn Conference, particularly over a period that extends beyond 2014. Development aid from the U.S., the largest aid donor, dropped from $3.5 billion in 2010 to about $2 billion in 2011. Aid to support democracy, governance and civil society dropped by more than 50 percent and from $231 million to $93 million in the same period.[23] Amidst such decline in aid giving, exploring avenues for revenue generation and development of indigenous economic base remains critical.

## Economic Opportunities, Trade, Investment and Connectivity

While the chicken and egg (security vs. development) dilemma continues, the hasty announcements of 'exit' by the international community, has exacerbated the anxiety and fear of 'abandonment' among the Afghans. It is thus imperative to change and build on the narrative of opportunity to prevent the reversal of gains. What is striking is the demand by the Afghans for more assistance and investment in rebuilding the local indigenous economic base. Contrary to the media propagated myths of backwardness and inward-looking tribes that reject modernisation, the civilians in places like Kandahar are yearning for more assistance in the health and education sector.[24]

The discovery of huge reserves of minerals and natural gas has raised hopes of possibility of revenue generation, foreign investment and employment opportunities. Its underdeveloped yet significant agricultural and human resource potential, and its strategic geographical location at the crossroads of Central, South, West Asia and Eurasia, offer vast opportunities for foreign investment, trade and transit connectivity. Such potential can be harnessed by an assimilation of economic interests of regional countries through a mutually beneficial inter-dependent framework. The convergence of such interests could be the best leverage against slide of Afghanistan into instability. It would also mitigate the risks of negative zero sum competition among regional countries and build stakes for long term economic engagement in the region.

In the long run, this could pave the way for the transformation of the Afghan economy from a prolonged phase of being aid-dependent to self-reliant. Most of the international aid, being donor driven and delivered through alternate delivery mechanisms has done little to build on the state institutions' capacity to deliver, resulting in diminishing credibility of the state. International financial assistance comes with a string of conditionalities (mutual accountability), which are often difficult to adhere. Moreover, in a scenario of dwindling financial assistance, there is a real danger of economic downturn. In such context, without building on the state's revenue generation capacity through large scale investments, combined with funds and capacity building programmes for entrepreneurship and employment, particularly in the social sector (health and education), agriculture, small and medium enterprise (SME), the dangers or reversal of gains are imminent.

In this context, the New Delhi Investment Summit of June 28 sought to establish a critical link between the recently held and forthcoming international conferences on the future of Afghanistan. While the 21 May Chicago NATO Conference underlined the need for international support and assistance for Afghanistan's security and the 14 June Kabul Ministerial Conference focused on regional confidence-building, the 8 July Tokyo Conference focuses on Afghanistan's development and governance, the New Delhi Summit was intended to showcase Afghanistan's economic, resource, trade and transit potential to usher in foreign investment and augment the role of the private sector as an alternate approach to bring in long term stability in the conflict ridden country.

The Afghanistan International Investment Conference of 30 November 2010 held in Dubai and the Brussels Euro Mines Conference of 26 October 2011, aimed at promoting economic investment in Afghanistan, made valuable recommendations, but they essentially put the onus for investment on actions to be initiated by Afghanistan. The New Delhi Summit, taking into consideration the realities and needs on the ground, explored near and long term possibilities in the current environment and at the same time, sought a mechanism to address the needs of foreign and private sector investors and the government of Afghanistan. This is reflective in the efforts geared to catalyze investment decisions and forge cross-country and international partnerships to promote cooperation and greater collective confidence. A collective view of security for foreign investors would emerge from the reality of venturing together, rather than being externally provided to the individual investors risking an uncertain environment all by themselves.

The New Delhi Investment Summit, in addition to addressing the critical gaps that marred the past efforts was based on the premise that short-gestation investments in agriculture, small and medium enterprise (SME), social sector (health and education), telecommunications, IT and so forth will broad-base economic development at the grassroots and provide the necessary counter-point for big-ticket investments in newer ventures and long-term gestation projects like mining and hydrocarbons that can together address macro-economic issues such as revenue generation, fiscal viability, and help build a sustainable economy. It would also propel Afghanistan to work on improving its investment climate, particularly on its legal framework, arbitration and dispute resolution mechanisms. For companies from the west, with concerns about security and cultural impediments, it would be an opportunity to partner with companies and business houses of regional countries like UAE, India, China and others, already working in Afghanistan. Investments and collaborative partnerships among regional countries would work as an economic confidence building mechanism (CBM). It would go a long way in restoring the confidence among local, regional and international investors and promote the viewpoint that there is an alternate way of making Afghanistan a highly lucrative business and investment destination.

Haseeb Humayoon, whose chapter has not been included in the book, in his presentation on *Economic Opportunities, Investment, Trade, Connectivity and Transition Economies* provided an overview of the promises that many fail to see in the economic opportunities Afghanistan offers its people as well as the potential investors. He pointed out that returns on investments in Afghanistan are real, although fraught with uncertainty. The rich mineral wealth as well as energy and trade transit potential of the country are promising, and can spur economic growth. Investments in agriculture processing, media, services and telecommunications sectors have prospered and could sustain in the long run.

However, largely dependent on the purchasing power of the foreign militaries, and the flow of aid dollars, Afghanistan faces challenges in creating alternative and indigenous economic engines. The recognition of the need to offset damaging economic impact of the international military drawdown with attracting investments can serve as a healthy stimulus for reform of the investment climate. Heightened political risk and rudimentary legal and infrastructural frameworks and absence of equitable enforcement stand as the dominant challenges to reaping Afghanistan's potential. Haseeb points out that in the short-term, with increased uncertainty about the future of the country, the danger is that present investors in the market are likely to diversify their risks by channeling investments into regional economic hubs such as Dubai, if not completely withdraw from the Afghan market. The longer-term investment attraction and economic growth of the country depends on the confidence in stability of the Afghanistan market, as well as reform of access to essential factors of production (power, finance, land), security of property rights, as well as Afghanistan's clear-eyed pursuit of its comparative advantages in the region.

## Strategic Communications and Information Campaign

One of the crucial cornerstones in the long term stabilisation campaign is the role of information. In Afghanistan, the near absence of reporting of positive and success stories and dominance of stories of violence and destruction has fed into the insurgent propaganda. The need for building on the nascent Afghan media as part of the information campaign and strategic communications strategy is critical to build on the public trust and confidence. Radio remains the most accessible media for Afghan households. Other communications technologies such as television, mobile phones and computers are significantly more accessible in urban areas. Ownership of mobile telephones continues to increase in 2011 compared to previous years. A survey conducted by the Asia Foundation found that two thirds of respondents of the survey have access to mobile phones, although there is a large divide between urban and rural areas.[25] Information and communications technology has exploded to such a degree that some are envisaging a new "Digital Silk Road" with Afghanistan acting as a hub.[26]

In the chapter *The Role of Traditional and Modern Forms of Strategic Communication and Public Awareness in Actualising Transition,* Muhammad Sabir Siddiqi discusses the crucial role of strategic communication and public awareness with a focus on the agenda and mechanisms to be established for the transition process. His paper examines the performance of the government of Afghanistan and its allies in implementing policies and utilising channels and networks for dissemination of messages and communication of agendas and processes. Siddiqi argues that the lack of a well-coordinated and well-designed communication and public awareness strategy has led to public distrust. The government and its international allies have not used the modern communication tools optimally. Moreover, they also have ignored the traditional mechanisms, networks and tools to communicate the messages and policies. As a result, the government and the allies have failed to 'win the 'hearts and minds' of the people. The paper puts forward recommendations for establishing effective mechanisms of strategic communication and public awareness that would smoothen the transition process and yield the desired outcomes.

***Section Four*** of the book delves into the *Regional and International Community's Perspectives on Transition.*

Afghanistan's tragedy lies in the fact that time and again its internal contradictions have got trapped in the external power agenda. With the intensification of the search for the 'end-game', a regional solution is seen as a way out of the imbroglio. In understanding the contours of a regional solution, it is important to understand the perspectives of individual countries on the transition process and prospects of long term stabilisation of Afghanistan.

## Regional Solution, Consensus or Compromise?

Although regional consensus remains elusive, what remains to be seen is whether forging greater cooperation or reverting to competition would be beneficial for regional countries in the face of decreased international troop presence in Afghanistan. One way of building a cooperative regional architecture is through greater trade and transit, investment opportunities, including energy pipelines. The projected gain from the Turkmenistan-Afghanistan-Pakistan-India

(TAPI) gas pipeline has the potential to create a win-win deal among regional stakeholders in Afghanistan.

While regional cooperation has been an important plank of the Afghan foreign policy, the Istanbul Conference for "Afghanistan: Security and Cooperation in the Heart of Asia", held on 2 November 2011, provided a new agenda for regional cooperation by placing Afghanistan at its centre and engaging the 'Heart of Asia' countries in sincere and result-oriented cooperation for a peaceful and stable Afghanistan, as well as a secure and prosperous region as a whole. The emphasis was on regionally owned process led by Afghanistan with support and collaboration from its near and extended neighbours, and reiterating that, to reinforce the regional ownership of the process, decisions must be made through close consultation among the 'Heart of Asia' countries.

## Afghan Perspective

Haroun Mir in his paper *Is Regional Consensus on Afghanistan Possible?*, posits how the regional dimension to the Afghan conflict has always been a dominant factor. Afghanistan has been the theatre of a New Great Game since early 1990s. Although a regional approach to the conflict, led the U.S. policy makers to highlight the role of regional stakeholders in the 2009 U.S. strategy for the country, little progress has been achieved in building a regional consensus on Afghanistan.

The Afghan government has engaged in long-term strategic partnerships with India and the U.S. despite strong objections from Pakistan and Iran. In addition, Haroun Mir points out that the possibility of U.S. long-term military presence in the country after 2014 has alarmed regional stakeholders, which will fundamentally shift the regional balance of power. In light of these new ground realities in the region any short-term multilateral diplomatic effort to reach a regional consensus on Afghanistan will be futile. Being a part of three regional security complexes, it will be difficult for Afghanistan to regain its former status as a buffer state. A long-term option for Afghanistan is to strengthen its strategic partnerships while conducting vigorous bilateral diplomacy and exploring common opportunities rather than dwelling on differences.

## View from Pakistan

Professor Rasul Bakhsh Rais provides *Pakistan's Perspective on the Afghan Transition*. He reiterates that no other country has been affected by developments in Afghanistan and has been so much affected by the cycles of war in that country as Pakistan. Although it can and will play a key role, over the past decade, major powers—the U.S., its NATO allies, and India-have taken much of the initiatives. Pakistan's relations with the U.S. and Afghanistan have got mired in deep mistrust that leaves the former on the margins, even after making massive sacrifices in the war on terror. Over the years, Pakistan has silently advocated negotiations with the Taliban at home and within Afghanistan, a view that seems to be gaining traction. As U.S. and other powers transfer much of the responsibility to the Afghan government by 2014, Pakistan finds itself on the sidelines. Prof. Rais explores what role Pakistan can play toward the 'endgame', what are the interests that drive its Afghan policy, what are its perceptions and concerns of other powers. He argues that transitioning Afghanistan toward a stable, peaceful and normal state needs to be a collaborative, multilateral effort in which Pakistan can play a major role. Pakistan may need a proactive diplomacy to be heard, understood and accommodated in the future schemes about Afghanistan.

## Indian Perspective

Professor S.D. Muni in his presentation on the *Indian Perspective of the Afghan Transition Process* focuses on the civilisational aspects and strategic stakes India has in Afghanistan. India concluded its strategic partnership deal with Afghanistan in October 2011, to underline its will and capacity to be relevant to the unfolding developments in Afghanistan. India would like to see a stable, moderate and independent Afghanistan. With the prospect of U.S. and NATO departure from the country, a formidable challenge before "India now is to sustain the stakes pitched and obligations undertaken." He suggested that a regional arrangement could be worked out to ensure this, but the "haste and confusion under which the war on terrorism is being terminated, as also the contradictions and divergence in the interests of the regional stakeholders spanning from Iran to China and India to Russia have not allowed it."

In the chapter on *India's Engagement with Afghanistan: Developing a Durable Policy Architecture,* Daniel Norfolk seeks to map the contours of Afghanistan's geopolitical landscape in anticipation of the U.S.-NATO withdrawal, scheduled for 2014. Occupying a unique position as Afghanistan's leading regional development partner, India is poised to play an instrumental role. Without postulating Indian reactions to the myriad contingencies that may arise, this chapter concentrates on India's strategic objectives, constraints, and the evolution of New Delhi's Afghan policy framework. It examines the ways in which India has sought to position itself so that it might be indispensable to whatever circumstances emerge in Afghanistan throughout the inevitably turbulent transition period and beyond.

## Chinese Perception

Professor Dr Xuecheng Liu, whose paper could not be included in the book due to understandable difficulties and sensitivities back home, in his presentation on the *Chinese Perspective on the Afghanistan's Transition* highlights the fact that with the withdrawal of the U.S. and NATO-ISAF by 2014, all the Afghan domestic forces will struggle to seek their political/military presence in the future Afghanistan. The future of Afghanistan beyond 2014 will face great uncertainty and will witness three possible scenarios. One scenario is a sovereign and independent Afghanistan with a governing authority recognised by the international community; another scenario is the Taliban-dominant regime isolated by the international community; and the third is the divided country ruled by local warlords and ignored by the international community.

The present international efforts focus on creating the first one. However, looking at both the post-Qaddafi situation in Libya and the post-U.S. occupation turmoil in Iraq, and reviewing the post-Soviet withdrawal chaos in Afghanistan, the occurrence of the second and the third scenarios may not possibly be avoided. To succeed in national reconciliation and reconstruction in Afghanistan, there are three preconditions the international community should make efforts to establish. They are the United Nation (U.N.)-led peace-keeping operations, the Afghanistan-led regional coordination and cooperation, and the governing authority based on national reconciliation.

In advocating for the lead and coordinating role for the U.N., Dr. Liu states that given the successful case of the U.N.-led peace-keeping mission in Cambodia in the 1990s, the international community should support the U.N. role in coordinating international assistance to Afghanistan and ensuring a stable transition in Afghanistan beyond 2014. The international community should respect and accommodate the legitimate interests and concerns of neighbouring countries in the region. The international community should continue to support Afghanistan in capacity building so that it can take over the responsibility of maintaining peace, security and stability in the country by helping Afghanistan in advancing political reconciliation through its own efforts, he argues.

In Liu's view, China, as a friendly neighbour of Afghanistan has played an active part in supporting and promoting Afghanistan's reconstruction process and provided assistance to Afghanistan. China will, working with other partners, continue to take concrete steps to help Afghanistan with its peace and reconstruction process and support the development of resources, transport, energy, infrastructure and other sectors in Afghanistan. To strengthen Afghan governing capability is crucial to the future stability of Afghanistan. China is willing to make its own contribution, and is working with other stakeholders, to develop various training programs in this field. That China and the United States have implemented a joint training program of young Afghan diplomats at a Chinese university is an encouraging start in the Afghan reconstruction efforts within the framework of international cooperation.

### U.S. Perspective

Professor Marvin Weinbaum's chapter on the *U.S. Perspectives on the Afghan Transition Process* provides an American perspective of the Afghan transition process. He states that after more than a decade of involvement, the U.S. has committed itself to military disengagement and Afghanistan's transition toward becoming a more self-sufficient and sovereign state. This transfer of power and responsibility leaves many uneasy and uncertain of the success and sustainability of this process, especially over the longer term. The transition process began when in announcing a military surge in December 2009, President Barack Obama also declared that American troops would begin their withdrawal by the end of 2011. The blueprint for the departure of forces gained further definition with the agreement among NATO countries in Lisbon in November 2010 that their military commitments would extend only through the end of 2014. Left open is the speed of the American troop drawdown. The Obama Administration has lacked clarity over whether the transition militarily will be governed by fixed deadlines or be condition based. But whatever the pace, a large number of civilian advisors are slated to leave along with the military's departure, and the massive spending for Afghanistan, most of it in support of military operations, is destined to trail off.

This chapter examines the goals that have mainly guided U.S. involvement in Afghanistan and the shifting strategies employed to pursue them. It gives particular attention to reconciliation and regionally focused approaches intended to ease the departure of U.S. forces and leave behind a peaceful and stable Afghanistan. The chapter further examines the inevitable financial hurdles Afghanistan faces with declining foreign assistance and how U.S. aid policy is setting priorities that it hopes can minimize the impact. Drawing from these discussions four distinctive scenarios are suggested for how Afghanistan may fare in the transition process. They carry varying degrees of probability, but all have a reasonable degree of plausibility. Taking into account U.S. strategic objectives, the chapter concludes with a set of policy recommendations that might improve chances for a smooth and effective transition.

This book brings together diverse Afghan and regional perspectives on the prospects for the long term stabilisation of Afghanistan. A number of international conferences on Afghanistan have made numerous pledges and commitment, the implementation of which has been lacking. While the second Bonn conference on "Afghanistan and the International Community: From Transition to the Transformation Decade." held in December 2011 has set an extended period of international assistance: 2014-24 and has termed it the 'transformational decade', the contours of international assistance and engagement remain highly unclear. A series of international conferences seem to miss the crucial essence of stabilising Afghanistan by devising quick fix solutions and setting arbitrary time lines that do not meet with the needs on the ground. This disconnect runs the inherent danger of reversal of gains as the international community's prepares to transfer authority to the Afghans. The present volume looks beyond 'conference oriented solution's by addressing the critical gaps in making the *inteqal* an Afghan led and owned process and suggesting alternate course of action for bringing in long term stability from an Afghan and regional perspective.

## Notes

1. Gilles Dorronsoro, *Afghanistan: The Impossible Transition*, The Carnegie Papers South Asia, Carnegie endowment for International peace, June 2011, http://www.carnegieendowment.org/files/impossible_transition.pdf. Accessed on 10 June 2012.
2. Anthony H. Cordesman, *Afghanistan: The Uncertain Economics of Transition*, Center for Strategic & International Studies, April 2012, http://csis.org/files/publication/120418_afghanistan_uncertain_economics_transition.pdf. Accessed on 10 June 2012.
3. *Media Availability with Secretary of Defense Leon Panetta*, U.S. Department of Defense, February 1, 2012, http://www.defense.gov/transcripts/transcript.aspx?transcriptid=4967. Accessed on 23 April 2012.
4. *Lisbon Summit Declaration*, North Atlantic Treaty Organisation, November 20, 2010, http://www.nato.int/cps/en/natolive/official_texts_68828.htm. Accessed on 21 April 2012
5. Helene Cooper and Matthew Rosenberg, "NATO Agrees on Afghan Security Transition in 2013", *The New York Times*, 21 May 2012, http://www.nytimes.com/2012/05/22/world/nato-formally-agrees-to-transition-on-afghan-security.html?pagewanted=1&_r=1&smid=fb-share. Accessed on 23 May 2012.
6. *Chicago Summit Declaration on Afghanistan*—Issued by the Heads of State and Government of Afghanistan and Nations contributing to the NATO-led International SecurityAssistance Force (ISAF), 21 May 2012, http://www.nato.int/cps/en/natolive/official_texts_87595.htm. Accessed on 23 May 2012.
7. According to data by the United Nations, 2011 "was the deadliest on record for civilians in the Afghan war, with 3,021 killed as insurgents ratcheted up violence with suicide attacks and roadside bombs". See Kay Johnson, "U.N.: Afghanistan civilian deaths at peak", *Navy Times*, 4 February 2012, http://www.navytimes.com/news/2012/02/ap-afghanistan-civilian-deaths-at-peak-united-nations-says-020412/. Accessed on 20 May 2012.
8. *ISAF Monthly Data: Trends Through March 2012, April 22, 2012*, North Atlantic Treaty Organisation: International Security and Assistance Force, 22 April 2012, http://www.isaf.nato.int/images/20120422_niu_data_release_final.pdf. Accessed on 24 April 2012.
9. Bilal Sarwary, "Analysis: What Kabul attacks say about Afghan security", *BBC News*, 16 April 2012, http://www.bbc.co.uk/news/world-asia-17725266. Accessed on 16 April 2012.
10. *Statement by NATO Secretary General on Afghan Transition Announcement*, North Atlantic Treaty Organisation, 27 November 2011, http://www.nato.int/cps/en/SID-656CC458-77FAA000/natolive/news_81068.htm. Accessed on 20 April 2012.
11. Chicago Summit Declaration on Afghanistan. op. cit.
12. Julian Glover, "Few politicians say it, but most think it: our Afghan war is a disaster", *The Guardian*, 11 April 2011, www.guardian.co.uk/commentisfree/2011/apr/11/afghanistan-strategy-failed. Accessed on 11 April 2011.
13. Yaroslav Trofimov, "Afghan General Sounds Alarm," *The Wall Street Journal*, 18 February 2012, http://online.wsj.com/article/SB10001424052970204059804577229081438477796.html. Accessed on 20 April 2012.
14. Thomas Johnson and Matthew Dupee, "Transition to Nowhere: The Limits of 'Afghanisation'," *Foreign Policy*, 22 March 2011, http://afpak.foreignpolicy.com/posts/2011/03/22/ transition_to_nowhere_the_limits_ of_afghanization. Accessed on 5 April 2011.

15. Gilles Dorronsoro, *Afghanistan: The Impossible Transition*, The Carnegie Papers, South Asia, Carnegie endowment for International Peace, June 2011, http://www.carnegieendowment.org/files/impossible_transition.pdf. Accessed on 20 May 2012.
16. *Despite Improvements in MoI's Personnel Systems, Additional Actions Are Needed to Completely Verify ANP Payroll Costs and Workforce Strength*, SIGAR (Office of the Special Inspector General for Afghanistan Reconstruction), 25 April 2011, www.sigar.mil/pdf/audits/SIGAR%20Audit-11-10.pdf. Accessed on 22 May 2012.
17. C.J. Radin, "Afghan Local Police vital to General Petraeus' strategy", *The Long War Journal*, 26 March 2011, www.longwarjournal.org/archives/2011/03/afghan_local_police.php. Accessed on 29 March 2011.
18. Caroline Wadhams, Colin Cookman & Brian Katulis, *Afghanistan Transition: Elevating the Diplomatic Components of the Transition Strategy at the Chicago NATO Summit and Beyond*, Center for American Progress, 17 May 2012, http://www.americanprogress.org/issues/2012/05/afghanistan_transition.html. Accessed on 20 May 2012.
19. Thomas Barfield, "Afghanistan's Ethnic Puzzle: Decentralising Power before the U.S. Withdrawal", *Foreign Affairs* (September/ October 2011).
20. Javid Ahmad, "Election 2014: Afghanistan's chance to get it right?", *Foreign Policy*, 10 May 2012, http://afpak.foreignpolicy.com/posts/2012/05/10/election_2014_afghanistans_chance_to_get_it_right. Accessed on 20 May 2012.
21. Ruth Rennie (ed.), *Afghanistan in 2011: A Survey of the Afghan People*, The Asia Foundation, 2011, http://asiafoundation.org/resources/pdfs/TAF2011AGSurvey.pdf. Accessed on 15 May 2012.
22. Valerie M. Hudson, "What Sex Means for World Peace", *Foreign Policy*, 24 April 2012, http://www.foreignpolicy.com/articles/2012/04/24/what_sex_means_for_world_peace?page=0,2. Accessed on 20 May 2012.
23. Julian Borger, "Afghanistan conference promises support after troop withdrawal", *The Guardian*, 5 December 2011, http://www.guardian.co.uk/world/2011/dec/05/afghanistan-conference-support-troop-withdrawal. Accessed on 20 May 2012.
24. Shanthie Mariet D'Souza, "Kandahar's transition woes", *Open Democracy*, 16 December 2011, http://www.opendemocracy.net/opensecurity/shanthie-mariet-dsouza/kandahars-transition-woes. Accessed on 20 May 2012.
25. In a survey conducted by Asia Foundation, more than four fifths (81%) of respondents said they possess a functioning radio in their household, but there is a difference in access between rural (83%) and urban (73%) areas. Just under half (45%) of respondents use radio most often to get news and information, while just over a quarter (28%) use television". Ruth Rennie (ed.), *Afghanistan in 2011: A Survey of the Afghan People*, The Asia Foundation, 2011, http://asiafoundation.org/resources/pdfs/TAF2011AGSurvey.pdf. Accessed on 21 May 2012.
26. "Afghanistan: Is There an IT Fix for Kabul?", *Inter News*, 9 May 2012, http://internews.org/our- stories/news/afghanistan-there-it-fix-kabul. Accessed on 10 May 2012.

# SECTION I

# SETTING THE AGENDA: AN AFGHAN PERSPECTIVE

# 2

# The Challenges and Prospects of Transition in Afghanistan

*Ali A. Jalali*

In the next two-and-half years Afghanistan is expected to undergo a complex process of transition (*inteqal*) in the security, political and economic spheres. The country is scheduled to take over full security responsibility by 2014 as the bulk of the NATO troops draws down. The dynamism of these intertwined shifts will shape the end-state with a long-term impact. The transition process comes against a backdrop of many years of poorly resourced and ill-coordinated reconstruction efforts leading to continued insecurity and violence that gradually peaked to the highest level since the removal of the Taliban from power in 2001. From the outset, the reconstruction goals were too ambitious and the resources dreadfully limited. An under-resourced and inconsistent state building drive amidst a rising insurgency failed to match the real challenges and realities on the ground.

The flawed project was followed by a troop intensive counterinsurgency (COIN) strategy supported by a military surge in 2009-10. The move made security gains in key areas. But such a strategy required patience and time to succeed. Political pressure and financial constraints in donor countries have eroded support for an extended counterinsurgency effort leading to a calendar-driven drawdown of U.S. forces by 2014. Putting a timeline of military operations in a counterinsurgency environment usually leads to uncertainty pushing the insurgents and regional actors into a hedging behaviour that could prolong the violence. Now, a new strategy of 'advise and assist' to achieve a 'sufficient" degree of stability in Afghanistan, allowing the withdrawal of international military forces, is winning wide support in NATO circles and has influenced policy decisions at the NATO summit in Chicago in May 2012. The Summit decision calls for the beginning of full transition in all parts of Afghanistan by mid-2013 with the Afghan forces taking the lead for security nation-wide. Meanwhile the ISAF will gradually and responsibly drawdown its forces to complete its mission by 31 December 2014.[1] This situation has shifted international focus to the political solution of the Afghan conflict.

In Afghanistan, political leaders missed emerging opportunities and failed to rise above factional and ethnic rivalries in the interest of building national institutions, upholding the rule of law and stabilising the country through democratic solutions. Despite significant progress in state building and steady economic growth, the politicisation of donors' aid and their alliance with abusive power brokers and warlords in the war against terrorists and insurgents undermined the development of effective state institutions and the rule of law. Consequently, the government now lacks credible institutional and political muscle to offset the influence of local power brokers. The situation promotes corruption that permeates not only governance but also the political and economic sectors and becomes a major hurdle in the way of achieving security and development. The main factors that plague the Afghan political scene today include weak state institutions, strong insurgents and opportunistic non-state patronage networks.

Therefore, the strategic context where the transition takes place is complicated and multi-dimensional. The interplay between the Afghan government, the armed opposition forces, the U.S.-led International Security Forces (ISAF) and other domestic and foreign actors who are aligned directly or indirectly with the three major players will shape the future of Afghanistan as a state and as a geographic area with the potential to prevent or facilitate trans-national terrorist attacks. A military-security transition in 2014, therefore, is not a guarantee for peace and stability in Afghanistan without a meaningful reform in the Afghan government. Nor does a peace deal with the Taliban by itself promise sustainable peace in the region.

Sustainable peace in Afghanistan can be achieved only through the establishment of an 'end state' that is acceptable to the Afghan people while it does not undermine the legitimate security interests of other actors in the region and beyond. This necessitates addressing legitimate national, regional and international concerns emanating from the Afghanistan situation. Given the local and regional political and security dynamics, the transition process is going to be multi-dimensional, complex, and nonlinear.

The key to achieving this goal is predicated on a number of assumptions:

- The Afghan National Security Forces (ANSF) attain the capacity to deal with the security threats independently or with a reduced presence of U.S. troops
- The reconciliation process in Afghanistan moves forward to a point that leads to a reduced level of threat

- Taliban sanctuaries in Pakistan are removed or minimised through cooperation of Pakistan Government
- Progress toward implementing political reforms pledged by the Afghan government as part of the *inteqal* process and making the government accountable and representative.

## Building Indigenous Security Capacity

The U.S.-led military strategy envisions reversing the momentum of the insurgents and drawing them to the negotiation table allowing a gradual drawdown of U.S. forces and shifting the security responsibility to the ANSF as they progressively become more capable of doing the job. The projected target date for this shift is 2014.[2] Establishing long-term security will therefore require a professional, enduring, self-sustaining ANSF. The U.S.-led counterinsurgency strategy supported by a military surge in 2009-10 has blunted the insurgents' momentum in key areas and helped significant buildup of ANSF. These gains are real but reversible.

Despite a major effort by the NATO Training Mission in Afghanistan (NTM-A) in recent years, the development of the institutional capacity of the ANSF will take years. It has only been since 2008 that serious commitments have been made and adequate resources invested to create an effective Afghan National Army (ANA) and Afghan National Police (ANP); so the force has a long way to go before it becomes fully capable of operating independently. The total strength of the ANSF in October 2011 reached 306,903 (170,781 soldiers and 136,122 policemen).[3] Future plans envisage an increase to 352,000 personnel (195,000 ANA and 157,000 ANP) by October 2012. Final ANSF end-strength post-2014, however, remains to be determined by prevailing security, political and financial conditions.

There are a number of major challenges facing the development of the ANSF. Achieving the goals of the transition depends on responding to these challenges:

**First,** given the training facilities, available funds and abundance of volunteer recruits, the ANSF development goals can be easily met numerically. But what will make the ANSF a formidable force is its quality, including its professional and institutional capability and its capacity to function in an unstable and conflict-ridden environment. Furthermore, its effectiveness also depends on simultaneous development of other government institutions. This means the ANSF is years away from becoming a fully effective force. There is no guarantee that the ANSF will be able to take the lead in fighting the Taliban by 2014. The ANSF is also handicapped by limited fire power and 'enablers'—particularly logistics, intelligence capability, protected ground mobility and airlift capacity. Building an effective air force will take much longer as the Afghan Air Force is expected to become a professional, fully independent, operationally capable, and sustainable force by 2016. However, it will be mostly for transportation and logistics, with no significant combat capability.[4]

A report on Afghanistan from the U.S. Department of Defense (DoD) states that the Afghan security forces remain too dependent on coalition forces. According to assessments made in October 2011, some 582 army and police units in Afghanistan required assistance from coalition forces. Only one unit is assessed as capable of operating independently.[5] Meanwhile, more than half of the police and army units require coalition soldiers to fight alongside them. Only one-third is effective with just military advisers in support.[6]

**Second,** while the Afghan National Army (ANA) is somehow ethnically balanced, it is not a universally representative force. The insurgency infested southern Pashtun provinces are not proportionally represented in the army. Further, factional leaders in the government compete in appointing officers from their patronage networks in key positions under the veneer of ethnic balancing. Consequently the perverted implementation of the ethnic balance system leads to factionalisation of the armed forces. This entails a potential risk of fragmentation of the ANA in case the government loses control.

**Third,** the professional capacity of the Afghan police is thwarted by several factors. While the NATO Training Mission in Afghanistan (NTM-A) has made major strides in building up security institutions, political influence of competing non-state patronage networks, power brokers, criminal networks and other interest groups has heavily politicized appointment of senior and mid-level police officials, which contributes to a decline of professionalism, job insecurity and corruption. Further, failure to dismantle illicit power structures with a criminal 'past—many of whom have legitimized themselves as 'private security companies'—adds to security risks and ineffective response to threats.

**Fourth,** the lack of cohesiveness of intelligence institutions and investigative policing has failed on many occasions to detect security threats in time and take preventive action. In 2008, the Taliban planned and successfully carried out a brazen attack to free prisoners from the main prison in Kandahar. The operation that took the insurgents weeks to prepare was not detected and might actually have been covered up by local and national intelligence agencies. Intelligence agencies are fragmented and spying on their own citizens while the police are being trained as a counterinsurgency fighting force.

**Fifth,** another challenge is the Afghan government's ability to sustain the ANSF. It is expected that by 2014 the annual cost of the security forces will amount to more than six billion dollars and 4.1 billion for a reduced ANSF by 2017, which is way beyond the Afghan budget. The International Monetary Fund (IMF) has concluded that the Afghan government will be incapable of paying ANSF costs until at least 2023.[7] This means that Afghanistan will need long-term international assistance to pay for its army and police unless it manages to work with a smaller security force, which is not likely in the absence of a peace settlement. Failure to pay the troops can have grave consequences with a possibility of disintegration along ethnic and factional lines.

**Finally,** the public allegiance to the government and its institutions is the key to success in controlling violence, crime and terrorism in counterinsurgency operations. Security cannot be achieved merely through creating police and army units. It also requires winning the trust of the population through addressing public grievances caused by the weakness of the rule of law and rampant official corruption. Corruption is fuelled by an 'accommodating' style adopted by the Afghan leadership and its international partners with local power holders and patronage networks. This approach is based on the mistaken belief that co-opting these groups can avert instability. Instead, pervasive levels of corruption are leading to resistance to reform, undermining state-building efforts, and contributing more broadly to instability. In April 2011, nearly 500 Taliban prisoners escaped through a long tunnel dug from outside the jail. The audacious move showed once again the lack of public trust in security forces and corrupt government officials. It took the militants more than five months to dig the 300-metre tunnel under the prison and ferrying more than 450 inmates out took over four hours. Yet there was no action from the prison guards, whom many suspect were bribed. No one from the local population bothered to report obvious signs of the militant activity to officials, whom they do not trust.

Given the long-term security commitment of NATO, including the residual presence of international forces beyond 2014; and assumed development of ANSF, there is strong hope that the government will not collapse as some pessimistic projections suggest. The least the ANSF can do is to build a capacity by 2014 to ensure survival of the regime. However sustained viability of the Afghan government depends on reform in governance that wins the trust of the people and generates hope for the future.

## Prospects for Political Settlement

The gap between the assumed level of threat and the capacity of the Afghan security forces to meet them by 2014 is expected to be wide and real. No equivalent and sustainable international forces will be available to fill the gap. Therefore, achieving a political settlement to end the conflict or make it manageable by the Afghan security forces is seen as a pressing need and a strategic imperative.

Prospects for political settlement are linked to progress in the military situation on the ground, addressing the grievances that fuel the insurgency and improvements in good governance and the rule of law. Cooperation from the neighbours, particularly Pakistan, where the insurgents' sanctuaries are based, is also essential for achieving peace in Afghanistan.

There are a number of uncertainties and challenges facing the reconciliation process. In spite of an increasing international momentum in support of seeking a peace settlement in Afghanistan the efforts so far have been fragmented, uncoordinated and lack transparency. The Afghan government has been involved for several years in contacting selective Taliban members with no tangible results. Even with the appointment of a 70-member High Peace Council (HPC), the Afghan leadership has failed to identify credible interlocutors, their agenda and their legitimacy for peace talks. Such contacts suffered a major setback in September 2011 with the assassination of the chief Afghan government negotiator, the former president Burhanuddin Rabbani, by a suicide bomber posing as a Taliban peace emissary.

Meanwhile, the insurgents are fragmented and influenced by Pakistani intelligence in varying degrees. Inside Afghanistan, the 'Taliban' has become a brand name for various groups who pursue different agendas. An array of opportunists ranging from political factions to criminal groups and tribal networks, as well as aggrieved communities and ill-treated tribes call themselves part of the Taliban not because they share their ideology and ethos, but to legitimize themselves and their struggle.

The main questions concern who represents the Taliban and what peace means to different parties to the conflict. The U.S.-backed move to open a Taliban representative office in Qatar, endorsed by Kabul and the Taliban representatives is expected to serve as a means to identify the armed opposition and its legitimate interlocutors.[8] Most importantly, the move could be used as a test of whether the Taliban are serious about peace or they are using the opportunity for tactical gains. In either case, the attempt is worthwhile. Only time will tell whether the Taliban are really interested in peace negotiation or they use the contacts with the U.S. to buy time and attain tactical gains. There is little evidence that the insurgents have changed their basic demands—they have publicly stated that the talks do not mean the end of violence and they are in no position to accept the Afghan constitution which is one of the main demands of the Afghan government and its international partners.

Washington's recent heightened sense of urgency to engage with the Taliban stokes up Afghanistan's volatile ethnic politics. Seen as a means of U.S. exit strategy and an instrument of maintaining power by President Karzai, certain opposition forces dispute the timing of the peace initiative, arguing that conditions on the ground are not conducive to achieving a desirable outcome via talks with the Taliban. They support a longer counterinsurgency operation by NATO in Afghanistan, and the creation of a much stronger and effective Afghan security force that will ensure negotiations are undertaken from a position of strength. There are other patronage networks in Afghanistan who fear losing their privileged status to a peace settlement, and who therefore oppose reconciliation with the Taliban.

Even those who support the peace talks have suspicions about the U.S. exclusive contacts with the Taliban in Qatar without Afghan government participation. The suspicions are mostly about the real purpose of the talks and whether a U.S.-Taliban deal to facilitate a NATO exit strategy is the real focus. Obviously peace in Afghanistan cannot come through a deal between the U.S.

and the Taliban although the Taliban prefer to engage the Americans for what other parties cannot deliver, i.e., easing military operations and freeing Taliban prisoners. So, if and when the legitimate representatives of the Taliban get engaged in serious talks for peace, the process should become an Afghan-owned and Afghan-led process with the participation of the U.S. and possibly Pakistan.

A political settlement in Afghanistan is an efficient means of achieving U.S. strategic objectives that seek preventing the use of the Afghan territory by international terrorism and securing sustainable stability in the region. The settlement will significantly lower U.S. short-term military costs in Afghanistan and its long-term financial expenses to sustain Afghanistan national security forces. However, given the reducing influence as the troops drawdown proceeds coupled with political and financial pressure at home, there is a narrowing window for the United States to achieve a negotiated settlement from a position of relative strength. This explains the urgency of recent U.S. efforts to push for negotiation with the Taliban. Given the U.S. rush for a deal from a weakening position, where is the real incentive for the Taliban to seriously negotiate? There is a risk of realities being eclipsed by bureaucratic achievements.

There is a close link between the political strategy of negotiation and military action on the ground. Historically, negotiated ends to insurgencies have taken an extended amount of time and have been conducted in parallel with ongoing combat operations. So, in either strategy, talks and fighting are likely to go on simultaneously for some time until an environment conducive to a sustainable settlement, including local or general ceasefire, is created. This concept underpins the so-called 'fight, talk and build' approach recently promoted by the United States.

Still there are real risks that the peace process may not succeed by 2014, either because of Taliban disinterest or a lack of commitment to the process by local and regional actors. In this case the strategy should anticipate a longer and greater international engagement until it achieves a military situation that can be managed by the Afghan security forces. This highlights the strategic significance of the recent strategic partnership pact between the United States and Afghanistan that was signed in May 2012.[9] The pact is expected to be supplemented by a Bilateral Security Agreement within a year that could include a residual U.S. military presence (possibly 20,000 to 30,000 troops) beyond 2014.

Obviously peace talks are simply a means to an end while the end is a peace settlement that is legitimate, inclusive and sustainable; a settlement that all Afghans are willing to accept and the regional countries endorse. Any settlement needs to address grievances that fuelled the insurgency, such as corruption, injustice, political exclusion, and marginalisation. Such an accord is not just about a deal with the Taliban or Pakistan. The settlement should clearly define an end-state that Afghans are willing to support. Covert talks with the Taliban by armed parties (including the U.S. and Afghan governments) could alienate a substantial portion of the country's leadership and be extremely divisive. The lack of public trust in the Kabul government and deepening suspicions among the Afghan political forces require multi-level negotiations that are a part of any peace talk strategy. The Afghan government needs to become reconciled with its own people in order to create a strong constituency for supporting a peace settlement.

## The Role of Regional Actors

The role of Afghanistan's neighbours—particularly Pakistan—and other regional powers is essential in reaching a sustainable peace settlement. Despite the regional support for peace and stability in Afghanistan, the reconciliation process has been mired in the complexities of regional and global politics. The main challenge is how to overcome the competing security interests of regional actors in support of a coordinated regional engagement. Islamabad is seen as a most influential player in ending the insurgency in Afghanistan because of its links to Afghan insurgents that use safe havens in Pakistan in their cross border attacks. India and Pakistan see stability in Afghanistan in the context of their regional geopolitical interests. Pakistan would support a peace settlement that provides Islamabad with some political leverage in Kabul and limits Indian influence in Afghanistan. India opposes a political settlement with the Taliban that would lead to a surge of Pakistani influence there. Iran sees the situation in Afghanistan in the context of its frayed relations with the United States and maintaining a sphere of influence in Afghanistan. Like India, Iran would also oppose a political settlement in Afghanistan that empowers the Taliban in parts of the country bordering Iran, and which leads to Pakistani influence in the area. Other regional powers including China, Russia and the Central Asian states support a peace settlement in Afghanistan if that will stabilize the country and deny space to militant groups for potential transnational acts of terrorism.

Meanwhile, the spectre of possible regional instability caused by the chaotic situation in Afghanistan following the withdrawal of U.S. forces has created a new momentum for regional cooperation in support of transition in Afghanistan. Nevertheless, regional actors continue to hedge their bets amidst the uncertain future in Afghanistan. The lack of clarity of U.S. long-term strategy in the region fuels these doubts. While most countries in the immediate neighbourhood of Afghanistan do not favour a fast-paced withdrawal of U.S. forces, they have questions about the purpose of the American residual presence in the area. Both concerns could work in support of cooperation in bringing stability to Afghanistan, and sustain it by building indigenous capacity in the country.

While creating a regional mechanism to facilitate the end of war in Afghanistan is not expected to come any time soon, bilateral diplomacy between Afghanistan and its immediate neighbours coupled with strengthening international security and financial commitment to Afghanistan far beyond 2014 may change the strategic calculus of regional actors in support of peace and stability in Afghanistan. This underlines the significance long-term strategic partnership between the United States and Afghanistan and similar agreements with other major NATO countries including U.K., Germany, France and Italy.

## Government

Reform and improvements in the structure and function of the government in Afghanistan is the key to stability and peace. During the past 50 years, insurgencies have most often failed to defeat effective governments. Governments defeat themselves more often than they are defeated by a dominant insurgency.[10] The failure of government to address the root causes of the insurgency, as well as its loss of control over territory—particularly rural areas—helps the insurgents.

Emerging from decades of war and violence, Afghanistan is confronted with an array of interrelated political, administrative, economic, and social challenges. During the past decade, the country has made major strides in its political transition to democracy and in rebuilding state institutions such as its national security forces. The government's legitimacy has been supported by the political participation of all domestic stakeholders in adopting the constitution and holding presidential and legislative elections. Yet the inability of the government to deliver services and exert influence throughout the country has eroded its structural legitimacy. Consequently, government administration is far from effective, and suffers from a number of systemic and institutional weaknesses, particularly at the sub-national level, where the vacuum is filled by insurgents, militia commanders, and local criminal gangs, all of whom undermine human security, local governance, democratic values, and the provision of basic services.

For the Afghan Government to become a key factor in mobilising the Afghan people to bring in peace and stability, it needs to reform itself. The reform should be based on what the Afghan Government pledged during the Kabul International Conference in the summer of 2010 to implement a new approach termed as a 'whole of the state' approach and 'whole of government' path to national renewal. The essence of the 'whole of the state' is constitutionalism: to strengthen each of the three branches of the government and to reinforce the constitutional checks and balances that guarantee and enforce citizens' rights and obligations. However, little change has occurred so far. The long drawn stand-off between the executive, legislative and judiciary last year has created a serious constitutional crisis in the country that threatens the very foundation of democratic institutions.

The essence of the 'whole of government' approach is structural reform to create an effective, accountable and transparent government that can deliver services to the population and safeguard national interests. Together, these complementary approaches, by putting people at the core, are the key to stability and prosperity.[11] In concrete terms, government reform requires a series of short term and long-term corrective measures, including: improving the centre–periphery relationship; establishing checks and balances on executive power; improving government service-delivery capacity; enforcing the rule of law; and fighting corruption.

The peace settlement in Afghanistan will inevitably entail changes in the structure and functions of the government and state institutions. Such changes should lead to an end state that all Afghans can support not as a deal between the U.S. and the Taliban or a deal between President Karzai and the insurgents. Unless the peace settlement guarantees the major political, social, and economic achievements of the past ten years there is little hope that any peace deal would sustain.

The security transition in 2014 coincides with the Presidential election in Afghanistan. As the Afghan constitution does not allow President Karzai to run for a third term, a smooth transition of power to a new elected president and an expansion of the political basis of the government will have a positive impact on the democratic stabilisation of the country. Any attempts by the government to delay the elections as part of a deal with the Taliban or some other 'creative' measures such as a staged 'Loya Jirga' to rubber stamp an unconstitutional move, the country could slide back into its troubled past when leaders were reluctant to transfer power peacefully, plunging the country into renewed civil strife. A serious effort by national and international actors is needed to lay the groundwork for a trouble-free transition.

There are also calls by some political forces for amending the constitution to change the presidential government system to parliamentary system and elect local governments through provincial and district elections. There is also strong opposition against such drastic shifts in the absence of strong national political parties, lack of security and the dominance of the political scene by corrupt patronage networks and abusive power brokers. There is a need to look at possible changes in the context of current political situation in Afghanistan and the lessons from the country's immediate past.

Traditionally, Afghanistan has had a unitary state system. The central government has often been weak, but the peripheries were weaker and favoured the presence of some central authority as a power balancer and political arbitrator. The breakdown of central authority, during three decades of conflict and violence, stimulated a socio-political transformation which vitalized regional patronage networks under the leadership of regional commanders who often invoked ethnic references to legitimize their leadership. This situation, in the absence of a viable state, fuelled ethno-regional competition for power and resource distribution. However, abuse of power and infighting among local strongmen eroded their legitimacy and diminished support for decentralisation of power. This was clearly reflected in the overwhelming support for maintaining the unitary state structure led by a powerful president via the new constitution adopted in 2004. The constitution gives wide authority to the president, including the appointment of all mid- and senior-level officials down to the district level, and nearly all revenue generation powers are retained by the central government.

The Afghan government system suffers from negative impacts of centralisation and decentralisation of power at the same time. A too centralised power structure is not capable to deliver services to the peripheries while provincial and district governors have the opportunity to tap into non-state patronage networks and act outside the rule of law with relative impunity. The government consists of a wide range of formal bodies at the presidential, parliamentary, provincial, district, municipal, and community levels. However, these bodies and leaders are largely ineffective at governing owing to conflicting roles and responsibilities, a highly centralised decision-making and appointments authority, and few means for the Afghan people to hold their central and local leaders accountable for their actions.

In order to empower local government, including provincial and district governments, there is a need to delegate some administrative and fiscal authority and service-delivery resources to the periphery. This will give resources to local governments to respond to immediate local needs and deliver services in a more effective and efficient way. In the short-term, it can be done within the existing constitution. In the future, more drastic changes may require constitutional amendments, particularly in the context of the national reconciliation process. In order to establish meaningful checks and balances on executive power, the role of parliament and other elected bodies such as provincial, district and village councils (*shuras*), as well as the civil society should be expanded.

## Setting the Agenda

Given an array of deep-seated domestic, regional and global issues surrounding the Afghan conflict, Afghanistan's transition to a peaceful end-state is expected to be a complex, lengthy, and multi-faceted process. Nevertheless, the spectre of ever-increasing instability in the region, caused by continued insecurity in Afghanistan, has created incentives at local and international levels to pursue a more comprehensive and consistent strategy to end the conflict.

The strategy to achieve this goal must be an inclusive, fully-resourced and flexible response with realistic timelines. Flexible response to face security challenges in Afghanistan and shaping the strategic environment for a sustainable transition to peace requires an integrated approach combining the military strategy with political and developmental strategies. A political strategy of negotiation should not be seen as an alternative approach but rather as a complementing effort. A political strategy is not making a deal with the Taliban but should address the root causes of conflict and drivers of insecurity to include the state structure, governance and economic development that contribute to sustainable peace.

Finally, there is a need to emphasize on the development of sustainable and effective national security forces, good governance and the rule of law, and to address the key grievances that fuel insurgency. In concrete terms, government reform requires a series of short-term and long-term corrective measures, including: improvement in the centre–peripheries relationship; establishing checks and balances on executive power; improving government service-delivery capacity; enforcing the rule of law; and fighting corruption.

## NOTES

1. *Chicago Summit Declaration on Afghanistan—Issued by the Heads of State and Government of Afghanistan and Nations contributing to the NATO-led International Security Assistance Force (ISAF)*, 21 May 2012, http://www.nato.int/cps/en/natolive/official_texts_87595.htm. Accessed on 23 May 2012.
2. "Obama's Address on the War in Afghanistan" at the U.S. Military Academy, West Point, NY, 1 December 2009, transcript published in *New York Times*, 1 December 2009, http://www.nytimes.com/2009/12/02/world/asia/02prexy.text.html#. Accessed on 23 May 2012.
3. *Year in Review November 2009-November 2010*, NATO Training Mission in Afghanistan (NTM-A), pp.7–8; and *Report on Progress Toward Security and Stability in Afghanistan*, U.S. Department of Defense, April 2012, p.13, http://www.defense.gov/pubs/pdfs/Report_Final_SecDef_04_26_10.pdf. Accessed on 23 May 2012.
4. *Year in Review, November 2009 – November 2010*. op.cit. pp.4–5.
5. *Report on Progress Toward Security and Stability in Afghanistan*, U.S. Department of Defense, October 2011, pp. 43–45, http://www.defense.gov/pubs/pdfs/October_2011_Section_1230_Report.pdf. Accessed on 23 May 2012.
6. *Report on Progress Toward Security and Stability in Afghanistan and Unites States Plan for Sustaining the Afghanistan National Security Forces*, U.S. Department of Defense, April 2011, pp.14–17, http://www.defense.gov/news/1230_1231Report.pdf. Accessed on 21 May 2012.
7. *Sustainability: Hidden Costs Risk New Waste*, Commission on Wartime Contracting in Iraq and Afghanistan Special Report, 3 June 2011, p. 3.
8. "Taliban Say Office in Qatar Has Been Agreed", *Reuters*, 3 January 2012 http://www.reuters.com/article/2012/01/03/us-afghanistan-taliban-idUSTRE8020EJ20120103. Accessed on 21 May 2012. and Matthew Rosenberg, "Taliban to Open Qatar Office in Step Toward Peace Talks", *New York Times*, 3 January 2012.
9. *Enduring Strategic Partnership Agreement between the United States of America and the Islamic Republic of Afghanistan*, http://www.whitehouse.gov/sites/default/files/2012.06.01u.s.-afghanistanspasignedtext.pdf. Accessed on 21 May 2012.
10. Ben Connable and Martin C. Libicki, *How Insurgencies End*, RAND Corporation, 2010, p.153, http://www.rand.org/content/dam/rand/pubs/monographs/2010/RAND_MG965.pdf. Accessed on 21 May 2012.
11. *A Renewed Commitment by the Afghan Government to the Afghan People* and *A Renewed Commitment by the International Community to Afghanistan*, Kabul Conference communiqué, Kabul, 20 July 2010.

# 3

# Peace, Reconciliation and Reintegration in Afghanistan: Challenges and Milestones Facing Peace Talks, Transition and Stability in the Region

*Mohammad Masoom Stanekzai*

## Introduction

After nearly a decade of joint efforts by the Government of Afghanistan and the international community to rebuild the war-torn nation, Afghanistan is entering one of its most crucial phases. To date, considerable progress has been made on several fronts, including infrastructure development, governance, institutional reform, health, education as well as in the political environment enabling Afghans to participate in the political system through democratic processes. However, enormous challenges remain ahead.

Despite notable progress in the security sector and building the capabilities of Afghan national security institutions, provision of security to Afghan people which is their fundamental desire and a national priority still remains a goal yet to be achieved. In fact, with each passing year since 2005, the efforts to expand the authority of the central government beyond the provincial centers were challenged by increased levels of security threats which expanded to areas that were previously peaceful.[1] As President Karzai acknowledged in his speech at the Traditional Loya Jirga[2] on 15 November 2011, "While we made much progress in many areas that we can be proud of, I must admit that we failed to bring security to our people". Efforts to reverse this trend were largely reactive and disconnected from broader governance, justice and political processes, including the pace of economic development and job creation.

It was, however, only in the beginning of 2010 that the international community started to align its efforts behind the vision that was laid out by President Karzai in his inauguration speech for his second term in office. This vision was largely defined by five strategic goals: (1) achieve Afghan sovereignty through transition of responsibility to the Afghan security forces and strengthen the capacity and capabilities of civil-military institutions; (2) initiate an inclusive political process that provides opportunities for Afghans to reconcile and reintegrate to their communities and live in peace with each other; (3) improve governance at the national and sub-national levels through building human resources and fighting corruption; (4) provide increased investment opportunities in key sectors such as agriculture, water, mining, energy, infrastructure health and education as well as promote private sector growth; and (5) strengthen regional cooperation and international long-term partnership.

In 2011, for the first time, the deterioration of security started to reverse as a result of a pragmatic approach, emergence of consensus for peace, and proactive initiatives around these key strategic goals including military surge by the Afghan and international forces combined with wider efforts to improve governance and development.

In the search for lasting security and stability in Afghanistan, it is important to bear in mind that the conflict in Afghanistan is driven by a combination of external and internal factors that interact in complex ways. It will, therefore, be simplistic to attribute the conflict to one militant group and its support system across the Afghanistan-Pakistan border. Key factors include rampant poverty, unemployment, poor governance combined with social and political problems, the lucrative illicit drug trade, criminal networks and grievances related to the legacy of the past three decades of war inherited by the current administration. Mistakes committed by international military forces during night raids and search operations resulting in civilian casualties has been another important external factor that contributed to the public anxiety and has been widely used by insurgents in their propaganda to attract young recruits.

Perhaps the most pervasive and seemingly intricate factor remains the support to the insurgency from syndicates of extremist networks operating with or without the direct support of state actors in Pakistan. Their cross border operation seriously challenges the efforts to achieve durable peace in Afghanistan. Despite consistent bilateral, trilateral, multilateral initiatives and international diplomatic efforts to build confidence and encourage Pakistan to change its duplicitous policy towards Afghanistan, insurgency continues to enjoy support and access to safe havens on the other side of the border. This situation is further complicated by rivalries among regional players with conflicting interests seeking to achieve strategic positioning by using Afghanistan as battleground.

Moreover, given the inter-linkages between the issues in Afghanistan and the outside world, global events may also play a part in shaping the current and future political environment in Afghanistan. 2011 was also a turbulent year for many countries in the region and around the world. In addition to the continuation of violence in Afghanistan and Pakistan, the global economic crisis, the spread of violence in the region, and the Arab Spring are factors that in one way or another, have impacted on the developments in Afghanistan. Recent events such as the political and social upheaval arising in a number of Arab countries, for instance, have captivated the attention of the international community especially Afghanistan's key western partners which could potentially result in shifting priorities and resources.

Recent developments (both positive and negative) have led to a paradoxical situation where there is a mixed perception of progress and challenges in stabilizing Afghanistan. On the one hand, reduction in violence and improvement in security largely due to combined political and military efforts demonstrates progress; on the other hand, the increased number of spectacular attacks by anti-government elements (AGE) on high profile targets in large cities, including assassinations of senior government officials, political and tribal leaders, and religious scholars aimed largely at spreading fear and gaining media attention shows the severity of challenges ahead and undermines the perception of progress.

Afghanistan entered the year 2012 after a series of significant domestic roadblocks, such as issues related to the 2010 parliamentary elections and the protracted Kabul Bank/IMF crisis. However, events such as the Traditional Loya Jirga, the second Bonn Conference and most recently the Chicago Conference where the international community reaffirmed its commitment to remain engaged well beyond 2014, provided a powerful message regarding the future of Afghanistan. The outcome of these historic events which emphasised Afghan sovereignty, strong future partnership and inclusiveness of the political process, serve as a warning to spoilers not to wait for 2014 as the endgame.

There is a broad consensus among Afghans that security and stability as well as Afghan sovereignty cannot be achieved only through military means, so there is a need to end the decades-long conflict through combined social, military and development efforts and an inclusive political solution that is led and owned by Afghans. The underlying belief is that Afghanistan cannot afford another failure and cannot go back to the experience of the 90s, as it will also have dire consequences both for the region and for the rest of the international community. Thus, the more realistic the political process becomes, the greater the prospects for ending the war and violence. Reconciliation efforts that can pave the way for a possible political settlement[3] under the Afghan constitution must therefore be accelerated. The more the peace negotiations are delayed; the higher the cost for securing a lasting peace. In light of the outcome of the Traditional Loya Jirga in November 2011, time is now ripe for serious efforts towards launching high-level peace talks.

Thus, 2012-14 are crucial years for Afghanistan to successfully implement the transition process, which was endorsed at the North Atlantic Treaty Organisation (NATO) Lisbon Summit in November 2010. Undoubtedly, the year 2014 will be of special importance as the security and economic impact of drawdown will surface, elections will be held, and rivalries among key regional players will intensify for re-positioning of power and influence in a post-2014 scenario. Both the Afghan government and its international partners must therefore work closely and pursue joint efforts to ensure that this transition is smooth and that these processes are not undermined by spoilers.

Following this period and as agreed at the Bonn II Conference, the period between 2014 and 2024 will serve as the "Transformational Decade" to reach a goal of a sovereign and peaceful Afghanistan. Achieving sustained stability and durable peace in Afghanistan will require meaningful progress in the five strategic areas outlined by President Karzai in his 2009 inaugural speech as well as initiatives to secure public confidence and change perception of the populace. There is a need for joint efforts to address some of the potential challenges of the period up to and beyond 2014.

Some of the immediate measures may include: First, building public confidence as an essential step to move the peace, reconciliation and reintegration process forward through extensive and sustained outreach efforts. Second, replacing the current violence with meaningful negotiations and overcome the environment of fear and terror. Third, engaging the Afghans in a constructive dialogue on a number of strategic issues. This could include efforts to promote understanding between Afghanistan and the regional countries about the intention of the international security forces' presence in Afghanistan; providing assurances that Afghanistan is not occupied nor the presence of the international forces will be a threat to other countries, and that they will leave Afghanistan based on an agreed framework. Fourth, mobilising Ulema and religious leaders across the country to promote the message of peace and stress that the continuation of fighting in Afghanistan cannot be justified as *Jihad* but rather it is a *Fitna*.[4]

These efforts, combined with both top down and bottom up approaches by the government, will contribute to the success of the peace process, however, real success can only be achieved when Afghanistan's neighbours stop interfering in its affairs and support the peace process; and the international community stands by its commitment not to abandon Afghanistan once again.

This chapter provides a brief overview of the current Afghan peace, reconciliation, and reintegration process, including some of the achievements, challenges, and future prospects. It will also offer some insights on the key measures and priorities for the Afghanistan Peace and Reintegration Program (APRP) that can act as "enablers" for achieving a successful transition. Finally, it will conclude with some possible scenarios of what Afghanistan will look like in the near term (2012-14) and long term (2014 and beyond).

## Afghan Peace, Reconciliation, and Reintegration Process

In his inauguration speech in November 2009, President Karzai declared peace and national reconciliation as the central priority of his second term in office. The initial concept of the Afghan-led peace, reconciliation and re-integration program was presented in January 2010 at the London International Conference where an agreement for establishing a Trust Fund to support peace initiatives was also reached subject to the development of a detailed program document. Later in the same year, the government held a Consultative Peace Jirga (CPJ) in order to seek consensus from Afghans around the country to pursue a political solution to the enduring conflict in Afghanistan. At the CPJ on June 2-4, 2010, the Afghan representatives agreed that the government and all the parties in the conflict should negotiate an end to the violence by working together with all stakeholders, including civil society, in the interest of peace.

While past efforts at achieving peace through political talks and reintegration of combatants had fallen short largely due to inconsistency of efforts, lack of political will, resources and more importantly the predominant belief and insistence on military solution to the conflict,[5] the consultative Peace Jirga, called for a new commission composed of respected tribal elders, religious and political leaders, women, and prominent Afghan personalities to guide peace efforts. This was reaffirmed at the Kabul Conference in July 2010, attended by over 70 foreign ministers from around the world, where the government presented a new program to revitalize and support peace efforts—the Afghanistan Peace and Reintegration Program (APRP)—which would be led by the HPC and supported by the international community.

Importantly, the Kabul Conference also presented the broad outline of 22 National Priority Programs (NPPs), which served as the government's three-year prioritised development plan to strengthen its capacity across a number of sectors to deliver services to the Afghan population. In many respects, the Kabul Conference represented a "transition moment" for the government in the non-security areas, as it called for 80 per cent of donor assistance to be aligned with Afghan priorities (as defined through the NPPs) and 50 per cent to be brought 'on-budget' and channeled through government ministries and systems. Though discussions between the government and the international community on transition were just beginning, the Kabul Conference was an important occasion to define support for Afghan-owned and Afghan-led initiatives and APRP was one of the most advanced and complicated NPPs. However, the Kabul process was negatively impacted by certain political and governance challenges including concerns about corruption mainly related to the Kabul Bank for the most part of 2011.

Fortunately, the Kabul Process has once again started to receive the attention it deserves and the Afghan people hope that the decisions of the Bonn-II will be translated into concrete sets of actions for successful transition and political stability. As follow up steps to Bonn–II, a series of events and conferences this year with focus on specific areas of support to Afghanistan—the Chicago Conference which took place in May was security focused where international support to ANSF was discussed, the Kabul regional conference known as the "Heart of Asia" held in June this year talked about regional cooperation and measures by key regional players in building confidence in the region, enhancing economic cooperation as well as supporting the political process in Afghanistan, and the Tokyo conference held in July this year where the International Community reaffirmed its commitment to Afghanistan beyond 2014 supporting economic development during the Transformation Decade. The announcement by the United States which came a day before the Tokyo Conference calling Afghanistan non-NATO ally, was another historic achievement for Afghanistan. These events will have both moral and material impact on the government's efforts for a peaceful future of Afghanistan.

## Formation and Structure of the High Peace Council

Following APRP's endorsement at the Kabul Conference and in accordance with the recommendations of the CPJ, the High Peace Council (HPC) was formed in October 2011 through a presidential decree. The HPC is a national-level body composed of respected *Jihadi*, political and community leaders, religious scholars, tribal elders, civil society and female representatives with the mandate to lead nation-wide political and social efforts in support of the peace, reconciliation and reintegration process. Although the structure, composition[6], and size of the council has been subject of constant debate, especially among civil society organizations (CSO), in particular after the assassination of its chair, the HPC has made notable progress in various fronts. Under the HPC's leadership, the APRP far exceeded its goals set for its first year of operations.

The HPC is a body of 70 members that has an Executive Board of 16 members, including a Chair and three Deputies, as well as a number of sub-committees to allow for expedited decision-making and follow through its initiatives. These sub-committees comprise of (1) Contact and Outreach committee, (2) International Relations committee, (3) Public Awareness committee, (4) Provincial Affairs committee, (5) Detainee Affairs committee, and (6) Grievance resolution committee. Nine out of seventy members of the HPC are women with various professional and academic credentials. They include women who are former and present parliamentarians, senators and members of civil society.

At the national level, HPC's efforts are concentrated on outreach, public awareness, confidence building and establishing contacts through engagement with provincial governors/officials, Ulema, religious scholars, civil society and local elders/leaders in order to promote public trust, communicate messages of peace and establish contacts with opposition groups. The underlying aim is to create conducive social and political conditions and provide opportunities for those who are willing to leave the vicious circle of violence and also to accelerate the process of transition.

The HPC is also extensively reaching out to the neighbouring as well as regional countries in order to build trust and promote cooperation in support of the peace process in Afghanistan. In this regard, its efforts supported by the international community over the past one year have generated a positive momentum in support of peace efforts and also in overcoming the obstacles that can stall a constructive dialogue among the Afghans.

Recognising the role of women in the peace process and given the importance of incorporating gender perspectives in the implementation of the program, women have played an instrumental role right from the design phase to the implementation of the Afghanistan Peace and Reintegration Programme (APRP). There is a strong emphasis within the HPC leadership that women's role and participation should not be symbolic, rather they should be involved in the decision making process as well as in the execution of the programs. In line with this view, a gender unit has been established within the APRP that works closely with the combined HPC-APRP-Civil Society Women Group (HACSWG). The group meets regularly to review progress on program delivery and make necessary recommendations. It has organised various forums and meetings with civil society organisations, women networks, Ulema, Academic Institutions, Youth groups and other national and international agencies. Members of the group have also participated in field visits and have travelled to various provinces.

Following the recent setbacks in the peace process, reconciliation and reintegration efforts are gradually gaining traction at all levels especially after the appointment of its new chairman, former HPC chairman Burhanuddin Rabbani's son, Salahuddin Rabbani. The long awaited appointment of the HPC chairman is seen as a positive step by the Afghan Government to revitalize peace efforts, streamline HPC activities and increase synergy of efforts. The approach of the High Peace Council in addressing the potential factors of conflict and instability in the country, to date, has been largely inclusive and comprehensive based on the underlying notion to end the decades long devastating conflict which has torn communities, destroyed infrastructure, and clouded the very aspirations of Afghans to harvest the fruits of a peaceful and stable country.

In accordance with the Afghan Government's peace and reconciliation strategy, peace efforts take place at two primary levels: (i) the strategic and political level, which include reconciliation talks with the senior members of the insurgency as well as mobilising regional cooperation and international support to the Afghan led peace process; and (ii) the national and sub-national level efforts, where the Afghan Government, High Peace Council, civil society and other stakeholders create a national support base and consensus around peace in Afghanistan and oversee reintegration of ex-combatants around the country. While HPC leads peace efforts at national level, peace committees are formed to lead these efforts at provincial level with provincial governors providing overall coordination and leadership.

Operationally, the APRP is managed in a phased approach and implemented in three main stages. (1) efforts are primarily focused on conducting outreach, establishing contacts, building confidence and undertaking negotiations; (2) demobilising ex-combatants, conducting vetting, managing weapon, and providing immediate support to those who join the peace process. This is a crucial stage for community engagement and addressing the grievances and peaceful reintegration; (3) APRP focuses on community recovery initiatives so that all members of the community where reintegration takes place can benefit.

Shortly after the establishment of the HPC, allies of the North Atlantic Treaty Organisation (NATO) and its partners to the mission in Afghanistan, which together composed 48 nations, convened in Lisbon, Portugal on November 19-20, 2010 to discuss the future of the international security mission in Afghanistan. The NATO members and the Government of Afghanistan reached an agreement that would pave the way for the transition of security responsibility to the Afghan National Security Forces (ANSF), the gradual drawdown of international troops, and their evolution to train and support mission. This process of transition (*inteqal*) began as early as mid-2011 and is expected to culminate in 2014.

The commencement of preparation for transition and its first initiatives coincided with the period when the APRP was setting up its program, recruiting staff, establishing provincial bodies, engaging with international partners, and seeking to build a national narrative for peace. When the announcement was made in June 2011 for the first tranche of provinces, districts and municipalities to be included in transition, conditions were mostly in place for the security responsibility to be passed to the ANSF, a shift that was marked in ceremonies in the seven designated areas. An increased coordination between the APRP and the Transition coordination commission has resulted in greater alignment of peace efforts with the transition priority areas, particularly for cities, districts, and provinces in the second phase of transition. Already anecdotal evidence suggests that a segment of combatants who are joining the peace process in recent months have done so because international forces have departed or intend to depart from their region. This shows tangible evidence of the synergy between the *inteqal* and peace process.

## Major Achievements of the Afghan Peace Process

Over that same period, the Afghan Government through the High Peace Council worked steadily to record achievements that would greatly exceed the expectations of the July 2010 Kabul Conference. APRP's goal for the first-year was to initiate program activities in eight provinces and officially enroll up to 1,000 reintegrees. Presently, the APRP is operating in every province, has established 31 Provincial Peace Committees (PPCs), which together with the Provincial Governors are responsible for the implementation of the peace process in their respective areas.

At the end of June 2012, the APRP has officially reintegrated over 5000 fighters from the battlefield, 10 percent of which is commanders and include high-ranking members of the Taliban and Hezb-e-Islami. These achievements have led to improvements in security conditions in certain areas, which is the real indicator of progress for the peace process. The challenge, however, is to prevent the reintegrees from returning back to the insurgency by offering meaningful alternative opportunities/livelihood at a time when provision of employment remains a key challenge for the government. The other challenge is to ensure the security and safety of those who join the peace process as conditions vary for ex-combatants who join the peace process in different areas of the country.[7]

One of the important components of the Afghan peace process is the community recovery programs (CRP) which provide both ex-combatants and the communities into which they reintegrate with locally planned and designed development programs in order to address their immediate development needs and lay the foundation for mid to long term development, providing a type of 'peace dividend.' Community recovery programs include both line ministry projects that work in support of APRP, as well as small grants projects that are designed and managed at the provincial level. These projects, in addition to those of line ministries, have directly benefited approximately 25,000 reintegrees and community members. Further, numerous outreach efforts by the APRP and the High Peace Council have taken place in the provinces to engage in local grievance resolution and build public confidence for the peace process.

As part of the HPC's efforts to engage non-governmental aspects of Afghan society and mobilize their support for the peace process, joint working groups (JWG) have also been established between the High Peace Council and civil society, academics, and parliament. These bodies provide a formal mechanism for the HPC to address certain concerns and ensure inclusion of alternate viewpoints on pursuing the peace process. While reintegration enjoys a relatively strong nation-wide support, there are still ambiguities and skepticisms about the reconciliation process at least among some civil society members and opposition groups. In an effort to partially address such concerns, as part of its outreach efforts, the High Peace Council has begun a consistent interaction with civil society organisations as well as Ulema and scholars by actively engaging them in debates, consultations and discussions. Representatives of these organisations meet regularly with HPC, discuss critical issues, exchange views and provide recommendations.

As an essential element of the government's campaign to promote regional cooperation in support of the peace process, HPC leadership has visited several neighbouring countries to build consensus and support for the peace process. This included several trips to Pakistan and high profile visits to Turkey, Turkmenistan, India, Iran, UAE, and Saudi Arabia. A Joint Afghan-Pakistan Peace Commission was established in March 2011, with the first official meeting taking place in Islamabad in June 2011, as an important confidence building measure to advance political discussions. Similarly, a Core Group (Afghanistan, Pakistan and U.S.) was established to review progress and recommend priorities for reaching a successful outcome of the peace process.[8]

Thus, the approach of the Afghan initiated and led peace process has been holistic, inclusive and comprehensive. In addition to actively reintegrating fighters, the APRP's outreach efforts have built confidence, mobilised communities, and promoted coordination and collaboration among state and non-state institutions both at the center and provincial level. These efforts were instrumental in creating momentum and a sense of urgency to end the decades-long violence and bloodshed, and restore peace and harmony to communities. Indeed, these important achievements within a short span of time have created great hope within Afghan society and its international partners about the prospects for moving forward in the political process. This does not necessarily suggest that the process will be simple. In fact, it is much more complicated than expected and achieving real progress will take time and effort.

## The Assassination of HPC Chairman Burhanuddin Rabbani and Future of the HPC

The tragic assassination of HPC Chairman Professor Burhanuddin Rabbani represented a serious setback to the peace process in Afghanistan, which reignited the debate within Afghanistan on the prospects for peace and the appropriate strategy toward that goal. On November 16, 2011, H.E. President Karzai placed this issue before the Traditional Loya Jirga, with the objective to formulate a national consensus on the way forward to advance the peace, reconciliation and reintegration process.

In the four days of consultations at the Traditional Loya Jirga, over 2,000Afghans from across the country including women and youth endorsed a number of recommendations regarding the future direction of the peace process and priorities for APRP, calling for more proactive measures, inclusiveness, and a practical approach informed by lessons of the past. The consultations at the November Loya Jirga resulted in a number of recommendations for the Afghan peace and reconciliation efforts.

As the peace process enters a new period following the Traditional Loya Jirga, the HPC will continue to evaluate its approach and progress. Success will be measured on the basis of overall improvements in security around the country, not simply the number of reintegrees. The underlying assumption of APRP is that peace process is an opportunity for all Afghans to participate in a political process, engage in the resolution of grievances, and mobilize support at the national and local levels, all of which will strengthen the position of the Afghan Government in negotiating peace.

Recent events such as the Istanbul Conference, Traditional Loya Jirga, Bonn II, the Chicago conference, were important opportunities for the government to reflect on its past policies and approach, particularly in light of the recent setbacks in peace efforts, and develop a consensus for a possible shift in the strategy of the peace process.

The recommendations that emerged from 2,000 participants at the Jirga became the new foundation for the way forward in Afghan political negotiations and the peace process in Afghanistan. Shortly after the event, the HPC General Assembly convened to discuss the conclusions of the Jirga and made recommendations to the President on the way forward in advancing peace efforts. The following principles, therefore, highlight important components of the government's new policy:

The peace process must:

- be Afghan-led and its outcome must reflect the desires of all Afghans;
- be inclusive and represent the legitimate interests of the people of Afghanistan, regardless of gender or social status;
- contain the renunciation of violence;
- include the cutting of ties with international terrorism;
- be guided by the Afghan constitution, including its human rights provisions, specifically the rights of women;
- offer due participation to all relevant forces; and
- be respected by regional countries, who should support the political process and endorse a political settlement.

The Loya Jirga also recommended greater focus at the sub-national level where reintegration occurs, including measures in strengthening local structures and capacity to lead the peace process and accelerating the delivery of community recovery programs to the ex-combatants and communities who have made the definitive choice for a peaceful future.

Moreover, the Afghan Government's new policy affirms that reconciliation and reintegration are integral parts of the Afghan-led political process, and that high-level negotiations for reconciliation will only be possible with authorised negotiators who have proven identities and a clear address. Equally important is the safety and security of those involved in peace talks and the assurances in this regard. Successful peace-building in Afghanistan requires sincere and close cooperation with Pakistan in order to build trust and confidence for ending violence in both countries, particularly given that most of the insurgent leadership is based in Pakistan. Other neighbouring countries must also be brought onboard to demonstrate concrete measures of support, as any peace settlement cannot be achieved without their genuine commitment in relinquishing support to different political and insurgent groups.

According to the 11-point statement issued by the Afghan Government in January 2012 regarding the government's principles for talks, to begin negotiations, violence and fighting against the Afghan people and Afghan and international security forces by the insurgency should be ceased[9] and ties must be cut with Al-Qaeda and all other terrorist organisations. Moreover, in the process of conducting negotiations, the achievements of the past 10 years must be preserved, which include respect for and preservation of the Afghan constitution, Afghan national sovereignty, territorial integrity and national unity. Peace negotiations must be led by the Afghan Government, held by known representatives of the insurgency, and supported by regional countries especially Pakistan. Finally, no country should intervene in this process, without the agreement of the Afghan Government as after all, it is an inter-Afghan dialogue and the outcome must be based on the desires of the Afghans while international and regional support will remain critical for a successful outcome.

In line with these principles, a number of practical measures that can help facilitate peace negotiations, include de-listing the Afghan Taliban from the UN Security Council sanctions lists who are engaged in negotiations, and the resettlement of Taliban leaders who wish to join the peace process. The government, with support from its international partners, should also ensure the safety and security of those Afghans who join the peace process and provide necessary transition assistance.

In tandem to any high-level peace negotiations, a national political dialogue must be conducted to facilitate greater inclusiveness, maintain internal political support for key initiatives such as the peace process and transition, and help bind people to the state. It is important to give all groups the opportunity to engage in political dialogue and help achieve their political objectives through peaceful and democratic means. Afghan Ulema and tribal leaders, women and youth must be encouraged and engaged as important national partners in promoting a culture of peace, helping to unite society, and further eroding the relevance of groups who continue to pursue their goals through violent means.

To support these efforts, deliberate and focused attention must be paid to address and resolve grievances which may continue to be motivating factors for combatants. Community recovery activities will continue to play an important role in this regard, as they solidify reintegration by meeting the economic and social needs of reintegrees and their communities.

Given that several national and international actors are involved in the process, it is important that there is an effective coordination and information sharing process which will help maintain unity of messages. Finally, to effectively manage the diversity of interests of international and regional partners, the Afghan Government will need to employ an active diplomacy based on the fundamental principles agreed and commitments made at the Istanbul process, Bonn II conference, Chicago and Tokyo conferences where Istanbul and Bonn conferences have focused more on the policies guiding joint efforts, Chicago and Tokyo represent tangible demonstration of long-term international support for Afghanistan, which also sent a strong message to insurgents who may prefer to wait out the international community's withdrawal from Afghanistan.

## Challenges Facing the Peace Process

For all the achievements in the past year and with a new strategy in place, the Afghan peace process faces significant challenges. First, although the Traditional Loya Jirga was an opportunity to forge a new way forward for the peace process and the appointment of the new HPC chair was an important step in regaining the confidence, greater efforts are now needed to reach out to people and restore confidence following the assassination of Professor Rabbani.

Second, the peace process involves a set of complex and multi-dimensional efforts which will face setbacks and require patience and perseverance by all Afghans. It has been challenged by expectations for quick results within Afghan society and the international community. At the time of writing, there are doubts, suspicions and concerns about the outcome of the high level political talks among political circles and members of the civil society, particularly the women groups. These groups maintain fears of possible secret deals or the unpredicted outcome of a deal imposed on Afghans and influenced by the agenda of other countries.

There is no doubt about the existence, in Afghanistan, of certain networks and groups who benefit from the continuation of conflict and instability. There are also groups who may not simply like to talk with their past rivals as there are those who still dream of monopoly and return to the past without taking into consideration the ground realties that all Afghans should be provided equal opportunities to become part of the political and social landscape of an improved and acceptable political system in the country. There are certain Afghan politicians who are generally supportive of the peace efforts and stress the need to be in a position of strength to participate in peace negotiations, however they often fail to understand that in reality, through their rhetoric, they weaken such a position by damaging the unity of efforts behind critical national priority initiatives. Thus, lack of understanding, absence of political maturity among some political figures, and highly varied interests driven by short term personal gains, challenge meaningful progress in issues of national importance.

Third, Afghanistan has become a 'chess-board' of conflicting regional interests and rivalries where regional countries continue to provide support to individuals, groups and networks to serve as proxies for safeguarding their interests by promoting militancy, extremism and efforts to divide Afghans. Despite strong cultural and historic ties, relations with Pakistan, whose sincere cooperation is indispensable in ending support to the insurgency and persuading its leadership to participate in peace talks, have been strained and relatively unstable. Pakistan's policy towards Afghanistan remains largely ambiguous and its sincerity to support the Afghan political process has been seriously questioned by Afghans as well as in most diplomatic settings. Although the Afghan government supported several efforts since 2007 to build confidence and actively engage Pakistan in the political process including through bilateral and trilateral interactions in 2011, no real progress was achieved as a result. Thus, consistent and sincere partnership to end violence in both countries remains elusive, which weakens the negotiating position of the Afghan Government vis-à-vis insurgent leaders operating in both countries.

Fourth, as the center for gravity of reintegration efforts shifts to the provinces, the Provincial Peace Committees (PPC) will face challenges to provide adequate leadership and take the necessary responsibility, as their current levels of activity and capacity vary considerably. The APRP, together with its close partners, has been working to address these capacity constraints, which will require time, resources and constant engagement.

Fifth, though much progress has been made, the delivery of development projects by the line ministries and provincial governments have not taken place as quickly as expected and will remain a key area of focus in the near term. These development programs which are expressly designed to help address inequalities that are the drivers of grievances must be accelerated.

Sixth, despite the fact that Afghans are embracing the peace process, many still lack awareness about the APRP or remain skeptical based on experience with previous efforts. Moreover, there is generally lack of an effective communication strategy or if it exists it is not commonly pursued both by the Afghan Government and its international partners. Messages are, thus, still largely fragmented which often leave doubts and uncertainty among people. While the government strives to synchronize security, governance, and development efforts, there is a need to pursue a vigorous public outreach campaign and effective strategic communication to ensure that a uniformity of messages by both the government and the international community with regard to the peace process exists.

## Role of Pakistan

Though briefly mentioned above, it will be appropriate to discuss in some detail the role of Pakistan in ending violence in both Afghanistan and Pakistan. Despite extensive efforts through diplomatic channels between the two countries as well as the international community to build trust and confidence, relations between the two countries remain largely shaky due to the policy of Pakistan's military establishment. For many years, the Pakistani military has consistently denied the presence of safe heavens in that country as well as its unabated support to extremist networks which has not only taken many lives, but has threatened the security of the entire region. The international community ignored this issue and remained relatively quiet.

Today, no one will doubt that Pakistan is home to nearly all leaders of insurgent groups who fight in Afghanistan and enjoy support there. Recent studies and independent analysis including the sequence of events that unfolded in the last several months, suggest that Pakistan's Afghan policy has contributed to further radicalisation of Pakistani society which will have long term consequences for the region. The recent statements of former senior as well as present Pakistani civil and military leaders are, indeed, shocking in terms of who determine politics.

Given past experiences[10], Afghans strongly believe that unless the two countries cooperate and address issues of mutual concerns through a constructive and honest dialogue, there will be no sustained solution. Moreover, if good intention and sincerity of efforts can be best judged by practical steps that produce desired outcomes, that has not been achieved yet. This is not to suggest, however, that there isn't any hope and so all efforts must cease. In fact, among other efforts, the existing high level joint commission can still be an effective mechanism for reopening a new chapter of constructive engagement to end the hostility in the region. This will also require commitment from all sides including the international community especially the United States to support certain measures that will address, at least, the following major concerns:

1. The existence, in Pakistan, of safe havens and support to insurgent groups engaged in cross boarder operations
2. The assurance of long term international engagement that will prevent the regional players to destabilize Afghanistan.
3. The suspicion of Pakistan in relation to U.S. presence in Afghanistan demanding necessary guarantees that there is no hidden agenda related to Pakistan's nuclear weapons and its territorial integrity.
4. International community's fears that if not dealt with or managed well, Afghanistan and Pakistan can be turned into safe havens for international terrorism.

These concerns can only be addressed with increased cooperation not through confrontations. In fact, stability will return to this region only when the current confrontation turns into economic cooperation that will impact the lives of people in both countries. There are no differences in people to people relations between the two neighbhouring countries and they will continue to be a positive factor in enhancing cooperation. Missing is a political wisdom that is based on the underlying principles of modern statehood characterised by respect to individual citizens, mutual cooperation and good neighbourly relations.

## Transition and the Peace Process

In July 2011, the Afghan Government and the international community began the process of transitioning the security responsibility of the country, province by province, to Afghan control. This process of *Inteqal* will culminate in Afghans taking overall security lead for their country by the end of 2014 through a phased and deliberate approach. The underlying assumption is that as the Afghan National Army (ANA) and Afghan National Police (ANP) increase in confidence and capability, international military forces will move from direct combat role to partner, advise and support.

Though transition is primarily a security-defined process, sufficient Afghan capacity in governance and development must also be in place to ensure that it is irreversible. The areas that would revert to Afghan responsibility in the third tranche of transition were identified in May 2012 shortly before the Chicago Conference. The third phase involves 25 provinces in total covering 75 percent of the total population. The key distinction between tranche 3 and tranche 1 and 2 is that it includes provinces and areas that are considered volatile and vulnerable such as districts of Jawzjan, Kunduz, Kapisa, Nuristan, Kandahar, Uruzgan and Helmand which means the ANSF will assume full responsibility for these areas when the transition completes. The provinces of Kapisa and Uruzgan will also see full transition. Tranche II for which Transition Implementation Plans (TIPs) have been developed and implementation is in process involves transfer of responsibility to Afghan forces for large cities and the major transportation corridors. Upon completion of this tranche, Afghan security forces will protect four of the country's five largest cities—Kabul, Mazar-i-Sharif, Herat, and Jalalabad.

The 13 May 2012 announcement constitutes a milestone toward the Afghan Government's assumption of nationwide control in the fourth and fifth tranches. Based on current expectations this is likely to begin in early 2013 and continue well into the following year. If this timetable holds, the security transition envisaged by the international community at Lisbon will be completed on schedule by 2014, when coalition forces will have the primary responsibility for training and supporting the Afghan security forces.

However, given the challenges ahead including concerns about the number and, more importantly, the capacity of Afghan forces (military, police, and intelligence) to independently conduct complex operations and maintain security, it is unclear whether the security transition will be successful on this timeline based on substantive measures instead of process measures. Despite significant improvement, the Afghan National Army (ANA) still faces considerable challenges to lead independent complex counterinsurgency operations, especially in remote areas. The same can be construed of the Afghan National Police, with the exception of a few elite components, such as the Afghan National Civil Order Police.

In contrast, the Afghan Local Police (ALP) have in some regions demonstrated great promise, but they are lightly armed, relatively small in number, with approximately half of the total 30,000 Tashkeel recruited to date, and not yet well disciplined. In some provinces, they are the major sources of problems as they act like militia forces. This situation has led to serious concerns among the local population particularly in relation to their loyalty to individual commanders, rather than the state and the possibility of shifting side once the international forces leave the country.

Thus, although the security transition will likely proceed on schedule, the Afghan Government may still have difficulty to independently face the threats posed by cross border insurgency who continue to enjoy sanctuary and support in Pakistan. Failure to neutralize such threats, as has been observed in some instances in Tranche I areas, will undermine confidence and could potentially lead to further civil strife and insecurity in the region.

It is imperative that advancements in governance and development move in parallel with the security transition. The Government's primary plan for doing so is under the framework of the Kabul Process (mentioned above) and the National Priority Programs (NPPs). The NPPs are planned on a similar three-year time frame as transition, but these programs also require adequate support and funding from the donor community. Roughly half of the NPP activities are already underway and have funding, but greater support is needed to be fully successful and consolidate the gains made in the security areas.

The government, donors and ISAF must avoid quick-fixes and easy solutions to 'check the box' in the governance and development areas in the name of transition. Indeed, strengthening the government's ability to serve its population is the central goal for transition in the non-security areas, and this must be done in a responsible manner, consistent with the commitments made in the July 2010 Kabul Conference and the principles articulated in the Bonn II Conference Communiqué. Only then, the transition process can be made irreversible.

## Role of Peace Process in the Success of Transition

Transition and the peace process are two inseparable processes, where the success of transition depends on the effectiveness of peace efforts to restore confidence among the Afghan communities. If utilised effectively, the APRP can be a powerful tool for a smoother transition process, because as international forces depart an area, a key grievance used by the insurgents will be removed, and outreach efforts may have greater resonance. The APRP may, therefore, act as an 'enabler' for transition in the following ways:

- **Strategic Communication:** Governors and Provincial Peace Committees (PPC) in a province under transition can open up new dialogue with the population to explain that the departure of international forces does not represent abandonment, but rather a symbol of the strengthening capacity of Afghan security forces and the Afghan state. Moreover, this is the beginning of a process that will ensure sovereignty and an end to dominant role of international forces. A province can take pride in the assumption of its security responsibility and demonstrate the ability of Afghans for defending their own people.

- **Outreach and Negotiations:** During the transition phase, Governors and Provincial Peace Committees may attempt to re-open dialogue with insurgent groups and potential reintegrees. This will require them to deepen their understanding of the grievances which have played a role in the insurgents' motives for fighting. Fighters who had grievances against the presence of international forces may be best candidates for reintegration during the transition process, though assessing the likelihood of certain fighters or insurgent groups joining the peace process must be done carefully, monitored closely and supported properly during the transition process, as the dynamic nature of the political and security landscape may alter rationale decision making.
- **Increasing Government Legitimacy:** As the provincial government becomes more active in implementing the peace process and mobilizes various stakeholders to become agents of peace in their communities, particularly in the effort to resolving outstanding grievances that have long plagued communities, the effect will serve to enhance the governing legitimacy of provincial officials and help fill the political space which is openly contested by the insurgency. Restoring harmony and repairing the fabric of Afghan communities, which have experienced years of trauma and conflict, is a basic but difficult governing function that will contribute to an enduring transition. PPC members, who include tribal elders, Ulema and religious leaders, civil society and women, can provide an effective and enduring mechanism for connecting provincial governments with local people.
- **Enhancing Internal Government Coordination:** The delivery of the peace process in a given area requires extensive coordination between both civilian and security institutions at the provincial and national level. Where APRP has been successful it has helped to increase internal government collaboration and coordination. For example, security institutions must be aware of outreach and negotiation efforts with potential reintegrees in order to not derail their success through military operations and at the same time must work to ensure that new reintegrees are not targeted and their security is maintained. APRP can act as an enabler for Afghan government actors to work together more closely, which is an important feature of Afghan governance in a transition area.
- **Enter into Meaningful Negotiation:** As discussed, this involves complicated processes that require effective coordination, facilitation and confidence building measures. The leadership of the insurgency has reached the conclusion that it will not be able to win militarily and even if it wins, it will not be able to run the country. Moreover, Afghanistan is not the same as it was ten years ago and Taliban no longer

enjoy popular support they enjoyed when they first appeared at the political scene. As such, it is now important to pursue an inclusive, multi-faceted and multi-level policy that takes into account both the internal and external factors as well as measures to strengthen regional cooperation and ensure sustained international community's support for an Afghan led peace process. The overall aim should be to create the "enabling conditions" for those who join the peace process. Thus a breakthrough in peace negotiation will accelerate transition to the Afghan authority.

## Possible Future Scenarios

Given the geo-political realities of the region and the multi-dimensional nature of the conflict in Afghanistan, the Afghan Government and the international community must adopt a collective, integrated and proactive approach informed by the lessons of the past. The peace, reconciliation and reintegration process must continue to remain an inclusive national priority supported by all actors. As recommended by the Traditional Loya Jirga, in order to strengthen national unity, and avoid further divisions among Afghans—important factors for achieving durable peace—the process must be led and owned by Afghans.

Factors and forces at the regional level will have a significant impact on the success of the peace process and transition in Afghanistan. The commitments made by the regional countries recently at several international settings to support an Afghan-led peace process are a step in the right direction; however these are still words on papers and must be turned into real and tangible actions. Any durable peace settlement in Afghanistan cannot be achieved without genuine commitment and concrete measures of the neighbouring countries, especially Pakistan. It is now time to reflect on the past experience which has shown that pursuing violent means to achieve influence and broader geo-political objectives cannot succeed and indeed can be self-destructive.

Taking into account the current social, political and economic realities both inside and outside Afghanistan, the following could be considered as possible future prospects and scenarios for Afghanistan up and beyond 2014:

1. Afghanistan with support from international community and regional players makes progress in all five key strategic areas as outlined in this paper (peace process, security transition, governance, investment in key sectors including a private sector led economic growth, strategic partnerships and regional cooperation). This will increase public trust on the ability of government to deliver and on the willingness of the international partners to remain committed. It will also ensure sustainability of the progress made to date and the stability of the current political system which is bound by numerous challenges. And finally, it will serve the interest of all except the spoilers who are obsessed with

only short term gains and are less concerned about the long term national interests.

2. Afghanistan reaches a breakthrough in peace talks and Pakistan stops providing sanctuary (and support) to different extremist networks within its territory carrying out cross border insurgency and as a result the level of violence drops dramatically which will ultimately pave the way for a timely withdrawal of international forces and an effective transition to the Afghan authority. As reconciliation succeeds, the challenge will then be how to accommodate the different groups within the political system to avoid internal divisions and promote political cohesion.
3. The talks fail but progress is made on all other fronts including reintegration and uniting Afghans behind a national movement of peace. The widening of the security box through reintegration efforts will open other opportunities in development and governance, further consolidating the conditions for long-term community recovery and peace. An effective peace, reconciliation, and reintegration process from 2012-2014 will thus lay the foundation for peace and stability beyond 2014. There is no doubt that in such circumstances, in the short term the spoilers will most likely increase spectacular attacks on high profile targets including peace activists as they did so recently to spread fears and change public perception. This state, even though temporary, will be difficult and could result in potential losses. In the long run, however, Afghanistan will become a stable country and the probability of collapse of the political system will largely diminish partly because national security and civilian institutions will then be better equipped and matured with increased level of public support.
4. The international community enters into direct talks aiming at facilitating withdrawal without the Afghan people and government ownership/leadership. In this case the peace talks will mostly likely fail to produce the desired outcome and instead could end up with catastrophic results as experienced in the 90s. It is also possible that peace talks succeed, yet Pakistani based militant groups and extremist networks will still be receiving support and new groups would continue to be mobilised to replace the old leadership that is expected to talk. This situation will further complicate the position of Afghanistan and Pakistan. Uncertainty in Pakistan will remain major sources of concern and will provide more room for instability in the region.

While it will be difficult to measure the level and extent of long term commitment of the international community, what remains true is that neither the Afghan people nor the international community wants to see the mistake of the 90s repeated. Both the Afghan government and the international community renewed their commitment in the second Bonn, Chicago and recently in Tokyo

Conference for working on the next phase to help Afghanistan transform to a stable and sovereign country. Moreover, the importance of stability in Afghanistan for the region and beyond as well as the growing interest in long term investment will justify the long term international engagement to support Afghan led initiatives. As such, the continuation of the status quo is not in the interest of making Afghanistan a stable and sovereign country. It is therefore crucial that the Afghan government and its international partners work together to make a positive change and put Afghans in the lead so that there is no room for spoilers to have any excuse for continuation of their fight.

The first three scenarios above are possible but each will require different timing and level of commitment as well as patience, thoughtfulness and necessary cautions as the process involves a great deal of sensitivity. While for some short-sighted politicians at the domestic level, the fourth option will seem an easy choice to strike a deal and achieve immediate gains, however, choosing this path will not be a wise decision and will most likely have consequences for the security of the entire world—something no one will ever want to do after all these years of enormous efforts and great sacrifices.

## The New Way Forward

After ten hard and difficult years of tireless efforts, enormous investments and tremendous sacrifices, Afghanistan is entering into its most crucial phase and decisive moments. While much has been achieved and considerable progress is made in several fronts, the challenges for the road ahead remain grave. It is critical therefore that decisions are not affected by emotions, personal judgments as well as the pressure of fatigue. Instead, they are based on a national vision that serves the long term interests of all Afghans. Key elements of this vision will be patience, flexibility, determination and political wisdom.

Afghans are tired of the continuation of conflict in their country and are desperately seeking a serious political process supported by regional countries especially Afghanistan's immediate neighbours as well as the international community. Moreover, there is a broad consensus among Afghans that security and stability as well as Afghan sovereignty cannot be achieved only through military means and so there is need to end the decades-long conflict through combined efforts including an inclusive political solution that is led and owned by Afghans. Thus, reconciliation efforts that can pave the way for a possible political settlement must be accelerated in light of the Afghan constitution. This is partly because the more the negotiations are delayed, the higher the cost for securing a lasting peace will be.

The scenarios presented above is an apt description of Afghanistan's trajectory for achieving the goals it has set out and how the peace process can play its intended role during the critical transition period prior to 2014. The Afghan Government, regional countries, the international community, as well as disaffected populations and insurgent groups must all do their part to make this a reality. An effective peace, reconciliation, and reintegration process from 2012-14, backed by a strong regional and international commitment, will lay the foundation for a positive and peaceful post-2014 national landscape.

Undoubtedly, the next two years will be critical to reclaim the national dialogue on peace and transition and reaffirm the Islamic underpinnings of the Afghan state to those who would question it, and demonstrate that the government will eventually assume its responsibilities as a sovereign state through the transition process. The path to this end state will likely encounter disruptions and require adjustments, but as the Traditional Loya Jirga confirmed, we must all make this choice for peace, even when it tests our faith and demands our sacrifice.

## Notes

1. These include some districts in the northern, northeastern and western provinces of Jawzjan, Faryab, Badakhsan, Kunduz, Baghlan, Takhhar, Balkh and Ghor.
2. *Loya Jirga* refers to the Grand Council, a traditional national consultative process, convened by the government of Afghanistan in November 2011 to consult on the strategic partnership with the U.S. as well as on the way forward in Peace and reconciliation process, following the tragic death of the Chairman of the High Peace Council (HPC) Professor Burhanuddin Rabbani.
3. Some measures by the negotiating parties in support of the reconciliation efforts may include—accepting the Afghan constitution, provision of safety and security guarantees, release of detainees, de-listing of names from UN Sanctions list, opportunity to participate in the political process etc.
4. As a noun, the word *Fitna* implies any act that creates division and disunity among a people.
5. Despite marking initial success, the Programme Tahkim Solha's (PTS) efforts failed largely due to inconsistency of efforts, lack of political and financial commitment and resources.
6. Following the death of its chair Professor Rabbani, serious debates about the effectiveness of the HPC resurfaced, given the large size of the organisation. In November 2011, Loya Jirga also called for a review of the current composition of the organisation and recommended possible downsizing.
7. In many cases, ex-combatants especially commanders who join the process cannot return to their villages or areas due to fears of being killed. So in addition to social and economic services, they require guarantees for their safety and security which at times necessitates their resettlement to other areas of the country. Recently both reintegrees and peace advocates including HPC and PPC members have become targets of insurgency and in some cases have greatly suffered from the brutal acts of terrorist groups e.g. the tragic assassination of Maulavi Arsalan Rahmani, one of the most active members of the HPC on 13 May 2012 as well as Mohammad Hashim Muneeb, the chair of the Provincial Peace Committee of Kunar Province in April 2012.
8. Despite these important measures, real progress in promoting regional commitment particularly from Afghanistan's neighbours was not achieved and in fact following

the assassination of HPC chair, both the Joint commission and Core Group suspended meetings. Following the high level events e.g. Istanbul, Bonn and Islamabad meeting, these forums resumed talks.

9. However, it was not a precondition.
10. This includes recent joint Afghan and international diplomatic efforts to encourage Pakistan to support the Afghan-led peace process, which did not yield fruitful results and thus, were put on hold following the assassination of Professor Rabbani.

# SECTION II

# SECURITY, POLITICAL PROCESSES & GOVERNANCE

# 4

# Security in Afghanistan Beyond 2014: Preparedness of the Afghan National Security Forces

*Arian Sharifi*

The 2014 deadline for the withdrawal of the international forces from Afghanistan has generated great concern both in Afghanistan and outside. Most observers, Afghan and international, are worried that the Afghan National Security Forces (ANSF) are far from ready to take up the security responsibility in Afghanistan once the international forces leave. Indeed, these concerns are real and understandable. Both Afghan and American authorities have continually acknowledged that the insurgents seem to become stronger, better organised, and bolder each year.

While a few years ago, the Taliban engaged in less sophisticated attacks, exploding bombs on the streets and in marketplaces, they now initiate well-coordinated and targeted attacks against high profile civilian and military targets. The attacks on the Serena Hotel, the Intercontinental Hotel, the American Embassy, the British Consulate, and many others in Kabul all suggest that the insurgents are not only becoming stronger, but also bolder and more sophisticated in target selection and attacks. At the same time, they are able to sustain battles against Afghan and international forces for much longer, and inflict more casualties on Afghan and international military forces in the countryside. The announcement of the international troop withdrawal from Afghanistan by 2014 has even further encouraged the insurgents to hold their positions, and sustain the war. With the talks of the majority of the international forces leaving Afghanistan by 2014, they are hopeful, that there is a chance of victory if they wait their time.

Meanwhile, the Afghan National Security Forces, which mainly consists of Afghan National Army (ANA) and Afghan National Police (ANP) are perceived to be ill-trained and under-equipped to be able to protect the populace against these attacks. Many observers argue that the ANA's morale is low, the retention rate of new recruits in the army is considerably low, they are minimally equipped, and their overall fighting quality is less than acceptable. The story with the ANP is even less encouraging in the above-mentioned areas. A high level of corruption in the police has diminished people's trust in the organisation, generating even further public support for the insurgents. In short, with the 2014 withdrawal deadline approaching, Afghanistan is facing an increasingly stronger insurgency, and a less-than-adequate national security force that could potentially withstand the onslaught of the insurgent attacks once the international forces leave the country.

Taking into account the above-outlined situation, most observers and commentators have a pessimistic view about the future of Afghanistan after 2014. There are serious doubts about the capabilities of the ANSF and their ability to provide security for the Afghan populace in the long term. While the situation is dire, and these doubts about the ANSF's capabilities are real and serious, the pessimists overemphasize the negative points, and seem to completely ignore some of the positive signs that suggest a rather optimistic scenario in Afghanistan after 2014.

Moreover, the phenomenon of transition and the withdrawal deadline of the international forces from Afghanistan by 2014 are vastly misinterpreted by many observers, particularly the media. Generally, the misinterpretations occur in two main areas:

- First, there is an embedded assumption that 2014 will be the end of the international forces' mission in Afghanistan. Many commentators assume that after 2014, Afghanistan will be left on its own, and the international community will cut all or most of its assistance to the country. This is not a realistic perception. Many coalition and NATO countries have already declared their long-term commitments to Afghanistan. Based on these commitments, international assistance to the Afghan National Security Forces will continue well beyond 2014.
- The other misinterpretation is that many observers ask the question as to whether or not the Afghan National Security Forces would be able to provide security for the country after 2014. The phrase "providing security", is too broad and little understood. It can mean everything from partial stability in major cities, to complete security across the country. It encompasses the handling of threats posed by foreign adversarial countries, by international terrorist groups, by domestic insurgent fighters, by large organised criminal networks, as well as by petty criminals. To assume that the ANSF would be able to secure the

Afghan populace at large against threats posed by all of these sources would be a misguided assumption. Afghanistan has never had a security force of such high quality, and such a scenario is unlikely for many years to come. Even with over 140,000 Western troops in the country at present, such level of security does not exist.

Therefore, there is a need to rephrase the question, and decrease the expectations of the Afghan National Security Forces to a more realistic level. More importantly, there is a need to be concerned with a more pressing issue—the survival of the regime beyond 2014.

Whether or not the current political regime (not specifically referring to the current administration, but the process and ideals upon which the Afghan political system was established in the late 2001) can survive beyond 2014 remains the crucial question. In the ongoing debate among the Afghans, as well as some international media outlets, four broad scenarios are speculated for Afghanistan after 2014:

(1) Soon after the withdrawal of the international military forces from Afghanistan in 2014, the government in Kabul will collapse and the Taliban will take over, as the ANSF will not be able to withstand the increased attacks by the insurgents. Afghanistan will revert to its pre-2001 status. The Taliban will establish their radical Islamic government in the country, and all of the achievements of the last ten years will be reversed.

(2) With the security vacuum created by the withdrawal of the international forces, former *jihadi* groups, particularly the non-Pashtun groups in the north, will feel vulnerable. To secure their own survival, they will start jostling for power. To gain more influence, they will encourage ethnic divisions in the country, and most of the Afghan populace will be divided along ethnic lines. In the meantime, the central government in Kabul will collapse, and another bloody civil war will follow.

(3) The central government will survive for two-three years after 2014 (as with the Soviet withdrawal in 1989), but insurgent attacks will increase as time goes, further weakening the government. Meanwhile, power struggle between the *jihadi* groups will intensify, and eventually the central government will collapse. Once again, the country will be divided—with some of the *jihadi* groups forming an alliance in the North, while the Taliban establishing a government in the South and the East.

(4) With financial, strategic and advisory support provided by the international community, the Afghan National Security Forces will be able to help preserve the current regime in the country for the medium term, despite the potential rising levels of insurgent attacks.

The latter scenario—the fourth one—seems to be more plausible, for many reasons:

> Contrary to how it is perceived, a considerable number of international troops will remain in Afghanistan after 2014. Many countries, including the United States, Great Britain, France, Germany and others have already declared that they would retain their military presence in Afghanistan beyond 2014, albeit a more limited presence. Although specific details are yet to be worked out, most likely, the international military involvement in Afghanistan would be based on bilateral strategic agreements between Afghanistan and these countries.
>
> The signing of the Afghan-American Strategic Partnership Agreement recently, which declared the continued commitment of the United States to Afghanistan until 2024, is a major step toward that end. Despite strong pressure from Afghanistan's neighbours, particularly Iran and Pakistan, both houses of the Afghan National Assembly ratified the treaty, and applauded the government for this major achievement. As part of this broad strategic agreement, Afghan and American authorities have one year to conduct negotiations on a Bilateral Security Agreement that would specify both parties' rights and responsibilities in the area of security. Like this Strategic Agreement, the Bilateral Security Agreement is also expected to be inked prior to 2014.
>
> Afghanistan direly needs the longer-term presence of American military forces on its soil. Afghan authorities are fully aware of the fact that without some American military presence in the country, Afghan National Security Forces do not have the capability to fight the insurgents, to maintain general stability and order in the country, and to preserve the regime. Meanwhile, American authorities know that if they completely abandon Afghanistan, it is more than likely that the Taliban would take power and turn the country, once again, into a training ground for international terrorists. This is a scenario U.S. would try to avoid.
>
> Afghanistan has also signed such agreements with many other countries, including India, France, Great Britain, and Germany, and is currently working with other European countries on potential similar agreements. The bottom line is that Afghanistan will not be completely abandoned after 2014, and that a considerable number of Western troops will remain in the country for the foreseeable future.
>
> How would this help to improve the security situation in Afghanistan? It can help in the following ways:

(a) The presence of international forces, even a limited number of troops, on Afghan soil would deter any potential, albeit not probable, invasion by one of Afghanistan's neighbours. However, the chances of Afghanistan being directly invaded by one of its neighbours are very slim. Nevertheless, the stationing of Western troops in Afghanistan through strategic partnership agreements would completely take that threat off the table, as the responsibility of the defense of Afghanistan's borders would certainly be part of these agreements. This would substantially ease the burden of responsibility on the shoulders of the Afghan National Security Forces, at least for the medium term.

(b) The presence of Western troops in Afghanistan would prevent the possibility of the break out of factional fighting in the country, and the potential toppling of the regime by one or more of the former *jihadi* groups. As a matter of fact, one of the biggest fears of most Afghans is that the *jihadi* groups might once again drag the country into the flames of factional fighting as they did in the 1990s. But with Western troops in the country, this threat would be substantially reduced for they would continue to support the central Government.

(c) The presence of Western troops in Afghanistan would also prevent the possibility of the Taliban taking over the country and re-establishing their regime. While the Taliban could become stronger, and their attacks could increase, with a considerable number of Western troops in the country, the Taliban's total victory would be inconceivable.

(d) The international forces would continue to provide the Afghan National Security Forces with training, guidance and assistance in the conduct of operations. The Afghan National Security Forces would take the lead, and the international troops would provide the needed strategic and tactical assistance to them. They would also continue to equip the Afghan National Army and the Afghan National Police.

The second factor suggesting that the Afghan National Security Forces would be able to help preserve the regime in the country after 2014 is that the coalition countries, particularly the United States, will continue to provide financial assistance to Afghanistan for the foreseeable future. The Afghan Ministry of Defense (MoD) estimates their financial needs between 5 to 7 billion dollars per year after 2014 and based on verbal agreements, they are confident about receiving that amount from the international community for many years to come. Currently, the presence of the international military forces in Afghanistan costs about 150 billion dollars per year. With a little over 140,000 troops in the country, that is roughly about 1 million dollars per soldier per year. If by 2014, troop levels would be reduced to about 40,000, that would allow for a cost cutting of over 100 billion dollars per year for the international community. Thus, providing 5 to 7 billion dollars every year as assistance to the Afghan National Security Forces should not be much of a burden for the international community.[1]

Finally, the Afghan National Security Forces are growing rapidly in number and quality, and by 2014, they will be a good enough force, capable of defending and preserving the regime. By October 2014, the combined Afghan National Army and Afghan National Police are foreseen to have a force of 352,000 personnel. While this number is still considerably lower than the recommended number of 20 security personnel for every 1,000 population in insurgency environments, it will be good enough to provide security and preserve the regime.

There are some areas of concern that need to be addressed. The Afghan National Security Forces at present lack an air force, as well as the capabilities of heavy weaponry and equipment. So far, only 5 to 10 per cent of what could be considered a modest air force has been established. These statistics have to do primarily with personnel training, and not with equipment, radar and air defense capabilities. The ANA lacks tanks, artillery and other such equipment.

But the international security forces seem to have become more serious about providing equipment and training for the Afghan National Security Forces. Their efforts at equipping and training the Afghan National Security Forces have considerably increased since the 2014 deadline was set. Further, with the type of missions the Afghan National Security Forces are expected to conduct for many years to come, i.e., mostly counter-insurgency operations, not a lot of heavy military equipment are needed. What is needed for such type of warfare is light and robust units that can move in and out of missions with ease, and have defensive capabilities against light, swift insurgent attacks. And that is what the Afghan National Security Forces are being trained and equipped for.[2]

## Challenges and Opportunities?

While there are reasons for optimism about the capabilities of the Afghan National Security Forces and the survivability of the Afghan political regime beyond 2014, there are several issues that could potentially undermine these optimistic scenarios. Some of these issues include the following:

(a) The potential of total withdrawal of the international forces at a time considered too soon from Afghanistan. Though there are indications that some international forces will remain in Afghanistan for several years after 2014, it will largely be contingent on the level of political will in the capitals of these countries. If the international forces leave Afghanistan earlier than they should, the earlier hypothesis would not hold and the Afghan government could collapse.

(b) Cutting of financial assistance to Afghanistan prematurely would have serious implications. Like the presence of the international forces in the country beyond 2014, the assumption holds that international financial assistance will also continue for the foreseeable future. Should the reality turn out to be otherwise, such a scenario would not hold.

(c) Leaving Afghanistan to its neighbours. Unfortunately, they would still continue to meddle in Afghanistan's internal affairs. Therefore, if they are given more leeway in Afghanistan, the Afghan government would become even weaker, and the possibility of its collapse would increase.

(d) The possibility of major popular uprisings in the country. At the moment, the gap between the Afghan government and its people is quite wide and increasing. If the Afghan government is not able to introduce major improvements in some of the main areas of its conduct, i.e., curbing corruption, decreasing the production and trade of narcotics, improving the rule of law, providing basic social services for the people, and others, it is possible some major uprisings against the government could occur. That would considerably weaken the government, further tarnish its legitimacy, as well as the credibility of the international forces, and would create large support base for the insurgents.

To conclude, the transition of responsibilities to the Afghan National Security Forces should be considered a positive sign. If Afghanistan is ever to stand on its own feet and provide the needed security for its population, it can only be realised through taking full responsibility. As the saying goes, *"one only learns how to swim by swimming,"* so would the Afghan National Security Forces learn how to provide security for Afghanistan only with assuming responsibility.

As Dr. Ashraf Ghani Ahmadzai, the Head of the Transition Commission stated *"The transfer of security responsibility is not the end but is the deepening of the mutual partnership between Afghanistan and the international community."*[3] As such, 2014 would mark the beginning of a new era of cooperation between Afghanistan and its international partners. Both sides have great responsibilities to fulfill in this new era. On the one hand, the international community must maintain its declared commitment to Afghanistan, and continue to provide strategic, advisory, financial and tactical support to the Afghan National Security Forces. On the other hand, the Afghan government must work to bring about better governance, curb corruption, curtail the production and trade of narcotics, improve its relations with its neighbours, and provide a better environment for investment and economic development in the country. The fulfillment of the parties' respective responsibilities would determine the fate of Afghanistan in the long run.

## NOTES

1. Interview with General Zaher Azimi, Spokesperson for the Afghan Ministry of Defense, Kabul, 2 January 2012.
2. Ibid.
3. Dr. Ahmadzai's speech was aired on radio and TV stations across Afghanistan.

# 5

# Political Reform and Peace-building in Afghanistan

*Ahmad Wali Masoud*

The creation of the modern state of "Afghanistan" in the mid-19th century by Ahmed Shah Abdali from the Sadozai tribe was followed by four decades of rivalries between the Sadozai and Barakzai tribes and two consecutive Anglo-Afghan wars (1839-42 and 1878-80). During the 19th century, rivalries among members of the royal family continued until Mohammad Daud Khan, a first cousin of the last king, abolished the monarchy and declared a republic in 1973. In subsequent years, Afghanistan was occupied by the Soviets, resulting in the Afghan *Jihad* to oust the Red Army. Victory, however, was short-lived. War soon erupted to unseat the new Mujahiddin Government in Kabul, and the country became a stage for regional as well as extra-regional rivalries. Tragically, the people of Afghanistan were the primary victims of these armed-conflicts. For centuries, they have been denied their right to peace and a legitimate political system.

The aim of this paper is to explain the fundamental causes of failure in Afghanistan's past and present. The paper suggests various ways to extricate the nation from the current quagmire. The root causes of the crisis are increasingly more evident. The paper is based on the hypothesis that for a recovery plan to succeed, the circumstances that led Afghanistan to its present state must be investigated. A recovery strategy that is not based on a correct analysis of the past, has very little chance of success and will lead the country deeper into the abyss.

As early as 2002, it was more than evident that we were heading in the wrong direction. In 2003, I devised a comprehensive new strategy called 'The National Agenda' which proposed ways to foster a national identity and strengthen the confidence-building process. The strategy stressed upon the fundamental values of human rights and democracy, security and the establishment of a national unity government led by a sound leadership.

Regretfully this strategy was largely ignored by the Afghan establishment as well as foreign powers, and the outcome is very clear today. Afghanistan's internal conditions are fast deteriorating to an all time low. Individuals with outdated modes of thinking have dominated the decision-making apparatus and have already inflicted irrecoverable damage to the country. Putting an end to their monopoly over power might reverse this ominous trend. After a long and bitter experience, the people of Afghanistan can no longer afford to let pass the present opportunities for peace and should use these opportunities to legitimize the political processes in the country.

Throughout the history of Afghanistan, ruling elites have fuelled political and social insecurity in a bid to preserve their own grip on power. A succession of centralised autocratic administrations has prevented the emergence and development of an effective civil society. They have chosen to promote tribalism at the expense of the general population's right to self-determination. Therefore, before it is too late, measures must be taken to mend relations between the people and their government, and consolidate the rule of law, promote civil society, and provide the conditions for people to enjoy their inalienable rights to a life of dignity and prosperity.

## The History of War and Peace in Afghanistan

King Abdul Rahman Khan's autocracy, King Amanullah Khan's constitutional monarchy, Mohammad Zahir Shah's so-called decade of democracy, the socialism of the People's Democratic Party of Afghanistan (PDPA), *Jihadi* leaders' Islamic government and the Taliban's Islamic Emirate were all means to legitimize the various regimes that came to power in Afghanistan, but none of these ever reflected any fundamental changes in Afghan society. Differences of ideology and opinion among the ruling elite lacked roots and foundation among the ordinary people. The fierce rivalries for power among the Afghan elites cast a dark shadow over the history of Afghanistan.

The ideologies that were crafted by the elites were a diversion from what was essentially the traditional culture of politics in Afghanistan. The traditional politics of Afghanistan are based upon a set of intractable beliefs on the structure of family relationships. Those advocating formal ideologies are merely products of their traditional societies who have never been able to sever those social and cultural ties.

Foreign powers have exploited this self-destructive political culture throughout the history of Afghanistan and instigated regional games and rivalries in this country. For most of the rulers, the patronage of foreign countries has been pivotal. That is how foreign countries, whether from North or South, have imposed 'amenable' regimes in Kabul, and the people have not had the opportunity to participate in the decision-making process that shape their lives. By taking a brief look at the history, it is evident that in the context of 'The Great Game', the will of Britain and to some extent of the Soviet Union played a determining role in establishing the political direction of Afghanistan.

Power-mongering among the elites throughout the modern history of Afghanistan rendered the country an optimal ground for rival external players to jockey for regional influence by proxy. Dependence on external powers thus has become a necessity for rulers throughout Afghanistan's modern history. None of the central governments were able to exert control and administer political and social affairs without the patronage of foreign powers. The case is no different today.

Efforts to establish a strong centralised power in Afghanistan have repeatedly resulted in failure. But with the intervention of foreign powers, the rulers to some extent were able to bring parts of the country under the control of the central government. However, these governments continuously suppressed the will of the people, which accounts for the marked absence of political and social institutions in Afghanistan.Every government or political movement in Afghanistan enjoyed support in accordance with tribal and ethnic affiliations. Successive conflicts, oppressive policies and Afghanistan's failure to become a sovereign country inflicted severe damage to the nation, the consequence of which was to relegate Afghanistan to a state of backwardness and stagnation.

After the coup d'etat of 1978, the pillars of traditional legitimacy, laden with the potential of crisis, were demolished, and Afghanistan entered a new phase. But the government's monopolisation of power eliminated community councils and as a result, there was no linkage between the state and the people. The political system was divided, so was the society. Ideological extremism along with tribal politics was used by elites to establish the link between government and society.

## Emergence and Ascent of Taliban Movement

The political expression of the Taliban movement differed from other Islamic and non-Islamic parties and organisations in Afghanistan. From its very inception, the movement shared a practical and theoretical disposition towards organisations such as the Al-Qaeda, in its pursuit of specific objectives in the region and the world.

The stated objective of this group was to establish a political regime based on traditional and local beliefs. The leaders were proxies of foreign political institutions and intelligence services, particularly that of Pakistan's Inter-Service Intelligence (ISI). Thus, the Taliban is an extremist, that poses an enormous threat to the region. Some analysts state that the foot soldiers of this group include ordinary people who were fed up with warlords and joined this group to replace the social, economic and military regime in the south of Afghanistan. These foot soldiers, analysts posit, believe that they have a God given responsibility to fight against the oppressors, and even to lay down their lives for this cause. This group therefore does not follow tribal and ethnic rules of the wealthy persons (Khan) or local leaders (Malik).The leadership of this radical group is located on both sides of the Durand Line (the disputed border between Afghanistan and Pakistan), and this has added to the complexity. While the level of local leaders' adherence to the ideology of the organisation varies, the fact remain that they are extremists, brutal and violent.

It is difficult to define the Taliban's world view; its interpretation of state, nation, democracy, civil rights, equity, tolerance, human rights and other values shared by the wider international community. From their own narrow religious viewpoint, all these values are un-Islamic and therefore have no place in their political culture. Hence, anyone opposing their view is considered an enemy and they have the sacred obligation to fight them endlessly. Targeting civilians and military people of different age groups, gender, local or expatriate, Muslim or non-Muslim, in every location even in mosques and schools stem from this extremist point of view.

In the National Agenda document, I had warned that any attempt on the part of the then-vanquished Taliban to regroup and reemerge could lead Afghanistan to another serious crisis. From the very beginning, it was evident that there were efforts to keep the re-emergence and expansion of the Taliban a secret. The government of Afghanistan in order to find an excuse for its failures to be responsive and accountable to the international community, had to show that they were grappling with dire internal conditions. In order to overcome political opposition, the government essentially gave the Taliban the green light. It was a risky venture and a policy that destroyed all constructive efforts in Afghanistan. Today, not only has the government pushed the country into the abyss, but the Taliban is well organised, well equipped and have an upper-hand in the ongoing psychological warfare. The Taliban are more vocal than ever before, they terrorize, claim victory and speak as the victor.

## The Bonn Conference and the Beginning of a New Era of International Engagement

The overthrow of the Taliban regime and Al-Qaeda network in 2001 provided a historic opportunity to establish a new Afghanistan and move forward after years of under-development. The new era required a new strategy, a new vision and above all, legitimacy to connect Afghanistan with the rest of the world.

The Bonn Conference approved a list of these new arrangements based on which Afghanistan had to be governed under new political principles, a conventional political regime, and rule of law. Hamid Karzai was recommended and appointed as the Head of Interim Government by the United States. As mentioned earlier, three decades of conflict and struggle had disrupted the social structure in Afghanistan and by adopting new values, such as democracy, human rights, elections, freedom of expression, Afghanistan's political system needed to be redefined and restructured. The country needed the rule of law, sound policies and new political tools.

However, even after a decade of direct engagement of the international community in Afghanistan, little has changed. Individuals active in the political scenario of Afghanistan work as proxies of the bigger players in the region and the world, and try to expand their personal or their party's power base with tribal or foreign patronage. By painting a deceptive picture of Afghanistan's social and political developments, these individuals unabashedly pursue their personal or tribal interests. Although the political culture of present rulers and the opportunism of self-interested politicians to some extent continue as in the past, it has become evident that this process no longer functions. There is an inherent paradox between calls for returning to the past while planning for the future, and this has been a significant reason for the failure of the new Afghanistan in the past decade.

Only fundamental changes in the social structure combined with the introduction of new trends like democracy, human rights, women's rights, elections and free media, would help Afghanistan enter a new phase of political and social life in the 21st century. I stress upon the fact that the present-day Afghanistan should be governed by new principles and regulations. The policies and strategies experienced in the past decade were based solely on militarisation, funneling money, convening international conferences and creating councils that did not yield the expected results.

## The Peace Process and President Hamid Karzai's Approach to Reconciliation with the Taliban

To begin with, it needs reiteration that the Taliban are no longer the dispersed force they were ten years ago, and peace in the current political climate does not mean reconciliation and the end of war.The Bonn Agreement and other international conferences that were convened for the reconstruction and rehabilitation of a new Afghanistan were focused on components of Peace, Nation and State-Building (PNSB). One of its principles was to fight terrorism and bring stability. A decade has passed since the Bonn Conference. The Afghan administration seems to distort the process for nation and state-building and democracy in order to return to the past. The administration tries to sweep its failures under the rug, on the pretext of negotiation with the Taliban.

Ten years ago, Afghanistan was presented, for the first time in its history, an unparalleled opportunity to forge a future with peace and prosperity. There was general consensus and understanding both inside and outside country.

However, considering the performance of the Karzai administration over the past 10 years, it is evident that there was no plan of action to steer the country toward stability, security, tranquility and freedom. Years have passed since the negotiation with the Taliban was made public. This has raised widespread concern among the public, particularly women who make up more than 50 percent of Afghanistan's population. People from all walks of life question the objectives behind the rumours and secret policies to reach an agreement with the Taliban. How can the Taliban, responsible for the destruction of countless Afghan lives, now be credited as a viable negotiation partner?

If there were the remotest chance of peace with the Taliban, it would have happened when the late national resistance leader Ahmad Shah Masoud—in a historic and courageous move in 2006—visited the supreme council of Taliban in their command centre but returned empty handed. The Taliban not only persisted to fight but sent Al-Qaeda foot soldiers to assassinate Ahmad Shah Masoud in September 2001. Ten years after that assassination, they assassinated Professor Burhanudin Rabbani, head of High Peace Council in 2011. The assassin entered the home of the former president under the guise of a Taliban peace envoy, and then detonated his turban bomb. Can peace negotiations be conducted with such a group?

What Afghans witness today is considerably different from the promises they were given at Bonn. The Kabul administration's policies have engendered doubts and uncertainties about the process of peace, nation and state-building that were announced at the Bonn conference. Those who raised the expectations of the Afghan people at the Bonn conference with their lofty promises seem to have conveniently forgotten their commitment to act on behalf of the people of Afghanistan.

It is not the purpose of this paper to offer an opinion on whether or not any of the warring factions should join the peace process. After all, it is entirely plausible for any given faction to come to accept constitutional values, forsake war and join the peace process. What is critically important to the people of Afghanistan is to define the intention of reaching a peace deal with this group through a national framework, acceptable to the people of Afghanistan. Seventeen years after the emergence of the Taliban, not only have there been no changes in their strategy but the new generation of this group is far more extremist and fanatical in their beliefs and approach.

Peace talks with the Taliban, promoted by the Afghan administration, is nothing more than an attempt to bring back into the fold those individuals who have proven to be ineffective for the Taliban and have thus been ousted from the Taliban movement. It is also an attempt to bring in those groups which the administration for its own purposes wishes to incorporate into the government. These groups, after all, are the product of this administration's ambiguous diplomacy. In effect, there are a number of other opposition groups such as the narco-mafia groups, smuggler bands, groups opposed to provincial governors, commanders, dealers, groups created due to local hostilities and other such groups that benefit from labeling themselves as "Taliban" and misuse the good offices of the international community in the peace process. The Taliban equally benefit from such groups mainly in their propaganda war. In this context, such conspiracies not only deter the resolution of the problem but further complicate the situation.

The radical shift in the policies of the international community from combating terrorism and extremism to reaching a peace agreement with the Taliban has led to confusion. Different regional and global actors have their own definition of peace and pursue those agendas which are not consistent with the peace that the people of Afghanistan want and deserve. Any deal with the Taliban requires a national consensus; it cannot be subject to the whims and interests of certain individuals, parties, tribes or administration. The issue transcends even the jurisdiction of the national assembly. An opportunity should be extended to the people of Afghanistan to participate in making these decisions, particularly women who were the main victims of the Taliban and the Al-Qaeda ideology.

## The 2014 Deadline for Political Reform and Peace Building in Afghanistan

International forces have been stationed in Afghanistan for last ten years, and although the 2014 deadline for their withdrawal is looming near, there remain significant security challenges, and the people of Afghanistan are apprehensive about the future. In the Bonn Conference, the international community declared its commitment to supporting Afghanistan's fight against terrorism. World leaders promised to back the process of nation and state building in Afghanistan and assist the reconstruction, democratisation and establishment of rule of law in the war-torn country. Ten years after the first Bonn Conference, around 100 countries of the world gathered at the second Bonn Conference and the international community unanimously renewed its commitment in support of Afghanistan. At the same time, however, the international community underscored its intention to withdraw their forces by the year 2014 and transfer security affairs to the Afghan forces.

One would assume that after ten years of hands on experience in Afghanistan, the international community would understand that without political reform and fundamental changes in the prevailing power structure, the war on terror cannot be won. Such victory is entirely dependent on stability in Afghanistan. A hasty withdrawal of international troops without the aforementioned measures will inevitably result in the collapse of the Kabul regime, and the country will revert to being a bastion of terror it was prior to 2001. History is rife with such examples. Dr. Najibullah's leftist regime fell in 1992 after the Geneva agreement, despite the fact that the regime was more powerful and better organised than the current Karzai-led administration.

Political reforms must be undertaken on the basis of decentralisation of power. Power must be distributed as per the decentralised nature of Afghan society. Social and political justice must be ensured for all. Decision-making structures must be organised in way as to enable citizens to participate and know how matters of state are conducted. A moderate foreign policy, particularly with regard to the immediate region, must be formulated. A national strategy must be devised, beginning with wide-scale confidence building process. In this manner, the space available for terrorism and extremism would shrink.

In Afghanistan, political institution building must become a priority over any other development. Even the rule of law, which is a prerequisite for the emergence of democracy, is not possible without fundamental changes in the political system. Focus on individuals, tribes and families should be diminished. Even though political reform is a long term process and must be implemented gradually, the process of reform must be intiated.

Political reforms required in Afghanistan can be summarised as follows:

1. Fundamental reform in power structures;
2. Rule of law and institution building in Afghanistan;
3. Establishment and strengthening of political parties and civil society organisations; and
4. Free, fair and transparent elections and reform of the election mechanism.

## Fundamental Reform in the Power Structures

The perpetuation of outdated political systems and approaches, resistance to change and emphasis on inefficient practices and institutions are among the primary causes behind the failure of successive Afghan administrations throughout history to bring in reform. Today, Afghanistan is re-living numerous historic tragedies and calamities as a result of these outdated political principles. Instead of adopting new methods, the current administration has resorted to reviving archaic and ineffective systems.A brief overview of the political history of Afghanistan demonstrates the covert intentions of Afghan leaders, which has primarily revolved around their drive to maintain a grip on power. Their medieval tactics prevent the emergence of forces that might regulate and control the mis-use of power. These types of policies have led Afghanistan into a sea of turbulence.

After Hamid Karzai's appointment as head of the interim administration in the first Bonn conference, the United States committed its second mistake by imposing a presidential system on the country. This plunged Afghanistan into a new phase of crisis. The imposition of a centralised presidential system in the Constitutional Loya Jirga (2004) contradicts the understanding reached by the participants of the Bonn conference. Ten years on, the deficiencies of this highly centralised presidential system are amply clear. Contentions, conflicts between the elites and regional competitions that have been at the root of all calamities during the history of Afghanistan have re-appeared. Insisting on the preservation of this system will cement the continued failure of Afghanistan.

Neither the centralised government has the capacity for governance nor has it achieved the requisite legitimacy. The 2004 constitution paved the way for a highly centralised government based on the royal constitution of 1964. In a country where politics are decentralised in nature, its president has the authority of appointing provincial and district governors, chiefs of police, ministers, directors of so-called independent commissions, and all government employees. Moreover, the President controls the budget, expenses, and accounts.

According to the Afghan constitution, the parliament has the responsibility to audit, control and grant votes of confidence; however these powers have never been put into practice. If the government feels challenged, it has no qualms in taking action to quell this perceived threat, without fear of recrimination. The Supreme Court which should have acted as an independent institution, has never disagreed with the president on important affairs. There are many high ranking government officials and even the head of Supreme Court and some of its members who carry on their functions without having a vote of confidence from the parliament.

Eight years after the promulgation of the Constitution, the election of district councils as a complementary element to the Loya Jirga has not taken place. The president has withheld the launching of the district council elections in order to avoid the completion of Loya Jirga quorum so that he would be able to convene traditional Loya Jirgas. Similarly, the election to the municipalities have not been held, while the authorities of the provincial councils are yet to be specified. The current provincial councils hold no decision making and budgetary authority apart from advising government bodies. The provincial budgets are prepared by the government ministries at the central level and managed with direct orders by the president. Very often, decisions related to provincial budgets are politically driven.

The centralisation of power, budget and appointments from Kabul as well as the weakness of judiciary and legislative institutions, have led to widespread corruption and the emergence of a powerful economic mafia with nexus with the government. As a result, people have distanced themselves from the state and some even joined the armed opposition.

The following changes are required as part of the political reform in Afghanistan.

A. Cabinet ministers, members of independent commissions, (the independent election commission and election mechanism) and members of Supreme Court should be approved by and receive vote of confidence from parliament as per the Constitution.

B. Provincial Councils, local governments and municipalities are established as per the law.

C. Implementation of a bill which disallows appointment of incompetent individuals or criminals.

D. Indictment of drug and economic mafia currently holding positions in the government.

E. Guarantee the principle of separation of power.

Fundamental change in the political structures of the system, the principle of distribution of power with introduction of parliamentary system at the center, specifying the authority of the provincial and local councils, conducting the election of municipalities and district councils and as well as the election of the provincial governors are the critical priorities for Afghanistan.

In order to establish a strong and lasting national government, democracy should be strengthened from provinces to the capital. There is a need of a system containing the necessary balances and skills to prevent the accumulation and misuse of power in the hand of one person. Adopting a parliamentary system at the centre and holding local elections in the provinces are considered a part of the principle of the distribution of power. Delegating responsibility and authority to local councils and holding local elections would enable people to practice democracy and develop a respect for the law. These changes should constitute the natural and lawful rights of the people in the new era of political transformation.

## Rule of Law and Institution Building in Afghanistan

Historically, the desire of the Afghans for a legitimate political system stems from their chronic uncertainty and insecurity in the absence of a national legal framework. In the past decade, implementing legislations has been a learning opportunity for the elites but for the common man it is confusing, bewildering and mystifying. One recent example was the convening of a traditional Loya Jirga despite firm opposition from segments of civil society, political parties, and prominent individuals. By issuing a decree and acting above the law, the president not only undermined the legal system but proved that the government abides by laws in order to achieve its own political objectives. A weak, fragmented and ineffective parliament such as in place today in Afghanistan is the result of rivalries within the administration. The 2009 election in Afghanistan has resulted in the establishment of a monopolistic government, weak parliament and a dependent legislative system in Afghanistan. Tragically, the election itself was used as an excuse for authoritarianism. If this unbridled power is not checked, this might soon morph into a permanent dictatorship.

## Establishment and Strengthening of Political Parties and Civil Society Organisations

Historically, inter-elite rivalries and the lack of political and social institutions obstructed the state-building process and impeded the emergence of a broad-sweeping national identity. In modern times, Afghanistan's greatest obstacle to peace and stability is the perpetuation of the patrician system in the government. Afghanistan could have embarked upon a new chapter and political reform that would have led to the establishment of effective national political parties. But the international community failed to support those political parties who could have played a vital role in modernising Afghanistan. Political parties and active civil society organizations (CSO) should have formed the foundation of the democratisation process. By turning a blind eye to the Afghan administration's implementation of old policies and tribal assemblies, the international community is clearly vying to expedite its own exit from Afghanistan.

The calamitous potential of the personal, tribal and linguistic agendas of the present administration can only be averted by the empowerment of political parties in Afghanistan. Political parties convey the perspectives and the will of the people and help the government move towards that direction. Political parties will help people to put forward their agenda in a lawful manner, and avoid fracturing the country along ethnic, tribal or religious lines. Power has been the source of corruption in Afghanistan's centuries' old history and particularly during the last ten years. Afghanistan figures high up in the list of most corrupt countries in the world. Endemic corruption has spurred a rapid decline in political ethics. In today's Afghanistan, political parties are often defined by their leader and their agenda, reflecting the personal ambitions of the leader.

Another critical responsibility of political parties in Afghanistan is to review and define their political doctrine in order to avoid tensions and confrontations. They should have a precise definition of national interests, security, national unity, social justice, foreign policy and other components of their political doctrine. Only in this manner can the crisis of confidence be abated and national trust regained. So long as political players do not adhere to the rules of the game, politics will remain a sport for the narrow-minded self-interested individuals. Most of the non-partisan representatives who have succeeded in the national assembly have a tendency to focus on local and regional issues, and they are less loyal to the national interests of the country as they are dependent on local sources of support for re-election.

A series of weak excuses have been used to marginalize the role of political parties. The rationale was the political parties were not sufficiently organised to represent the people. This was one of the hardest blows to democratisation and political development in Afghanistan. Political parties supplement parliamentary democracy. Parliament could never play a significant role without the serious and active participation of political parties. As a feature of parliamentary democracy, the political weight within parliament should be proportional to its social representation, so that the parliament yields results in line with national interests. Else, such imbalances will provide fertile ground for social and political violence.

## Free, Fair, Transparent Election and Fundamental Reform of the Election Mechanism

Over the last ten years, Afghanistan has seen four elections—two presidential elections and two parliamentary elections. While elections and the right to vote are novel concepts in Afghanistan, the process is vital for the nascent democratic institutions in the country. Unfortunately, all four elections were marred by fraud and irregularities, and the process is now seen as nothing more than a charade that lends a veneer of legitimacy to the government.

The independent election commission, whose members were appointed by the president, serves the interests of the government. Similarly, the Single-Non-Transferable Voting system (SNTV) for the parliament has led to the establishment of a toothless parliament. Given the social composition of Afghanistan, this system does not produce a proportional representative system. There is neither accountability, nor responsibility. Parliament remains mired in internal squabbles, thereby making little impact on the country's legislative affairs, auditing or keeping checks on the government.

The best option would be the parliamentary electoral system of Proportional Representation (PR), which is compatible with the realities on the ground in Afghanistan with respect to the population, representation, and parties. Afghanistan needs good management, free and fair elections, a truly independent monitoring commission and a reliable census. The composition of the election commission and the integrity of the commission's members will affect the level of legitimacy it enjoys and in turn, that of the election results. An impartial judge faithful to the country's constitution must be empowered to give legal interpretations in the event of electoral fraud and irregularities, and uphold the rule of law and transparency.

## Conclusion

This paper by delving into the historical background of the state and institution building processes in Afghanistan has emphasised on the serious need for political reform, policy change and broad sweeping changes in political structures as a prerequisite for lasting peace in Afghanistan. Several inter-related issues nation and state building processes, confidence building, formulation of a national strategy and national security, together with issues such as foreign policy, and critical regional relations, are integral components to ensure lasting peace in the country. Although successive Afghan governments have endeavored to address these issues from time to time, due to the lack of suitable political mechanisms, a national government and legal structures, their efforts have been fruitless.

The politically motivated peace talks with the Taliban will not lead to a sustainable peace in Afghanistan. These are merely games played by intelligence agencies, which will only add to Afghanistan's historical problems. Any effort that does not begin by solving the inherent problems in political structure, establishing national political institutions or addressing core national issues, will certainly lead to a crisis of confidence and legitimacy. There is a need to replace terrorism and tribalism with the values and policies of a modern state. Traditional rule of politics, ethnic supremacy or monopoly of power held by certain factions and individuals must be dispensed with.

As Afghanistan approaches the 2014 deadline for the withdrawal of international troops, it becomes increasingly important to achieve some measure of political stability essential for establishing durable peace in Afghanistan. Launching the confidence building process, devising a clear vision for the future, and consolidating the political will to realize these goals, must be on the national agenda, in order to compensate for the lost decade since the first Bonn conference.

# 6

# Myths and Impact of Bad Governance on Stability in Afghanistan

*Shahmahmood Miakhel*

This chapter details specific events in Afghanistan during the last three and half decades. Many of these events have become part of the living history in Afghanistan.[1] The main focus of this endeavor is not to delve on the root causes of the ongoing insurgency in Afghanistan, but on the prospects of political, military, and economic transition leading up to 2014. The chapter dispels a few myths that exist among Afghans, as well as within the international community, regarding Afghans and Afghanistan. It is important to mention that these myths have not only become a part of the popular narrative and but have also significantly influenced policy formulation, albeit negatively. As former interior minister of Afghanistan, Ali Ahmad Jalali once said that "the Afghan government and international community are both partners in Afghanistan, but unfortunately neither side understands the other very well".[2]

## Myths about Afghanistan

There are two types of myths, one set circulating within the international community and the other set circulating among the Afghan elites. The myths within the international community including the so-called non-Afghan experts are:

- Afghanistan has never had a functional government;
- Afghans do not know how to practice democracy and see it as perfectly acceptable to make deals with warlords and power brokers or—in some cases—even with known criminals;
- Since the Afghan government is weak and does not control areas beyond Kabul, it is willing to make deal with the local warlords;

- The government cannot function because there is a lack of capacity and absence of laws and institutions to govern;
- Since Afghanistan's government does not function because of its ineffectual centralised system, it is best to ignore the central government and work with the peripheries; and
- Corruption is an inevitable part of Afghan culture.

Similarly the myths circulating among the Afghan elites are as follows.

- Counter terrorism is an excuse by the international community, especially the United States (U.S.), to control the region and have access to Central Asian natural resources;
- The U.S. wants to have a long-term presence in Afghanistan in order to curb Chinese influence in the region;
- The U.S. is in Afghanistan to have control over extensive mines and natural resources in the country;
- For the international community to stay in Afghanistan, it is imperative that they maintain the status quo—allow insurgency to fester—to justify their presence, even if it means supporting both the Taliban and Afghan government at the same time;
- The presence of international community is a conspiracy against the Pashtun ethnic group in the region, which explains why a majority of fighting is occurring in the Pashtun areas on both sides of the Afghanistan-Pakistan border;
- The prime objective of international community is to destabilize the region, which is why they support both the Afghan government and Taliban. This view is particularly widely prevalent in rural areas where there is a significant information gap; and
- The international community is in Afghanistan as part of a larger conspiracy to destroy Islam.

It is important to explain and dispel these myths. To begin, the myth that Afghanistan has never had a functional government and corruption is an inevitable part of the Afghan culture, is flawed.

Before 1978, Afghanistan had a functional government with opportunities for people to travel to different provinces, study in the universities, fulfil military duties, work as civil servants and also to address their grievances through the existing formal and informal institutions. All ethnic groups and educated elites had opportunity to serve in different parts of the country. In those times, for example, an unarmed police officer in a very remote part of the country could summon anyone who had committed a crime or against whom someone had lodged a complaint, to the local government office. The elders—*Maliks, Arbabs, Kalantar or Qaryadars*[3] were obliged to report all criminal activities to the government. Similarly, with the exception of the people of Loya Paktia,[4] everyone including sons of King Zahir Shah and President Daud, were not exempted from military conscription. The countryside was safe that one could travel to any part of the country during day and night without any dangers of physical harm.

In terms of accountability and transparency, most former senior government officials reached the highest positions by virtue of merit, especially in the decades of democracy—1960s and 70s. Examples of this trend include most prime ministers, ministers and governors who assumed positions after 1964 and who did not belong to the royal family. They reached these positions mostly through their skill and hard work.

Likewise, in Afghanistan the court system and rule of law remained functional and people had confidence in the system to address their grievances through the formal or informal justice system. Indeed, it was a sign of pride for most senior officials to be honest and poor rather than corrupt and rich. Even to this day, many people reminiscence of the value system of the previous regimes. Remarkably, despite all the ills committed by former members of Khalq faction of the People's Democratic Party of Afghanistan (PDPA), people praise them for not being corrupt, unlike the Mujahideen factions and warlords in later times. In particular, most senior officials of the Khalq regime still live under poor conditions, which show that they did not amass illegal wealth during their tenure in power.

A good example of the merit based, transparent and functional system is the story of Zarlashta, President Daud's daughter who failed to clear the examination in the Kabul University. According to Chief Justice Abdul Salam Azimi[5] who was former Chancellor of Kabul University, Professor Mohibi[6] of the Science Faculty refused to retract the decision against President's daughter. Chief Justice Azimi said that many people approached Prof. Mohibi to try to convince him to change his decision, but the professor insisted that she had to be treated at par with the other students. President Daud summoned the professor and expressed his appreciation for his fairness and courage and later appointed him as Minister of Higher Education. Such examples are indicative of the fact that Afghanistan did have a functional government and corruption was not an inherent part of the Afghan culture.

Another myth that needs to be tested is that Afghans do not know how to practice democracy. Many Afghans strongly disagree with this statement. In fact, principles of equality, representation and independence are strongly rooted among Afghans. Most of Afghanistan's local institutions are based on equal participation of people in day-to-day decision making processes. *Jirgas* and *Shuras* (two terms used for formal gatherings) are the best examples of how people make their decisions based on fair democratic participation. In most instances, all the men of a community have equal right to sit on councils like *shuras*.[7] Local political positions are not strictly inherited and elders must work to satisfy their followers or they risk losing their positions.

Unfortunately, in the past and especially since 2001, the international community has tried to impose non-democratic processes on a democratic society at the local level.[8] This is done by favouring certain local commanders and providing them with resources so that they no longer need to respond to the needs of the communities, thereby promoting a culture of impunity. For example, during the last decade, most of contracts in the security and construction sectors were awarded to warlords or to those who had support of the international community and not necessarily the support of the people.

The model of democratic governments might vary from country-to-country, but the essence of democratic process is fair participation of people in the decision-making process, governance and selection or election of their leaders. To this day, many Afghans testify that a majority of local leaders before 1978 were respected by the people, not because of their wealth or rules of inheritance, but for their impartiality, fairness and services. In essence, Afghans have given a fair chance to socialism, communism, *jihad*, and democracy as the norms of governance—but all these ideologies have failed because of the unfairness of the government and the breakdown of governance structures. The past two centuries of Afghan history have amply demonstrated that the prime reason for the fall of the regimes is rooted in the system of resistance such regimes develop towards allowing popular participation.

As Professor Barfield observes "while Afghanistan's Durrani rulers (1747-1978) may have originated in an egalitarian Pashtun tribal system, they employed a classical hierarchal model of governance to maintain power exclusively within their own dynastic lines. They abandoned the democratic and federal political institutions used among the Pashtun tribes at the local level, and replaced them with autocracy. Because of this, the relationship between the Pashtun tribes and their putative dynastic leaders was always a troubled one, in which cooperation (or conflict) depended on the issues involved.[9]

According to Professor Barfield, the rulers imposed classical hierarchal autocratic model of governance on the egalitarian society of Afghanistan thereby excluding people from decision making processes that impacted on their day to day life. Throughout the history of Afghanistan, people have resisted, both at national and local levels, attempts by rulers to impose non-democratic system or processes.[10] Such resistance has either been through armed opposition or through means of non-cooperation with the regimes. This is the reason why regimes have failed.[11] For example, Amanuallah Khan's regime was overthrown in 1929 after he tried to impose a new value system without consulting local communities. The same fate befell on the post 1978 communist regimes.

Since 2001, exclusion of people from decision-making processes or ignoring opinions of people in the political process has created a schism between people and the government of Afghanistan. This has, in turn, created a conducive condition for the growth of the insurgency.[12] The decisions taken in the Bonn

Conference (2001), Emergency Loya Jirga (2002), Constitutional Loya Jirga (2003), and in subsequent presidential and parliamentary elections in (2004, 2005, 2009, 2010) have been ignored and undermined by the government and international community.[13] Consequently, the results of each of these processes have faced credibility and legitimacy challenges. This chapter does not attempt to provide details about each of these processes.[14] In many of these instances participants were handpicked by the government, reinforcing the perception that the chosen lot were not the real representative of the country as a whole.

Another good example is the recent election fiasco in Afghanistan. Parliamentary elections took place in September 2010, but the results and legal stature of parliament are questioned even after more than one year, despite the fact that close to 120 million dollars were spent to ensure free and fair elections.[15] By way of contrast, back in the 1960s, when Afghanistan had less communication infrastructure, the results of elections would be announced on the same evening, and the whole process did not cost as much.

At present, elections in Afghanistan cost hundreds of millions of U.S. dollars and are mostly funded by donors. It is very obvious that such patterns of elections would not be possible to be held without international support.[16] However, it is possible to design the whole new election process in a way to reduce the cost to the level affordable by Afghan government in the long run. For example, in 2002, the election for the Emergency *Loya Jirga*, in four eastern provinces of Kunar, Laghman, Nuristan and Nangarhar, cost less than U.S. $100,000 in which about 2400 representatives were elected by the people in first round of election. That election was more representative and legitimate in the eyes of people compared to the recent elections.[17] In fact, the complications and slow announcement of results has raised concerns that the election results are being manipulated by high level officials.

Some commentators argue that lack of capacity and absence of institutions are the main problem of service delivery in Afghanistan. However, facts prove otherwise. Afghanistan may need to improve capacity and some procedures in the administrative system. But the actual problem is that of lack of vision and political will to use the existing capacity and to appoint competent, honest people to administrative positions. Incidentally, the reforms process in the Security Sector, Judiciary, Economic and Civil Service sectors have created enormous job insecurity. Many qualified people have been removed from the system in the pretext of reforms.

Arguably, the administrative system of Afghanistan is more sophisticated than the UN system[18] and the current work force is not capable of addressing the needs of the people. They can serve as useful advisors to senior officials rather than appointing foreign civilian advisors who are not familiar with the Afghan system. However, the views of such qualified, honest and dedicated workers in the country have not been taken into account. In many instances, they have been replaced by incompetent and dishonest officials from the government machinery due to favoritism, patronage, ethnic politics and corruption.[19] In 2003, the local governance and administration department of the Ministry of Interior (MoI), had three foreign advisors. The MoI decided not to renew their contracts because none of them were able to help and advise the department of local governance and administration. They lacked the field knowledge which is relevant for governance. On the contrary, the local directors who knew the system, rules and regulations, and carried out most of the work were found to be more suitable than the foreign advisors.

Commentators argue that the current centralised system of government is a cause of instability in Afghanistan as it does not facilitate improvement of governance. This notion can be dispelled as well. Who is in charge of the model is more important than the model of the government itself. Models can be improved and that is a process in continuum. Despite the criticisms labeled against them, the current judicial and police system of Afghanistan have convicted some criminals. However, political interefence and influence of the mafia network ensured that they were released by Presidential decree. Example can be cited of the April 2009 release of five convicted drug dealers by President Karzai. These five men were allegedly close to the President's campaign manager in 2009.[20]

Many argue that the central government is weak and does not exercise authority beyond Kabul. The weakness in the government in Kabul is not because the Afghan government's enemies are very strong, but because the government in Kabul has become hostage to selected few who benefit from the war economy and instability. It could be argued that the current government of Afghanistan is the strongest government in the history of Afghanistan: it has national and international support, but unfortunately it is not able to use all this support for establishing a better system. According to the Asia Foundation Survey in 2011, the support for the government of Afghanistan is still much higher than sympathy for the armed opposition to the government.[21] Yet it is a pity that the government has not been able to deliver the basic services to shore up it's credibility.

Despite corruption, insecurity and mismanagement, people are still willing to give a chance to the current system. However, at the same time, there appears to be a complete failure of strategic communication from the government. In contrast, the Afghan government's enemies are more sophisticated in communicating their strategies. Their messages resonate more effectively among the Afghan people not because people agree with them, but because they are consistent with their messages and are able to implement their decisions, albeit ruthlessly. For example if Taliban issue a night letter to stop cooperation with the government and international community, people are aware of the implications of disobeying such a diktat.

On the contrary, the Afghan government and international community are seen to be failing in fulfilling their promises. For example, on the recent reconciliation talks, different government entities, representatives of the international community, and political leaders have been giving contradictory messages to the masses, thereby indicating that there is no consensus how to move forward with peace talks. The insurgents, on the other hand, have been better able to communicate through very clear messages and have shifted the narrative to their own advantage.

Regarding the second set of myths, there is no doubt that the international community has made colossal mistakes and lost many opportunities to succeed in Afghanistan. One of the principal reasons of their failure in Afghanistan is the lack of understanding of the human terrain, a total lack of preparedness for a long war and a lack of interest in institution building in Afghanistan. As Minister Jalali mentioned in one of his discussions, 'when there was more time, there were no resources to support institutions in Afghanistan, but then when there were more resources, there is no time to build institutions in Afghanistan'.[22]

General Caldwell, head of NATO Training Mission-Afghanistan (NTM-A) mentioned in his review that there were not sufficient resources before 2009 for Afghan National Security Forces.[23] Between 2003-2005, the total budget of the Ministry of Interior of Afghanistan, including IDLG, was around U.S.$ 129 million, but now the total budget of ANSF is more than U.S.$ 10 billion.[24] A brief scrutiny at the involvement of international community and disbursement of resources every year reveals that the international community especially the U.S. never had a long term plan for Afghanistan. Even now, the contradictory statements made by different U.S. government officials and politicians are indicative of the fact that the U.S. does not have a long term political strategy for Afghanistan.

The U.S. and international community have interest in the region for security and economic reasons. However, an unstable Afghanistan with the dangers that it might become a safe haven for the Al-Qaeda remains a concern to the international community, Afghanistan's distant and close neighbours. There is no doubt that the current policies of spending billions of dollars with little or no accountability will not bring stability to Afghanistan.

Some predict that the Taliban movement might initiate *Jihad* in Afghanistan. However, the opposite could be also true. The war in Afghanistan is not a religious war and those who support it do so for political reasons, using Islam or ethnicity as a rallying point. However, since the government has been ineffective, those who support the Taliban or exploit ethnic divisions have been able to use religious rhetoric to further their causes.

Undoubtedly, the international community has committed mistakes. Moreover, Afghanistan's neighbours, especially Pakistan, have been supporting the insurgency and have provided them sanctuaries. It is an open secret. As the famous English proverb says that good fences make good neighbours, the

Afghans have to protect their own interests. The same proverb, in the Pashtu language, says that, *Khapal mal wa sata aw gawandai ta ma waya chee ghala* ("Keep your property safe and don't call the neighbour as thief."). This implies that if Afghanistan does not take measures to protect its own interest, no one else will do the same. Likewise, as long as the Afghan people and government do not take responsibility, notwithstanding the support Afghanistan gets from international community, security and governance cannot improve in Afghanistan.

In 1973, leaders of an underground Islamist group, *Jawanani-Musulman* (Muslim Youth Organisation), including Gulbudin Hekmatyar and Professor Burhanuddin Rabani, Ahmad Shah Massoud, Moulavi Khales, Jalaluddin Haqani and others, escaped Afghanistan and crossed over to Pakistan. The then government of Zulfiqar Ali Bhutto in Pakistan trained and equipped them to stage war against the government of President Daud. These groups were sent into Afghanistan and attacked the government facilities in Kunar, Laghman, Panjsher, Nangarhar and Paktika provinces, but their uprising was immediately suppressed by the people of Afghanistan, who handed over most of the attackers to the government.[25] The local villagers arrested the leader of the Laghman group, Moulavi Habi-ur-Rahman and his followers and turned them over to government officials. This example indicates that as long as people of Afghanistan trust their government, external training, arms, sanctuaries and support for the Taliban cannot destabilize Afghanistan.

During the communist coup in 1979, the regime replaced the entire government machinery with their party loyalists and this led to a collapse of the system of governance. This time around, the same insurgent groups and individuals that had earlier been rejected by the people were able to destabilize Afghanistan. It can be argued that the reason for the Mujahideen success was because of the absence of legitimate government in Afghanistan and failure of governance. The same was true for Taliban after the civil war and incessant factional fighting. While ideology might have provided a tool, the absence of governance and Soviets' lack of understanding of Afghan society were the main drivers of the Mujahiden uprising, especially in the rural areas. In the present context, insurgency in Afghanistan derives its strength from the absence of governance and also the lack of socio-cultural understanding of Afghanistan by the international community.

## Recommendations

Both in the short and long-term, there is a strong need to focus on political transition leading up to 2014 to ensure that a smooth transition of power takes place, along with new momentum for better governance and accountability. The people of Afghanistan will not support a government which cannot defend the rights of all citizens equally. In order to pave the ground for smooth and peaceful transition of power in 2014, the space for positive political competition need to be made available for all the forces. Towards that end, the following steps need to be taken by the Afghan government and international community.

1. According to the constitution of Afghanistan, which specifies the date of presidential and parliamentary elections, these dates need to be fixed in order to open space for healthy political competition.
2. Once the date of elections are fixed, it would guarantee the space for many groups and individual to build their networks and coalition against each other and thereby ensure peaceful political transition.
3. By consultation with all political groups and potential individual contenders, an Independent Electoral Commission (IEC) should be appointed by the President of Afghanistan in order to guarantee credible election process.
4. The International Community, especially United Nations (UN), European Union (EU), Organisation of Islamic Countries (OIC) and other regional organisations (RO) and civil society groups (CSO) should ensure a good mechanism for monitoring the elections.
5. Earlier experience has demonstrated that holding the provincial election with the presidential election, provides opportunity for fraud and rigging of elections. It is strongly recommended that these two elections should not take place simultaneously.
6. The government of Afghanistan and especially President Karzai needs to provide guarantees to pave the way for peaceful and smooth transition and avoid undue interfere in the election process. A peaceful political transition is a legacy President Karzai should leave behind. Since Amir Abur Rahman Kahn (1880-1910) Afghanistan has not witnessed a peaceful transition of power.

In the absence of these measures, the credibility of the government would remain at stake. Such a government would not be able to command the support of the people and hence, its survivability would be in doubt. In the worst case scenario, Afghanistan might be forced to witness another civil war.

## Notes

1. Author has reported on these events in his various roles as a journalist, aid-worker, United Nations and government official.
2. Author discussion with Minister Ali Jalali on 31 of January 2012, Washington DC.
3. Chiefs of villages in different parts of Afghanistan are called by these names.
4. Exemption from military service was a reward to the people of Paktia who supported King Nadir Khan when he took over Kabul in 1929. While the men of Paktia did not have to join the army, they did serve in a local police force known as the *arbaki*, which had the responsibility for protecting their areas.
5. A USIP delegation including the author had a meeting with Chief Justice Azimi on 9 November 2009. During the meeting the author asked him to verify a story he had heard that President Daud's daughter was failed by a professor of Kabul University while he was chancellor.

6. He died in 2011.
7. There is less or no representation of women in *Jirga* and *Shuras*. Women also have less representation in the official government system as well as the judicial system.
8. The Maliks or local elders, who are the middle class of Afghanistan, have been suppressed in the last three decades by the PDPA regimes, the Mujahideen, Taliban and even now by the criminal-warlords-patronage system of the current regime.
9. Thomas Barfield, *Afghanistan: A cultural and political history*. Princeton University Press, 2010, p. 4.
10. For more details, see "The Rule of Law in Afghanistan: Missing in Action" in Whit Mason, ed. *Rule of Law and Human Security*, Cambridge University Press, 2011.
11. The communist regimes of PDPA, Mujahideen, Taliban have failed and even the current regime is on the verge of failure, due to imposition of non-democratic system in Afghanistan.
12. Insurgency grows only when internal conditions are conducive and the insurgents groups have outside safe haven and chain of support militarily and financially.
13. For further details, see Shah Mahmood Miakhel, *Emergency Loya Jirga and Election Process in Eastern Provinces* in Pashtu Language, Pir Printing, Kabul, 2006. and Shah Mahmood Miakhel, "The Importance of Tribal Structures and Pakhtunwali in Afghanistan: Their Role in Security and Governance,", in Arpita Basu Raj, ed. *Challenges and Dilemmas of State-Building in Afghanistan: Report of a Study Trip to Kabul*, Shipra Publications, New Delhi, 2008, pp. 97-110.
14. However, as a participant of some of these Jirgas and elections, I have witnessed firsthand that the decisions of the people were undermined by means of coercion and fraud For more details see Shah Mahmood Miakhel, *Emergency Loya Jirga and Election Process in Eastern Provinces*, Pir Printing, Kabul, 2006.
15. Pierre Tristam, *Bullets, Not Ballots, in Afghanistan's Parliamentary Election*, http://middleeast.about.com/b/2010/09/19/bullets-not-ballots-in-afghanistans-parliamentary-election.htm. Accessed on 18 October 2011.
16. In spite of expenditures running into hundreds of millions of U.S. dollars, district, village and municipal elections in Afghanistan have not been not held in the last 10 years.
17. The author of this paper was served as advisor to election of Emergency Loya Jirga in eastern provinces from April-June 2002.
18. The author of this paper worked as Deputy Minister of Interior, in charge of local governance department (2003-2005) and Governance Advisor to UNAMA (2005-2009). The local governance department was separated from the Ministry of Interior in 2007 and thereafter names as Independent Directorate of Local Governance (IDLG).
19. Author book; *Ministry of Interior: Challenges and Achievements: A Personal Account, Published by Author in Pashto language*, Kabul, 2011.
20. Karzai released dangerous detainees: WikiLeaks, 30 November 2010, http://www.cbc.ca/news/world/story/2010/11/30/wikileaks-karzai-.html. Accessed on 19 October 2011.
21. *Key Findings—Afghanistan in 2011: A Survey of the Afghan People*, http://asiafoundation.org/resources/pdfs/KeyFindingsAGSurveyBookFinal.pdf. Accessed on 20 October 2011.
22. Author discussion with Minister Jalali on 31st of January 2012 in Washington DC.
23. NTM-A: Year in Review, November 2009 to November 2010, http://www.defense.gov/Blog_files/Blog_assets/NTMAYearinReviewFINAL.pdf. Accessed on 19 December 2011.
24. Ibid.
25. The author was a high school student and his father worked in Laghman province as Director of ID. He witnessed this operation and arrest of the attackers.

# SECTION III

# AID, GENDER, DEVELOPMENT, ECONOMIC OPPORTUNITIES, TRADE, INVESTMENT,CONNECTIVITY & STRATEGIC COMMUNICATION

# 7

# Afghanistan in the Course of Transition: Civilian Surge, Aid Coordination, War Economy and Alternative Livelihood

*Najeeb Ur Rahman Manalai*

Transition of security responsibilities to Afghans, as a process cannot be actualised in quick time. The success of the process will require support of Afghans throughout the country as well as long term assistance from the international community. Recognising the role of the international community in the last decade, many Afghans agree that much has been achieved in terms of progress towards democratisation and development, though some highlight that more needs to be done to bring in 'peace and stability'. Their expectations of the international actors assisting Afghanistan include optimal use of the resources and preventing the reversal of gains. The demands of Afghans include ensuring meaningful participation of the people in the peace process and other crucial decisions, continuation of the assistance to the country until it can stand on its own feet, and enable the Afghans to achieve tangible progress towards democracy and stabilisation of their country.

## Understanding the Dynamics of the Transition Process

Transition of lead security responsibility from the international military (IM) forces to the Afghan National Security Forces (ANSF) has been the goal of the government of Afghanistan and the NATO troop contributing countries. The government of Afghanistan and the international community agreed at the Kabul and Lisbon conferences in 2010 that by the end of 2014, the ANSF should assume full responsibility for security across the country and the international troops are to be gradually withdrawn.

Transition as expressed by H.E. President Hamid Karzai in his speech in Kabul conference, implied that Afghan National Security Forces (ANSF) should lead and conduct military operations in all the provinces by the end of 2014. The international community has committed to provide the necessary support to train, equip, fund and assist the ANSF. The_international community also endorsed the plan for transition developed by Afghans in coordination with their NATO allies.[1] Transition had been envisioned since the beginning of intervention in Afghanistan by coalition forces. It refers to the last phase of operations of International Security Assistance Force (ISAF) in Afghanistan.[2] In fact, it is the Afghan security forces who would have the primary responsibility for security in the country. The role of ISAF was to support the Afghan government to ensure a secure environment for the reconstruction and development of national democratic institutions.

It is a well known fact that no government will be able to bring long term stability unless it secures the support of the people. For the Afghan government, to gain legitimacy and win the support of the people, delivery of services and establishing rule of law are essential. With one third of its population living under the poverty line, coupled with another one third slightly above the poverty line, Afghanistan continues to remain among poor countries of the world.[3] Poverty and unemployment have been identified as the driving forces behind insecurity and instability. Thus, there is a need for a comprehensive strategy of building on the social, economic and political components for actualising effective transition.

Although transition process has commenced, Afghans and the international community have concerns about the existing and future challenges. Apart from security concerns, financial sustainability of the Afghan government and lack of economic opportunities are some of the major challenges. In addition to delivery of basic services and ensuring viable livelihood, there is a need for infrastructure development, public awareness, education, creation of employment opportunities, and development of an indigenous economic base. If the international community fulfills their commitments and pledges, the *inteqal* process can be actualised effectively. Thus, in order to ensure real success of transition, the previous decade's experience of the Afghan government and its international supporters should serve as a guide to rectify actions and re-direct resources to meet the real needs of the ground.

## Aid Dependency and Nature of the Afghan State

Historically, Afghanistan has had a weak central Government which has not been able to extend its writ to all corners of the country. The central Government in Kabul has relied mainly on informal structures, such as tribal and other local leadership mechanisms, to maintain social order in remote areas. In addition, Afghan leaders relied on external support to rule the country as well as to manage economic development. But in return, these countries had some expectations that would ultimately serve their interests rather than that of Afghans. Even today, many Afghans believe that the countries providing aid have their own agendas.

However, the extensive aid-dependency of the Afghan government can complicate the process of transition. Afghanistan continues to receive significant amounts of aid since 2002. Although the pledges of the international community were much higher, only 57 billion has been actually disbursed by the end of 2010.[4] Though this assistance has helped the reconstruction and ensured considerable development in building infrastructure, education, health, communications, there is a need to address gaps in other critical areas.

Despite the decade long financial assistance provided to Afghanistan, neither Afghans nor their international partners are satisfied with the outcome. More than half of the money channeled to Afghanistan has been spent on security related activities mainly by the international actors. Over 80 per cent of the total aid has been spent by the development partners, bypassing the Afghan government with little or no involvement in planning, implementation and monitoring of the development efforts. The geographical distribution of the development aid reveals that the insecure areas have received most of the aid—Helmand, Kandahar and Nangarhar provinces being the major recipients of aid money after Kabul. This in turn has reinforced perceptions about aid serving military objectives rather than actual development needs. Moreover, relatively stable and peaceful areas in the north and west, received little aid resulting in these areas swaying towards instability.

## Improving Aid Coordination and Effectiveness

Efforts have been underway to address the challenges of aid coordination and effectiveness in Afghanistan. The development of Afghanistan National Development Strategy (ANDS) which serves as a five year poverty-reduction strategy of the country (2008-13), the initiation of National Priority Programs (NPPs) supported by Kabul Conference of 2010, establishing mechanisms for improving aid coordination among all development partners and enhancing accountability by the Government of Afghanistan and international community are among the positive steps taken to improve coordination and ensure aid effectiveness. These efforts include commitment of the aid providers and donors to deliver aid through the Afghan budget, and a plan to maximize aid effectiveness and benefits from off-budget assistance to promote alignment of the off-budget assistance with Afghanistan's development needs as reflected in the Afghanistan National Development Strategy.

It was recognised by Afghanistan and international community in the London Conference of 2006 that effective coordination and monitoring mechanism are key to the success of the London Compact. Thus, a Joint Coordination and Monitoring Board (JCMB) with participation of senior Afghan

Government officials appointed by the President and representatives of the international community was established. The Board is co-chaired by the Afghan Ministry of Finance and by the Special Representative of the UN Secretary-General for Afghanistan. In addition, the Afghan Government developed various plans and programs for better coordination and monitoring of development efforts in order to ensure aid effectiveness. These initiatives include National Priority Programs (NPPs) in line with ANDS, and other measures taken by the Ministry of Finance, such as better public financing system, regular public expenditure review to ensure transparency, the ministry's strategic plan, developing donors coordination report and so forth. Further, the international community, upon request of the Afghan government, agreed that by the end of 2012, at least 50 per cent of the international aid will be provided to Afghanistan through the government's budget.

However, there are still major concerns about the emerging financial deficiencies and fiscal sustainability. A country continues to be aid dependent when it relies on external funding to cover its day-to-day operating (recurrent) costs and development expenditures.[5] External aid comprises up to 70 per cent of Afghanistan's GDP, which implies that it is an aid-driven economy[6]. However, the aid money is not the only base of the Afghan economy. Afghanistan has a real economy as well which was running even before the aid money was channeled to the country, though it was weak. When the levels of aid have reduced, the GDP has shown a relative rise indicative of a potential for economic independence. But this cannot be accurately gauged because of the irregular inflow of aid money. For instance, in 2006-07, 2008-09 and 2009-10 although the aid flow declined from its previous years, the GDP denotes a rise.[7]

However, the decline of aid will not directly affect the economic growth of Afghanistan to the levels as projected by experts. A large proportion of the money that comes to Afghanistan is not spent inside the country. Instead, it leaves Afghanistan in the forms of expatriates salaries, fees and outward remittances. With regard to the outflow of aid money, locals in southern provinces express opinion that the foreign military personnel, particularly the Americans, come to Afghanistan without passport and any government involvement and leave the country the same way in military planes. The Afghans in the south who engage with the Americans say that they take huge amounts of money with them.[8]

Surely, the sudden cessation or significant reduction of aid money will have a disastrous effect on the Afghan economy. In order to stabilize economy of Afghanistan, alternatives to aid should be sought. One of the main sources of revenue is extraction of the mineral resources and oil and gas. The issue of extracting mineral resources and mines could be very sensitive in the first few years. It could either be a blessing or a curse depending on the utilisation and benefits to the local people and economy.

## Demographic Bomb

Afghanistan has a young population which is growing in large numbers that could create a youth bulge. Over 60 per cent of the population is capable of work and can contribute to the country's economy. On the other hand, the same proportion of the population if not employed will have negative implications. With a population growth rate of 2.8 per cent, the over 30 million country's population may reach to 40 million or more in the course of a decade. While this being the case in almost all countries in the region, including South Asia and Central Asia, a viable solution would be creation of a common labor market that would provide employment opportunities in the region.

The economies of these countries are intricately linked to one another. For instance, while South Asia has great need for energy, Central Asia has energy resources but no markets. Therefore, despite many problems between and among the countries of the region, there is a need for regional economic cooperation framework that will build on Afghanistan's potential as a 'transit country' and benefit the region. Turkmenistan, Afghanistan, Pakistan, India (TAPI) gas pipeline project, Central Asia South Asia Regional Electricity Market Project and the New Silk Road Intiative are good examples of such opportunities.

## The Troop Surge and Civilian Surge

In 2009, the U.S. president Barak Obama announced sending additional troops to Afghanistan in order to implement the counterinsurgency ("clear, hold, build and transfer") strategy as enunciated by General McChrystal, Commander of ISAF and Commander, U.S. Forces Afghanistan (USFOR-A). Defined by General Petraeus, this strategy means focusing on reconstruction of the areas 'cleared' from the insurgents control and 'holding' on the area by improving delivery of services to the people and strengthening local government institutions.

President Obama announced in 2009 that civilian surge was equally important to the military surge. Thus, the U.S. administration decided to send federal civilian officers along with the military to foster civilian reconstruction efforts, known as 'civilian surge'. Specific funds were allocated to ensure positive changes in the areas retaken from the insurgents. Therefore, the number of the U.S. civilian experts increased by three times until June 2011, an increase from around 300 to 1,040 and it was planned to further increase the numbers to around 1350 by the end of 2011, though this has not been achieved so far. The U.S. has spent about $2 billion on the civilian surge and it is predicted that the costs may even go higher in the coming years with the withdrawal of the U.S. troops, to provide security to these deployed civilians and the plan to open new consulates out of Kabul. The question of whether and to what extent this civilian surge has worked is debatable. Most of this money has been spent to cover the deployment costs of these federal employees which reached $ 410,000 to $ 570,000 per person.[9]

The role and utility of these civilians on the ground is also questionable. The need for protection measures restrains their mobility and most of them cannot leave their secure compounds in Kabul. An additional negative factor is deployment of one year period provides little time for design and implementation of any kind of long term projects. Reports indicate an estimated cost of supporting every civilian rising from $507,000 in 2009 to $667,000 in 2010 and possibly $694,000 per person in 2011.[10]

From an Afghan perspective, there are huge gaps in both the reconstruction projects and civilian surge. First, involvement of the military personnel and civilians in close connection and protection by the military has led to a rise in the hidden costs of the development projects. Second, the reconstruction efforts were not supplemented by proper messaging to the people and thus, the outcomes of the development projects remained unrecognised by people, leading to failure in achieving the objective of 'wining the hearts and minds of the people'. For many Afghans, it is difficult to differentiate the military personnel from the civilians. Even the Provincial Reconstruction Teams (PRT) are considered to be military bases for planning and launch of military operations in the field, rather than civilian reconstruction agencies. Therefore, any reconstruction project implemented by the PRT or other U.S. civilians is seen as part of the military operations of the foreign forces with a hidden agenda, rather than genuine contribution to development of the area.

## The War Economy and Alternate Livelihood

Although Afghanistan has been in conflict for over three decades, the character and extent of the present of conflict is different from the previous two decades. The international military (IM) operating with or without the involvement of national security forces, the change in the identity of the fighters, the type and motivations of the insurgents groups, the interest and engagement of the international community are some distinguishing features from the past conflict. Although presence of the IM is seen as the main driver of the current conflict, their presence has helped channel billions of dollars into the country. It is true that not all of the aid money is spent in Afghanistan, but the proportion spent is still a huge amount.

At a rather lower scale, the employment of Afghans by the IM directly to support their work as interpreters, advisors, and logistics providers and other service staff, or through the development projects has been a means of regular income for many Afghans. Many Afghan private companies, receive funds from the IM for development projects or other long term contracts for logistics and security for supply routes and convoys. The economic value of such contributions may not be very high, but it provides economic opportunities in rural areas. As a local from a remote village in Nangarhar province says: "*The money these young villagers get from the foreign military is not much, but it has kept them busy. Otherwise, only ten people can destabilize the whole village and pose serious security threats."*[11]

For the unemployed local youth, the money offered by the insurgents is considered a means of subsistence. A young man from *Kuchi* (Afghan nomadic community) in Logar province says: *"We have lost our cattle which was the main source of income for us. If I am lucky, I may find the opportunity to work as daily laborer in construction projects and earn Pak Rs.300-400 (U.S.$4-5) a day while this is only available two or three times a week. But, the Taliban offer Pak Rs.1,000 to 1,500 (U.S.$12-17)to me to implant a mine on the roadside at night. Why shouldn't I do that?"*[12]

These are major concerns that in the absence of improving legitimate means of livelihood and lack of economic opportunities might further complicate transition. There is a need for immediate and concerted effort in three sectors to help improve the situation:

> First, there is a need to build on the agriculture sector as it constitutes the livelihood for over 90 percent of people. There is a need to establish storage capacity in the rural areas, enhance productivity and improve market access of the products. The absence of storage facilities has constrained many farmers. Throughout the year, Afghans witness flow of fruits to the neighbouring Pakistan at a very low price when crops are collected, simply because of storage capacity. Later during the year, this fruit is imported back from Pakistan at a significantly higher price.
>
> Second, promotion of trade and transit will contribute to economic development of Afghanistan. Moreover, the absence of sustainable and legitimate means of livelihood has a crucial role in the maintenance of insecurity. It is anticipated that if trade and transit improves livelihood and economic opportunities, it will have a positive impact on the security.
>
> Third, the problems of Afghanistan need to be seen in the regional context and therefore, regional cooperation could be a mechanism for binding countries together. Currently, Pakistan's and Iran's involvement are evident in the conflict in Afghanistan. Discussions and talks between Afghanistan, Pakistan and Iran have not achieved sustainable results to help stability. The main reason is that there is no guarantee and means of pressure to bring about cooperation. But if the countries of the region continuously engage, then it is possible to provide some guarantees to all parties and convince every country to cooperate genuinely.

## From Time Bound to Condition based Transition

The process of transition will certainly take time. As this process needs to be 'conditions-based' and not 'time-bound', it is vital that a suitable environment should be prepared for transition. This can be achieved by combining security transition with economic and political transition. There are many plans and programs underway, some of them are being initiated while others are yet to be disclosed. The following initiatives could be seen as efforts to pave the way for transition while addressing serious concerns as well.

### *A. The Afghanistan Peace and Reintegration Program (APRP)*

Grounded in the Kabul Conference and Afghan traditional Peace *Jirga* in 2010, the Afghan-led program for peace is an important development that secured support of the international community. The program focuses on reintegration of the foot soldiers, small groups, and local leaders who form the bulk of the insurgency at the operational level, while at the strategic level, the efforts focus on reconciliation with the leadership of the insurgency. APRP is seen as a source of hope for many Afghans to bring stability and viable peace in Afghanistan.

### *B. Building Afghan National Security Forces*

Expansion of the training and recruitment of the Afghan National Army (ANA) and Afghan National Police (ANP) were accelerated in order to ensure replacement of the international forces heading out. Currently, the ANA levels has reached 180,000[13] and is estimated to reach 240,000 by the end of 2014. In addition, the Ministry of Interior shows the number of ANP at over 140,000[14] and expresses commitment that besides focusing on increasing the numbers, efforts are underway to improve the quality of ANP through specific training programs in the country and abroad.

Backed by the U.S., and launched in August 2010, another initiative for boosting the government's defense capacity is the formation of Afghan Local Police (ALP) also known as local militia or "Arbakai" in some areas. The ALP provides community based self-defense in areas with little or no ANSF presence. ALP is designated to function under the Ministry of Interior (MoI) for two to five years to fill the gap until the ANSF takes the responsibility. The communities and the police chief of the district are responsible for vetting and appointment of ALP. The idea is that ALP could be absorbed by the ANP. In Uruzgan province, twenty members of the ALP transitioned to the Afghan National Police force in the Shahid-e-Hasas district in June 2011[15] Otherwise, they will be sent back home upon completion of the program and the responsibility of the stabilisation of the area will be handed over to the ANSF.[16] The government has recruited over 8000 ALP in 51 sites and there are plans underway to increase it to 30,000 to serve in 100 sites throughout the country.[17] In the districts guarded by ALP about 300 men receive uniforms, salaries, AK-47's, and training from U.S. Special Operations Forces.[18]

The Afghan government and the U.S. claim that ALP has been effective in providing protection to the villages where they are deployed. But, ordinary people express mixed opinions. In some areas, particularly in the South and South-East of Afghanistan, many people are satisfied with the security provided by ALP. For instance, a local Afghan from *Marja* district of Helmand province that was retaken from the insurgents by joint Afghan-Coalition operations

*"Mushtarak"* in 2010, in response to the question about usefulness of ALP says: *"ALP in some parts of Marja was very effective and able to provide relative security. The reason is that the local young boys who were fighting as Taliban in the area are now serving as ALP and do not fight the government and the Americans."*[19] However, it is yet to be ascertained as to what extent this is grounded in reality and portends well for the future.

## Feasibility of the Transition Process

### *1. Security*

The task of providing security and curbing the insurgents' activities is the biggest challenge for both Afghans and their international supporters. It is common knowledge that the armed opposition, fighting the Afghan government and coalition forces, has gained strength. Although, the expansion of the insurgents' area of activity from their weak and patchy presence in the first few years to the current levels, raises questions about intentions, as well as capability, of pro-government forces, who have failed to curb the insurgency. Analysts have put forward different reasons for this failure, such as, underestimation of the insurgents' capability, failure in delivering on-time support, policies of light foot-print, delay in disbursement of aid and so forth. The following factors are the other shortcomings which allowed the insurgency to grow faster and expand widely.

#### *(i) Sub-contracting the War*

In the initial years of fighting the insurgency, the coalition forces, particularly the U.S. forces, in order to maintain a small security foot print, sub-contracted the war to the national and international private security firms. The International Military (IM) found this option so useful that from guarding important premises to protection of the supply convoys, security of highways, security of high profile persons, and at times, security responsibility of wider areas, and even training of ANSF have been sub-contracted to the private security companies (PSC). This approach, though useful to reduce the casualty of the IM by reducing their exposure, increased the costs of operations by many folds. Moreover, many Afghans share the view that some of these security companies pay the insurgents and other armed groups for protection. This is particularly true about security companies guarding convoys supplying logistics to the military bases in insecure places. This in turn, has helped fill in the coffers of the insurgents' and criminal groups, enabling them to expand in numbers and control wider area through networks to derive more benefits. Therefore, sub-contracting has proved to be counterproductive and needs to be reviewed. Currently, the Critical Infrastructure Protection (CIP) is seen in this light.

*(ii) Ignoring Local Realities and Cultural Sensitivities*

The current high level of violence in the country is linked with lack of understanding of the local realities and cultural sensitivities by the International Military. For instance, in south Afghanistan, some of the local people could engage with the IM sooner than others. As frictions among local community members and family feuds are part of the day-to-day life of the Afghan people, many individuals who had good relations with the IM or Afghan security personnel, particularly the intelligence, used this acquaintance as a tool for revenge by providing wrong information about their rivals. In many cases the accused people were formerly affiliated with the Taliban but had laid down arms to assume normal life. In the absence of awareness of the motives of the informants, particular people were targeted by coalition forces and Afghan authorities. This led to resentment in extended families of the victims. In a discussion with elders from *Panjwayi* district of Kandahar, elders gave examples that many people fled the village just because the intelligence and the coalition forces raided their houses frequently. According to a local elder from Kandahar, *"It is because of those operations that now all of his family members have joined the Taliban"*[20] Likewise, search operations, civilian casualties and night raids are among the serious concerns. Despite continuous protests from the local people and civil society organisations (CSO) against these operations, the IM largely relies on these tactics in their operations.

*(iii) Boosting the Afghan Defense Capability*

*(a) Retention and Attrition*

Retention of troops has been a major challenge for expansion of ANA and ANP. Many Afghans believe that young men join the security forces ranks only for salary. An Afghan analyst points out that the number of soldiers in the summer decreases when these young men find jobs in the agriculture sector, and some of them escape to avoid participating in the military operations as the insurgents attacks increase.[21] For instance, the annual attrition of 52 per cent in 2009 in the civil order police reduced to 24 per cent in a year's time in 2010,[22] as a result of pay reform by the Ministry of Interior in December 2009.

*(b) Financing the Sizeable Security Forces*

With the total government income of $3 billion per year, Afghanistan may not be able to fund a large security force. It is estimated that $6 billion is needed annually to maintain ANSF at the current level. This means that ANSF will need substantial amount of external support. Currently, the funds provided to the ANSF come mainly from the U.S. Although, the ANSF receives some funding from the Afghan government, other NATO nations, including dedicated Law and Order trust fund funded by Japan, these contributions are small in comparison to the U.S.[23] Therefore, in order to ensure smooth security transition, funding the ANSF should be continued until the government of Afghanistan is able to assume the responsibility. So far, there is no clarity on how this support will be continued.

In informal discussions, Afghans are skeptical of the current size and further expansion of the ANSF. They emphasise on the need for strategic planning to cope with the internal and external security threats.[24] Afghanistan will not be able to resist an invasion by any country, particularly by its neighbours. Therefore, Afghanistan needs to seek and rely on international guarantees for protection against external agression. To this end, Afghanistan does not need a big army. The ANA currently exert functions of police. To tackle the current insurgency, as the insurgents are using unconventional and guerrilla warfare, the country needs a strong, well equipped and highly trained and capable quick reaction force. This will be more effective and financially viable for the Afghan government in the near future.

*(c) Concerns about the Afghan Local Police (ALP)*

A major concern regarding this program is that the budget has been approved only for three years. In case, the program is suddenly discontinued, the ALP will create many problems both for the government and for the local communities, as many may turn to criminal groups and illegal armed groups, a process that goes in the opposite direction of Disbandment of Illegal Armed Groups (DIAG) and Disarmament, Demobilisation and Reintegration (DDR) programs.[25] Another concern is that the ALP in some parts of the country have engaged in illegal taxation, carried weapons outside their villages and in some cases committed assault. The recent Human Rights Watch report brings to light the human rights violations committed by the ALP in some parts of the country.[26] A third concern about formation of the ALP is that this process weakens recruitment of ANSF. The youth who could join the ANSF, particularly in the remote and rural areas, will prefer joining the ALP as they need not move to another province.[27]

**2. *Governance***

The problems associated with promoting good governance and rule of law are complex and inter linked. The following are some of the challenges in this regard that concerns many Afghans.

*(a) Corruption*

Corruption in Afghanistan could be assessed in three levels:

(i) Paying in return for services—This traditional kind of corruption exists in many developing countries where people have to pay in return for services. The economic burden of this kind of corruption is minimal but it alienates people. Tackling this level of corruption needs long term efforts and requires behavioral and cultural changes. Civil Society organizations (CSO)can significantly contribute to this change.

(ii) Funds secured by individuals and firms abroad to be spent in Afghanistan—Individuals or agencies secure funds in other countries and partner with agencies and organizations in Afghanistan for spending the funds. They fund projects which might not meet the needs on the ground.

(iii) Corruption at higher levels of the government—Aid appropriated for development of the country leads to loss of significant amounts of the resources. This is difficult to address and it could happen regardless of the aid being on-budget or off-budget. The higher the amount of aid, the more opportunity of corruption. The only means to control this corruption is holding the government accountable. The capacity of government should be built to institute useful mechanisms of accountability and transparency.

*(b) Rule of Law*

The law enforcement institutions in Afghanistan are perceived to be weak to enforce the rule of law. Therefore, the government should rely on other initiatives, such as using traditional justice mechanisms namely *Shura* and *Jirga*. The government should try to incorporate these mechanisms in the formal system. It is common practice in other countries, including Europe, for government to delegate some of the responsibilities/authority to the lawyers known as Notary or Notary Public and the court endorse their decisions. In Afghanistan, a good example is the Property Dealers, who manage many of the deals related to properties without involving the government. If everything is to come to the court, then it will increase the workload of the court as well as increase the possibility of corruption and delay justice. But, if the courts endorse the decision of the people outside the judiciary circle, then it will decrease the chances of misuse of power of the court.

*(c) Capacity building*

It should be recognised that in the last decade capacity of Afghans has been built to a significant level but it is not utilised in optimal manner. For instance, the Ministry of Finance alone, might have appointed around 150 medical doctors.[28] However, the existence of parallel institutions, such as International organisations and Non-Governmental Organisations (NGOs), that employ a big proportion of professionals, leaving the Afghan government short of its required professional staff, remains a big problem. Another problem in terms of capacity building is the near absence of vocational institutions that are required to train skilled workers.

## Success of the Transition?

There exists several ambiguities regarding the time-lines of hand over, type of NATO/ISAF support, mechanisms of replacing IMF and positioning of the

ANSF in the areas of transition. Skepticism and concerns about tackling the future security challenges by Afghan security forces remain. There are many Afghans who talk about possibility of fall of the current government and the loss of gains with the withdrawal of international forces, and therefore question feasibility of transition.[29]

Despite these ambiguities and concerns, the commitment of the international community demonstrated at the second Bonn conference of 5 December 2011 to support Afghanistan after 2014 and the U.S.-Afghan strategic partnership can be seen as guarantees for the Afghan transition and transformation. In addition, Afghanistan has signed an agreement of strategic partnership (ASP) with India for providing long term support to Afghanistan.[30] There are also plans to sign other strategic partnership agreements with France, Italy and UK. Many Afghans also seek regional cooperation to end their country's problems. Therefore, it is imperative that the international community should mobilize, help and encourage regional actors to genuinely support and cooperate in the peace and stabilisation efforts of Afghanistan. While transition gathers momentum, it is crucial that the international community continue their financial and military assistance for the stabilisation of Afghanistan.

## NOTES

1. *Kabul Communique,* 20 July 2010, Ministry of Foreign Affairs, Government of Afghanistan, http://mfa.gov.af/Content/Media/Documents/FinalEnglish Communique-KabulInternationalConferenceonAfghanistan-20July2010278201112315 8940553325325.pdf. Accessed on 1 May 2012.
2. NATO mission in Afghanistan consists of five phases—Phase 1: Assessment and Preparation, including operations in Kabul (completed), Phase 2: Geographic expansion, Phase 3: Stabilisation, Phase 4/5: Transition / Redeployment [if needed], http://www.nato.int/isaf/docu/epub/pdf/placemat_archive/isaf_placemat_071205. pdf. Accessed on 1 May 2012.
3. *Human Rights Dimension of Poverty in Afghanistan*, UNAMA, March 2010, Kabul, http://unama.unmissions.org/Portals/UNAMA/human%20rights/Poverty%20 Report%2030%20March%202010_English.pdf. Accessed on 21 May 2012.
4. *Development Cooperation Report*, Ministry of Finance, Government of Afghanistan, p. 1, http://mof.gov.af/Content/files/Development%20Cooperation%20Report%202010. pdf. Accessed on 21 May 2012.
5. Ibid.
6. Ibid.
7. Ibid.
8. Author interview with H. Kausary, Deputy head of research, Center for Conflict and Peace Studies (CAPS), Kabul, 25 December 2011.
9. Susan Cornwell, *"U.S. civilian surge to Afghanistan cost $2 billion: report", Reuters*, 8 September 2011, http://www.reuters.com/article/2011/09/08/us-usa-afghanistan-aid-idUSTRE7876NF20110908. Accessed on 21 May 2012.
10. Ibid.
11. Author interview with a farmer, Nangarhar province, 20 December 2011.
12. Author interview with Kuchi nomad, Logar province, 20 May 2010.

13. General ZahirAzimi, spokesperson of the Ministry of Defense of Afghanistan, VoA news Dari website, 21 December 2011, http://www.voanews.com/dari/news/afghanistan/Afghan-National-Army-136006043.html. Accessed on 21 May 2012.
14. *Shabaka-e Etla Rasani Afghanistan (Afghanpaper.com),* news article published in Dari, 16 July 2011, http://www.afghanpaper.com/nbody.php?id=24546. Accessed on 21 May 2012.
15. "Afghan Local Police Transition into the Afghan National Police in Shahid-e-Hasas", *ISAF*, 8 July 2011, http://www.isaf.nato.int/article/isaf-releases/afghan-local-police-transition-into-the-afghan-national-police-in-shahid-e-hasas.html. Accessed on 2 May 2012.
16. *Afghan National Security Forces (ANSF)*—Media Backgrounder, NATO—Public Diplomacy Division (PDD), 8 June 2011, http://www.nato.int/nato_static/assets/pdf/pdf_2011_06/20110608_backgrounder-ANSF.pdf. Accessed on 2 May 2012.
17. Luke Mogelson, "*Bad Guys vs. Worse Guys in Afghanistan*", *New York Times,* 19 October 2011, http://www.nytimes.com/2011/10/23/magazine/bad-guys-vs-worse-guys-in-afghanistan.html?_r=1. Accessed on 12 May 2012.
18. Ibid.
19. Author Interview with a local elder from *Marjah* district of Helmand Province, 18 December 2011.
20. Author Interview with elders from *Panjwayi* district of Kandahar, 13 November 2010.
21. Author Interview with Afghan analyst K. Sartor, Kabul, 20 December 2011.
22. *Afghan National Security Forces (ANSF)*—Media Backgrounder, op.cit.
23. CJ Radin, "Funding the Afghan National Security Forces", Long War Journal, 16 September 2011, http://www.longwarjournal.org/threat-matrix/archives/2011/09/funding_the_afghan_national_se.php. Accessed on 12 May 2012.
24. Notes of Group discussions conducted by Afghan civil society organisations under "People's Dialogue on Peace", during October 2011.
25. Author Interview with A. Ahrar Ramizpoor, 11 December 2011, Kabul.
26. "Just Don't Call It a Militia", Human Rights Watch, September 2011, http://www.hrw.org/sites/default/files/reports/afghanistan0911webwcover.pdf. Accessed on 23 May 2012.
27. Author interview with Afghan expert M. Nabi Tadbir, Kabul, 16 October 2011.
28. Author interview with Mr. Najibullah Manalai, Advisor to the Minister of Finance of Afghanistan, Kabul, 12 November 2011.
29. Author's discussions with the Afghan civil society members, June – December 2011, in Kabul and other provinces.
30. Anjana Pasricha, "*Afghanistan, India Sign Strategic Partnership Pact*", *Voice of America,* 4 October 2011, http//www.voanews.com/english/news/asia/Afghanistan-India-Sign-Strategic-Partnership-Pact-131074568.html. Accessed on 12 May 2012.

# 8

# Aid, Development, Women, Non-Governmental Organisations: A grass-root perspective

*Rangina Hamidi*

Afghanistan has transformed. Since 2001, the international community has poured more money into development and reconstruction efforts in Afghanistan than ever before in its entire history. Several accomplishments have been made: there are more paved roads; there are more schools—both in the cities as well as in the districts for children to attend; opportunities for higher education and training to enhance skills in many sectors such as management, finance and accounting. Much of the recent aid packages have invested in the on-going training of police and military personnel while a heavy focus has also been placed on "good-governance" initiatives to prepare the Afghan government for smoother transition by 2014.

However, in spite of these developments that have taken place in Afghanistan since 2001, many questions still remain unanswered. As the international community focuses on its departure year of 2014, Afghans and experts on Afghanistan need to ponder upon some of these questions:

- Has the aid delivered in Afghanistan since 2001 achieved its goals of helping the Afghan people? If yes, how effective has it been?
- What lessons can we learn from the past decade of development work to prepare Afghanistan for 2014 and beyond?
- What role can women play in developing their communities and the nation?
- What success stories or models exist to provide hope in the midst of a very chaotic and uncertain period in Afghanistan?
- What are the areas of concern or gaps in the international aid,

development, civilian reconstruction and surge (if any) that need to be addressed for effective transition by 2014?
- Have the non-governmental organizations (NGO) been effective in the aid delivery process? If not, what steps need to be taken in improving aid delivery and civilian reconstruction for effective transition?

This paper aims to address these issues to help policy makers and analysts to make better and informed decisions for Afghanistan in the near term, 2012-14 and in the long term, beyond 2014.

## History of Aid Giving in Afghanistan

Aid delivery in Afghanistan has not been without political connotations. The initial assistance package made during the *Jihad* period beginning in the early 1980s was characterised by a complete lack of planning and coordination. The aid provided helped the Afghans become refugees mainly in Pakistan and Iran. The influx of refugees to these two neighbouring countries had created an emergency situation and aid was thus delivered on a war footing. The objective of aid at that time was to assist the Mujahideen and the refugees in the war against the Soviets. Thus, the aid had nothing to do with developing or helping to enhance the capacities or build institutions. Since almost everyone was occupied with either fighting the war or making adjustments to their new lives as refugees, there was no room for monitoring or making sure that the funds were spent in the right manner. The decision to use *Jihadi* commanders as the recipients and distributors of aid opened doors for not only for misuse of funds but it served as a training experience for such people to head NGO's who would later run programmes for Afghans in Afghanistan. In view of this new career option, many people sought full-time careers in this field of "self-managing" aid packages that were coming into the refugee camps.

When my family was forced out of the country in 1981 to go to Pakistan, my father's first job offer was to become "head of a refugee camp." This was a promising career as there was no monitoring system in place to make sure that aid reached the most vulnerable. However, my father, conscientious man with a will to work for his living, turned down the opportunity. Many others, however, grabbed the opportunity and the nature of such aid delivery promoted corruption and patronage systems. As the divisions between fighting factions grew and the war lingered on in the 1980s, so did the division of aid. Those fighters or commanders with more clout with the international community got more funds. Whether it reached the people or not was not an issue of concern or importance at that time.

If one can buy the argument that during the years of the war with the former Soviet Union (1979–89), the international community's focus was on winning the war in Afghanistan and not on development of Afghanistan, a close look at the years following—first, during the Mujahideen era followed by that of the

Taliban—shows little change in the policy on how aid was delivered after 1989. During the Mujahideen period, the focus did shift to development in the midst of factions fighting each other. The United Nations (UN) and other international aid organisations implemented development projects primarily in rural Afghanistan where it was a bit more secure to work than in the cities, which were still under the control of the falling communist regime. However, even during this time, the UN filled the coffers of the Mujahideen commanders and other influential leaders in the region. The name and reputation of individuals helped win aid bids rather than their qualifications and track records. This way of aid giving continued through the 1990s.

A good example of how this relationship worked is the case of Mullah Naqib, the *Jihadi* commander in Kandahar. Naqib hailed from Arghandab district and exercised total control over the district until the Taliban resumed control. Mullah Naqib was the 'point man' (key contact) for projects and programmes that needed to be carried out in Kandahar. The reality was that he only knew how to fight, with very little experience of rebuilding what he destroyed. The international community, however, granted him the power to make decisions about development projects in the entire region. Not surprisingly, since the last twenty years, very little in terms of development is visible when one travels through these remote areas of Afghanistan.

Ill experienced and self-appointed leaders sprang up through out Afghanistan. This happened when the focus of development in Afghanistan actually meant mere creation of NGOs in the 1990s. The Afghans in a jocular vein caricature such NGOs, rhyming it with the word "GBO" which in Pashto translates to a 'pocket'. As more people set up NGOs to win contracts and bids for development work in Afghanistan, the NGOs were named as "N-GBOs"—entities which worked towards filling their own pockets, rather than a service to the people. This depiction still resonates with many Afghans throughout the country in 2012. The phenomenon of "N-GBOs" also means a lack of capacity among these NGOs. In stead of enhancing their capacity in select focus areas, NGOs became experts in 'all' fields, which ensured that their project proposals for grants accrue some funding, rather than being completely rejected.

I was compelled to start a women's NGO in Afghanistan, with headquarters in Kandahar, to work for the economic development of women in that region. After filing the application for registration with the Ministry of Economy, I took the application along with the appropriate necessary documents to register my organisation. After the head of NGOs section reviewed my application he asked me "why have you only marked the 'economic development' section in the field of work section?" My reply was simple "because I want to work in this field only." He smiled and said "you are new to this game—I suggest you check the areas of health, education, politics, etc. to make sure that you can win a bid from interested donors." I stood there shocked as I watched him check-mark the boxes for each of those fields that I was not going to work or had expertise. Though, I have not received donor funds for any of the above fields other than economic development, the organisation is registered in all of the other fields and donors can technically approach me for available funds in the field that I have no experience or capacity. This is an example of how the funding and donor driven agendas dictate the nature of work and activities of the NGOs in Afghanistan.

The problems in aid delivery continue in a similar fashion with the present regime. The same history of the Mujahideen and the Taliban era continues, but with new names and new faces. While there are no Mujahideen commanders dictating where and how aid funds should be spent, they have been replaced by warlords and corrupt government officials. Kandahar, for example, continues to be guided and directed by warlords within the government who have converted themselves to be community leaders and are pursuing ethnic and tribal agendas. The National Solidarity Programme (NSP) is a good example of how corrupt hands have reached the pockets of the development workers. The NSP, although a good programme in theory, gave the planning authority to old commanders and tribal leaders and put them once again in control of the funds for their villages and communities. While there might be success stories of projects in certain parts of the country through this project, the majority of the complaints from ordinary Afghans is that the commanders usually build infrastructure projects around their private homes or land to personally benefit from the programmes. It is thus not difficult to see the *Jihad* era of the 1980s repeat itself.

Donor countries argue that in 2001 to oust of the Taliban, Americans had no choice but to seek assistance of the warlords on the ground. Why the same tactic is being used after 10 years is not clear. Even if one has to buy the argument that there is no other way but to work with the warlords, the important question remains unanswered. Why must aid be closely tied to such politics? Two decades of failed experiment should provide sufficient lessons. Alas, Afghanistan is a different case.

In Kandahar, Gul Agha Sherzai, the first controversial governor after the Taliban was ousted, belongs to the Barakzai tribe. The tribe is one of the five major Durrani tribes in the Kandahar province. Sherzai treated Kandahar as the place only for Barakzai tribe members. Aid contracts, military contracts and government contracts all were distributed among his close friends and family and although no longer officially in power in the South, he continues to exercise his influence, with his illiterate brothers serving as the point of contacts. By continuing with such relationships and empowering corrupt officials with aid contracts, the international community is merely continuing with the vicious cycle of politicizing aid in Afghanistan. It diminishes the good work and sacrifices made by honest development and aid workers.

## Lack of Aid Coordination

In July 2005, a representative of the German Technical Aid Organisation, Deutsche Gesellschaft für Technische Zusammenarbeit (GTZ) came to Kandahar with a project of one million U.S. dollars for women. The money had to be spent by December 31, 2005. Not knowing what to do and having less than 5 months to complete the project, the GTZ invited NGOs to participate in the project. GTZ accepted applications from any organisation or group that promised to deliver something by the end of the year. A few organisations who received funding had never worked in Kandahar or in the South and had no staff or office for operation. They received funding in Kabul and implemented the projects from abroad with temporary staff who had no qualifications or understanding of the nature of work on the ground.

Eventually, when the faux pas was publicised, the Embassy of Germany in Kabul severed ties with the individuals who had brought this issue to the limelight. Instead of acknowledging and learning from their mistakes, officials attempted a thorough cover up and were successful as well. The net result of all this is that many aid organisations will use these methods for getting grants irrespective of the capacity or needs on the ground. This would perpetuate a cycle of corruption and result in absence of long term projects that can make an impact on the people's lives.

One more example of the GTZ's projects can also be cited. One of the projects that was initiated during that five month period in 2005 was to build a dormitory for girls at Kandahar University. At the outset it looked highly impressive. However, both the donors and the programme implementation agency had not made any assessment of the number of female students in the university. Out of 800 students, only eight were girls. Moreover, none of these eight female students were planning to live in the dormitory that was being built amidst great fanfare. By the end of 2011, the number of female students in the university has increased. However, none of them are living in the dormitory. The infrastructure remains unused. To add to the short sightedness, in 2006, United Nations Office for Project Services (UNOPS) Afghanistan decided to build another female dormitory for girls at Kandahar University, right next to the first one built by GTZ.

With two full-sized empty female dormitories, the Kandahar University remains without power and water. The engineers building the university structures had not taken into account the need to install a water system for the buildings. The university itself does not have the funds to provide electricity to students through a generator as the Kandahar city itself still does not have full time electricity. During the examinations, the university students study under the solar lights installed by the former Mayor of Kandahar City on the main streets.

In order to assess its true impact on the Afghan population, it is important to take cognizance of the popular perceptions about aid. Afghan psyche today has divorced itself from any responsibility towards its community and country. Many, understandably so, wait to be spoon-fed and want to cash in as much as possible today as for them, tomorrow is highly uncertain. The deteriorating security situation throughout the country over the past four years and the uncertainty about the future has shaped their mindset. Many want to prepare themselves for the worst and the lack of trust in the current Afghan government only adds to the complexities.

Lawlessness and the lack of accountability has lead to many to think that one can literally "get away with murder". In this milieu of utter lawlessness, siphoning off funds or grant money has become only a minute problem. Small NGO heads only follow what the corrupt ministers and governors are doing. This probably explains the lack of success in projects implemented by these organisations. Many NGOs, in spite of being blacklisted, continue to be given new projects. This is because the donors do not have the time to do their homework before granting the projects.

## Kandahar Treasure: A Case Study

Kandahar Treasure is the first private enterprise owned and operated by over 350 Kandahari women. For five years as a local non-profit organization, it received grants from various donors to run and manage its women's income generation project within the organisation. Year after year, the NGO would re-apply for funding and would receive grant money to continue its activities. The NGO had the vision to eventually spin off as a for-profit entity, but donors simply could not share this vision.

Today, Kandahar Treasure is soaring with business opportunities both inside Afghanistan as well as providing fine embroidered products outside the country. It has made profit for two years in a row. This is a success model for Afghanistan. It is also a great model for replication for other parts of the country. If this could operate successfully in war-stricken Kandahar, it can also be replicated elsewhere in the country.

Kandahar Treasure's uniqueness also lies in the fact that it is completely women run and operated, with the exception of some male-support staff. The world is finally awakening to the fact that women are better recipients of aid and contributors to their families and communities. Kandahar Treasure is a small example of what women are able to do to economically to help their families and communities. It took many years to convince the women working from their homes that this initiative was not a short-term project aimed at providing only training or short term job opportunity. From the beginning, the importance of creating a product that would compete in the world-market was emphasised. Bringing quality product to the world market would mean a heavy focus on quality control as well as crafting products that would compete in the vast ocean of choices available today. Communicating this thinking in the middle of many more organisations just trying to use donor funds to write good reports was not an easy task.

NGO projects do not revolve around quality. These are not linked to markets. The women beneficiaries could not differentiate between us and the other NGOs and would constantly ask, "Why are you so difficult to work with? The other organisations never required us to work this way." We had to persevere and continue to send the message over and over again that we are different and that we are not like the other organisations. Today, after nine years when most of the other organisations have left or shut down their activities, the women have emerged victorious. Through simple communication and consistent work we have relayed our message that we are serious about quality. If we can create quality products, the market will sustain our operations. The women operating with us did not need education or sophisticated training courses to make them understand that quality sells better.

Kandahar Treasure's success also lies in the strategy of how we work in our communities. Realising that Kandahar is a very conservative and traditional society, we consciously decided to ensure that women can work from their homes. Majority of Kandahari women do not have permission to leave their homes. So when women brought work to women inside their homes, the men could not reject the proposal. In fact, today many of the male family members of the women who work with us look up to Kandahar Treasure as a support system for the entire family and support our work as we move forward in a very difficult and politically volatile region. Our success lies with our women and their stories.

The following example would not be out of place. Maagul, a mother of six daughters and two sons is married to a lazy man. Her oldest son—the security for the family—has been convinced by his wife to leave his parents and sisters and have moved out of the house with his wife. Because her other son is the youngest, Maagul had no choice but to find work for herself and her daughters. Nine years ago, I met Maagul during a rainy night in the house of a women know to me. Maagul was crying for her misfortune of not having a place to live and not having any opportunity to earn. A room given to her family by a friend had only a plastic sheet serving as a roof. With rains the plastic sheet too came down. The family had to find shelter in the middle of the night and knocked on many neighbours' doors before someone could offer them temporary shelter. After our meeting, Maagul and her daughters immediately started working with Kandahar Treasure and within months they had saved enough money to consider renting a small one-bedroom home. Today, after nine years of working with us, Maagul and her daughters are the sole providers for the family's shelter, food, health and other needs. Maagul only has her hard work and Kandahar Treasure to thank for the change in her fortune.

The benefit for women working at Kandahar Treasure is not only about financial stability, but ensuring their participation in the small social changes that are also taking place. Girls in Kandahar are generally married between age twelve and fourteen and with poor families like Maagul's, the burden of one more mouth to feed often becomes the primary reason for considering such early marriages. Now, when suitors come to Maagul's home for her eldest daughter's hand in marriage, both Maagul and her husband delay it knowing that the daughter is a major source of income for the family. Finally, in 2011 Maagul agreed to get her eldest daughter married at the age 20 rather than at 14 like many of other girls in town. Without setting this as a goal, the work for Kandahar Treasure has changed the social norm for this particular family. It needs no reiteration that social change is a key ingredient for the development of a healthy and sustainable Afghan society.

The ability to work for a long term vision allows us to assess and record the changes that Kandahar Treasure brings to the women and society. We would have remained oblivious to our potential of brining in small but significant changes in society had we remained a short-term project implementing organisation driven by external funding.

## Looking for Solutions: Best Case and Worst Case Scenarios

The problems in Afghanistan are manifold. As an Afghan and more importantly as an Afghan woman, I believe that the world can no longer afford to hide itself behind traditional and cultural norms set in place to put women on the back burner. It is only fair to give women a chance to correct a lot of the wrongs in their communities, for which women have not been responsible. There is no better place for this change to take place than in the development sector.

From the economic point of view, women have proven themselves to be able contributors to their societies and families. Experts in this field are admitting that investing in women is simply smart economics. Kandahar Treasure is an example of this belief. In the education and social sector, it is the women who rebuild the fabric of the society by encouraging children to go to school rather than to fight and kill. It is the female politicians in Afghanistan who are raising their voices against the complete control of politics by warlords and corrupt government officials. Women do not seem to be as concerned about their safety when they decide to speak against corrupt officials. The grass-root efforts to raise the voice for peace has been initiated by Afghan women, be through peace prayers or marches against suicide attacks or participation in conferences and seminars to discuss how people can start working for peace from their homes and communities. Women are taking the lead in addressing these issues.

Afghan women of today are not the women of 2001 with times and circumstances pitted overwhelmingly against them. Afghan women are now educated in various fields and have received exposure and training to enhance their capacity. Their work and travel experience of especially the last decade has prepared many to handle very difficult tasks. Many women now have good track records for their activities and there are many more women joining hands to address the problem of corruption in Afghanistan.

As the world prepares for 2014 and envisions strategies for a smooth and transparent transition in Afghanistan, the following four points may be considered.

- Independent national and provincial planning and monitoring bodies to coordinate aid and projects throughout Afghanistan;
- The mission of aid and development should be long-term and not aim at being quick impact;
- Invest in new strategies and new partners. Break the cycle of corruption; and
- De-politicize and de-militarize aid.

If there is the political will to change the nature of aid giving and delivery in Afghanistan, a positive change will certainly come. The Afghan leaders and the international community need to put their fears and politics aside and join efforts to change the future of Afghanistan.

# 9

# Role of Strategic Communication and Public Awareness in Actualizing Transition

*Muhammad Sabir Siddiqi*

Afghanistan is in the process of transition (*inteqal*) as the United States and NATO hand over security responsibilities to the ANSF. The transition process, a critical juncture in the recent history of Afghanistan, is executed in the absence of an effective strategic communication and public awareness program which can turn the present gains into a strategic disaster for the allies and a victory for the Taliban.

The security transition process began in 2011 and is scheduled to be completed by 2014. While the U.S. Secretary of State Hillary Clinton stated, the U.S. pursues a three-pronged strategy of "fight, talk, build" during this period,[1] it is not yet clear what the U.S. and NATO mission and engagement will be in Afghanistan beyond 2014. In addition, there are contradictory messages emanating from high-ranking U.S. and NATO officials suggesting that they will not leave the country after 2014.[2] Similar contradictions are evident in the commentaries of the government communication agencies such as the Government Media and Information center (GMIC) which states "the 2014 is not the end of transition period, rather it will be the start of the process"[3]

This contradiction originates from lack of a clear vision for the future of Afghanistan combined with the absence of a coordinated strategy for communicating the right messages during the transition process. Such inconsistencies prove that the international community (IC) has not learned from the past decade, and continues to deal with the communication and public awareness as the less important side of the process. Strategic communication is obviously a critical challenge in politics and counterinsurgency as Galula asserts,

"If there was a field in which we were definitely and infinitely more stupid than our opponents, it is propaganda."[4]

To realize the usefulness of the strategic communication and public awareness programs for the transition process, there is a need to review the history of strategic communication and public awareness over the past decade and identify the reasons for the failure of the Afghan government and the international community in raising awareness, initiatives and programs to bring about a course correction.

## The Lost Decade: Lack of Strategic Communication Strategy

Since the establishment of the post-Taliban government in Afghanistan, the Government of Islamic Republic of Afghanistan (GIRoA) and the International Community (IC) have lacked a comprehensive, effective communication strategy to project their interests, policies, and objectives in the country. The GIRoA has failed to capitalize on the positive developments and win people's trust, confidence and support. One reason for this failure is the near absence of a sound, effective and realistic approach for sharing the agendas and goals with the people and providing them with reliable information to solicit their support and trust. Not only has the Afghan government failed to communicate effectively but it has also failed to establish a means by which people participate in the processes, express their opinion and receive feedback, thereby enlarging the space for establishing a true democratic system in the country.

The IC supporters of the GIRoA have also failed to inform the people about their agendas and programs. As the UK Ministry of Defence report states, "The (British) Government is not communicating key messages to the British or Afghan public about the purpose of its operations in Afghanistan effectively enough" and suggests that the UK Armed Forces have yet to optimally incorporate strategic communications and "information and influence" operations into their campaigns. Instead, the foreign supporters of the GIRoA admit the adeptness of the Taliban in "very successful and proactive" use of the media, emanating from Muslim and Arab TV stations and even improving their web presence. [5]

## Ignoring Traditional Communication Tools

In the previous decade, the GIRoA and the IC have mainly relied on modern communications such as TVs and Radios, ignoring traditional communication tools and networks (i.e. *mosques, madrassas,*[6] *jirgas*[7] *and other social and tribal forums*). The strategic communication of the GIRoA and the allied forces using modern communication, were simultaneously countered by the mosques, which indicates the failure of the IC and GIRoA to engage the traditional forums in their communication strategy. Since 2001, traditional communication tools are in the hands of the Taliban and neighbouring countries that use them to instigate people against the government of Afghanistan and the international allies. The Taliban and their supporters have used these traditional tools and networks to project their power and to strengthen their presence among the populace.

There are around 7000 mosques registered with the Ministry of Haj and Religious Affairs. These mosques normally should have been under the control of the government and supported the government agendas. However, the government failed to utilize this opportunity and consequently most of the mosques—including the mosques in Kabul are operating against any Western presence and at times, even against the Afghan government. There are more than 100,000 mosques in the country that are not registered with the Ministry of Haj and Religious Affairs and which are perceived to be in the hands of the Taliban.[8] Thus, the religious forum has been used effectively by the Taliban and other insurgent groups. The attempts of the GIRoA and the IC on building the religious medium, instead of yielding desired consequences, has resulted in targeted assassinations and elimination of a number of religious scholars who have worked to promote or support the GIRoA and IC policies and programs.

Moreover, the reason for the government's failure in this endeavour was the failure to recruit qualified professionals and scholars. Neither did the government attempt to address the shortcomings and gaps in these initiatives. Since the attempts and initiatives to use the traditional and religious mechanisms were flawed and underdeveloped, it yielded negative results and helped to develop a kind of Islamic orthodoxy and radicalism in the country.[9] Another problem in the government's communication strategy delivered through these initiatives was that they were naively or unskillfully linked with Islam. Since the GIRoA failed to link its messages with Islamic underpinnings, the public deemed its programs as un-Islamic, resulting in the rejection of such messages.

## Use of Modern Communication Tools and the Human terrain

While relying on modern communication tools, the GIRoA and IC were not successful in using these tools in an effective manner for myriad reasons. First, the GIRoA and IC fell short of understanding the social fabric of the Afghan society to tailor their programs according to the needs of the people. Consequently, their messages were interpreted differently on the ground. Second, they did not base their programs and initiatives on scientific foundations with undeniable reliability and validity.[10] The GIRoA, rarely use surveys and systematic approaches to gather and analyze information to make sound and well informed decisions.[11] Therefore, the GIRoA and the IC have based their conclusions on preconceived notions, instead of relying on scientifically and systematically gathered data.

Surprisingly, it has been the new generation of Taliban who have been adept in the use of the modern communication tools to communicate their messages much efficiently than the GIRoA and the international community. Hence, the

Taliban who previously banned the TV, Internet and camera, are now widely using mobile, internet and social media—SMS, E-mail, Twitter and Face book to convey their messages to the public in quick time.

The lack of optimal use of the modern communication tools has yielded sub-optimal results. The GIRoA has not established a partnership with the Afghan televisions, radio stations and the print media to inform the public of it's agendas and programs. As a consequence, the GIRoA and the IC have distanced the people and made them distrustful of the newly introduced concepts of democracy, human rights, social justice, to the extent that people have come to label these concepts as un-Islamic.[12]

The Afghan government and the allies have not adequately explained the meaning and connotation of the new terminologies and concepts used in their communication, which, in many cases, has caused the government's public awareness and communication programs to become counterproductive. An example is using the word "subject" instead of citizen in the almost all statements, announcements and other types of official communications, ignoring the difference between the connotations of the terms.

Similarly, the design of their communication and information campaigns have been inconsistent and do not match the realities on the ground. For example, the people in the south and southeast are traditional but their religiosity is not stronger than other groups in the country. However, the government and the allied forces wrongly labeled them as being strongly religious. Based on this flawed conclusion, the government and the allied forces linked their communication and public awareness programs with Islam and religious slogans, which were unskillfully crafted and inappropriately delivered. The consequence was the loss of people's support in the south and southeastern areas which indirectly, worked to the advantage of the Taliban.[13]

These poorly designed and inadequately implemented communication and public awareness programs also created room for Iranian and Pakistani propaganda communication outlets to flourish in Afghanistan. Under such influences, the public is compelled to embrace the creation of an environment by the hostile media conducive for the growth of Pakistani and Iranian positions against the government of Afghanistan and international presence in the country.

Likewise, there have been minimal efforts to create modern communication structures at the community level for achieving long-term strategic goals. The Community Development Committees (CDCs) established under the auspices of the National Solidarity Program (NSP) are not functioning effectively. Today, the widespread belief among the public is that the government does not have the capacity or the will to protect their rights and freedom. These beliefs discourage people to support the government agendas. For example, according to accounts of the local people, government authorities, including the intelligence officials and security forces, are afraid of the Taliban attacks and targeting. They are equally influenced by rumors and propaganda made by the Taliban and other insurgent groups.[22]

## Information Campaign and Role of the Afghan State

The Afghan government and the NATO forces have not been effective in the psychological warfare and the information campaign. On the contrary, the Taliban and other insurgent groups have demonstrated remarkable success in this area. The Afghan government and the allies have not answered the lingering questions and concerns regarding the legality and time frame of the presence of foreign troops in Afghanistan. Today, the overwhelming majority of people perceive the current government as no different from the Russian-backed governments of the 1980s. Nor do they perceive much difference between the Soviet occupation and the present NATO intervention. In fact, they argue the Russian occupation was an occupation by one country, however, today; Afghanistan is occupied by 40 non-Islamic countries.

Furthermore, the government did not bring the literature of modern state systems and modern concepts to Afghanistan. A good example of this is its failure to introduce the concept of citizenship and citizen rights embedded in the Afghanistan constitution. The government still calls its people 'subjects,' although the constitution of Afghanistan gives them the rights and duties of citizens.[14] This has resulted in negative perceptions among people and some even refer to the Afghan political system as a kingdom rather than a presidency.[15]

The performance of the government has been gauged negatively due to the lack of appropriate messages and statements of the government and its backers from the IC. The post-Taliban Afghanistan was envisioned to be a stable and peaceful country with a well-functioning political system and a social and political environment where the rule of law prevailed. Human rights and women's rights were to be respected and preserved, freedom of speech was to be safeguarded, and all citizens were to be aware of their rights and duties. In addition, the government was expected to encourage people's participation in the democratic process.[16] However, after a decade, surveys show that the above-mentioned goals have not materialised. Afghanistan is still unstable and insecure as the Taliban and other insurgent groups control significant parts of the country; moreover, the country continues to suffer due to serious political, social and economic dilemmas.[17]

Today, Afghanistan lacks a secure environment, a strong political structure, a reliable judiciary and a clear strategy for a stable and prosperous future. Moreover, the government is unable to provide basic services to the people.[18] Afghanistan's literacy rate stands at 28.1 per cent,[19] one of the lowest in the world. The education system lacks reforms and suffers from politicisation. Teachers and instructors are appointed on the basis of their political connections rather than merit. The management at the Ministry of Education (MoE) and in higher education is weak. No regulatory body has been established to monitor the quality of curriculum in the universities of Afghanistan. Research and scholarly work is hardly encouraged. Moreover, there is no cohesion between madrasas and public schools.[20]

Similarly, Afghanistan's justice system is "in a catastrophic state of disrepair," as described by Nick Grono, Deputy President of the International Crisis Group.[21] First, the system faces a political challenge as many power brokers benefit from a patronage based system. It enables them to buy and maintain loyalty. The second challenge is widespread and institutionalised corruption, which has become an integral part of the system. The third challenge is the lack of accountability and the culture of impunity. The government has not been able to pursue some of these offenders to increase its legitimacy in the eyes of its people and to undermine one of the claimed attractions of the Taliban—that it provides harsh, but fair and instant justice where none otherwise exists.

In addition, the justice system of Afghanistan suffers from structural inadequacies. The strong presidential system adopted under the 2004 Constitution has further the weakened the judicial institutions. The lack of a clearly defined arbiter of the constitution has undercut the authority of the Supreme Court and transformed the court into a puppet of President who has adeptly exploited the Court's relative weakness to blunt challenges from rivals and circumscribe the powers of other branches of government. The president has often turned to the Supreme Court to settle political disputes, substantially weakening perceptions of its independence. For instance, he has used the Supreme Court to block parliament's efforts to override presidential vetoes and assert its powers. Therefore, people do not believe that the justice system is there to protect their rights; rather they think the courts are a means to exploit them.

## Strategic Communications during Inteqal

The present situation is not any different from the past. The government does not have a clear and well coordinated strategic communications startegy. Moreover, the government by occasional public confrontation with some of its allies, give credence to the idea that this is not a transition, but it is a sort of exit under the cover of security transition. The decision for the transition and the handover of responsibilities have not been effectively communicated to the public. Consequently, most of the people do not understand what the *"Inteqal"* (transition) means and perceive the present process of withdrawal to be 'abandonment' by the foreign forces.

No local and citizen-friendly message of the process is provided to the people and the GIRoA and IC seem to miss the fact that "the importance of communication for change is not only informing, motivating and coordinating, but also managing expectations."[23] According to management theorists, failure to share information or to inform people adequately of what changes are necessary will have a highly negative impact on the process.[24] Hence, they suggest that leaders, while applying a change, should "take extra steps to ensure that every communication piece has a clear purpose and a target audience. This approach to communication helps set expectations, tells a coherent story, and fosters behaviour and attitude changes."[25]

The GIRoA lacks a coherent vision for the transition and post-transition periods. The lack of public-friendly policies in the transition period and lack of a clear and coherent vision for the post-transition period has confused the public about the process. Government officials representing the official view of the government explain the transition in such diverse and incoherent manner, which further adds to the public confusion and fears of being abandoned once again. Yet the government has not taken steps to address this problem. In addition, the government and its allies have not taken bold and decisive steps to counter the Taliban propaganda. All the incidents, attacks and other security problems have been attributed to the "enemies of Afghan people". However, this word itself is no less ambiguous than the policies of the government and its allies.

## Concerns and Challenges during Transition

As stated earlier, the message of transition has not been rightly conveyed which has resulted in confusion and anxieties of abandonment among the Afghans. Concerns among the Afghan people are acute in the following sectors:

### *Security*

The majority of Afghans express concern over the ability of the ANSF to handle the current situation on their own. They insist that Afghanistan is not ready for transition and the foreign troops must provide further training, as well as additional assistance in terms of weapons and other equipment to the Afghan security forces. These concerns are fuelled by overt failures of Afghan forces to handle situations in some of the provinces where security transitions took place. The results of the handovers have been uneven: some provinces such as Panjshir and Balkh are enjoying relative stability, while other areas, such as Kabul, Helmand, Bamiyan and Herat are experiencing further deterioration in their security. Barat Ali Barat, a resident of Bamian province, says that the security situation in Bamiyan has been worsening in recent months. "We ask the international community to not withdraw its forces from Afghanistan," he said. "The security situation is deteriorating by the day."[26] Even in the cases where ANSF has been successful, there has been little reporting which would have helped build the public confidence.

### *Governance and Political Transition*

Some ethnic groups that have no links with the Taliban insurgents perceive that the presence of foreign troops has helped maintain the fragile power balance in Afghanistan. They fear that a single ethnic group will amass absolute power, if the foreign troops leave the country which can trigger an ethnic war or even civil war. Since these groups are not connected to the Taliban, they tend to form or join separate armed groups. This in turn creates internal divisions that could be exploited by the neighbouring countries. Furthermore, it leads to further distrust and jostling for power, which will affect the stability in Afghanistan.

Currently, due to lack of transparent policies, people are divided along tribal lines and the dominant perception is that a single tribe dominates the government. There is a growing fear in Afghanistan that a single ethnic group is trying to restructure the offices and hold on to the key positions. This perception can propel other ethnic groups to withdraw their support and create or join anti-government groups. The second scenario is more likely because those with no ethnic linkages with the Taliban hardly trust this group and accept to join them.[27] To tackle this problem and regain the public trust, the government should introduce mechanisms to ensure equality, representation, balanced distribution of power and unbiased allocation of opportunities based on merit.

The government, with its short sighted policies and inadequate security management, indirectly aids the Taliban and its allies to have more impact on the daily lives of the people. Moreover, when people see that the government does not effectively counter the Taliban's attacks, they question the role of the government. In addition, when the government officials use armored vehicles for their personal safety and do not seriously condemn the Taliban attacks, the people tend to see a sort of connection between them and the Taliban. Those who are not ethnically linked with the Taliban perceive this as intentional policies to create conditions for more presence of those who are ethnically conneccted to that group in the power and the government.

## Recommendations

The Afghan government and IC need to build a well coordinated and coherent strategy to address the aforementioned concerns, communicate positive messages to the public about the transition, and thereby build on the public confidence. The lessons learned from the past failures suggest that having a comprehensive strategic communication approach places increased emphasis on the military—civilian interface by engaging people. This becomes a more serious priority during 'transition' to build on the public confidence. At a time, when the Taliban has shown a comparative advantage in this area, there is an immediate need to counter such insurgent propoganda. Communicating positive and reliable messages to create an public awareness would help prevent reversal of gains. According to Jürgen Habermas, "political action is steered by the public sphere, and that the only legitimate governments are those that listen to the public sphere."[28]

In order to have a successful security transition, the government must adopt reformist policies and effectively communicate its reform campaign to the public. The reform needs to occur in realistic timelines.

A. The GIRoA and the IC should systematically employ communications strategy to convey its messages pertaining to the transition effectively to the Afghan population. To attain this goal, the GIRoA and the IC should categorize the audience (rural-urban) and identify the most appropriate tools—both the modern and traditional communication tools for the U audience.

B. The GIRoA should unify efforts and have a common unified voice to ensure that different apparatus of the government—military, government officials and politicians do not create confusion by issuing varied statements. Such variation can arise in the absence of a coordinated communication strategy. It is up to the leadership to come up with a well coordinated communication strategy to find the equilibrium and send right messages.

C. The GIRoA and IC should endeavor to assure all segments of the population that transition does not imply transfer of power to a particular tribe or ethnic group. The process needs to be transparent and inclusive.

D. The government should adopt a clear and inclusive peace and reconciliation strategy. The GIRoA should make sure that the process is not deemed as a step stemming from the weakness of the GIRoA and the IC. Also, the GIRoA and IC should design justifiable goals and objectives for the process and communicate them to the people so that they do not regard it as power sharing with the Taliban or adopting policies to attract the support of those groups. Furthermore, the peace and reconciliation process should include well-designed and proven reintegration mechanisms to stop surrendered individuals and groups from rejoining the Taliban.

E. The government should adopt rational national strategies and policies, and should establish proper, suitable mechanisms to monitor, evaluate, and track the implementation process of these strategies and policies.

### Near-Medium term

The GIRoA and IC should take the following set of measures to counter the Taliban propaganda and effectively convey the messages of transition among the Afghan people:

1. One of the key messages that the government should disseminate among the people is that the government is capable of protecting their

rights and defending them against subversive forces. The government should reassure the public that no one can undermine the democratisation process in the country. Action-based messages should be communicated to the public about the capacity of the government and its stance to protect their rights and freedoms.

2. The GIRoA and IC, to win the support and trust of people and to counter the anxiety of withdrawal, should convey well-planned, coordinated and timely messages.
3. The GIRoA and IC should adequately enlist the support of the media and invest in the development of indigenous and local media in terms of putting out positive stories, sending right messages and facilitating public awareness.
4. The government should pay particular attention to traditional communication tools with a special focus on the mosques. In addition, there is difference between the audience at the urban and rural mosques. Furthermore, the audience may vary based on language and local culture. The government should make sure that messages are skillfully tailored to fit the target audience. In order to adhere to the local cultural norms, an active cooperation and regular coordination should be facilitated between the Ministry of Haj and Religious Affairs and the Ministry of Information and Culture.
5. The government should endeavour to create active interface between different types of modern communication tools, traditional communication tools and networks.
6. A survey of target audience and categorisation of modern and traditional communication tools and mechanisms based on coverage, reach, influence, reliability and acceptability should be conducted.
7. In order to reinforce the messages, the government should engage different forms of visual and print media such as newspapers, magazines and journals.
8. A particular emphasis should be placed upon effective and skillful use of telecommunication, mobile system and SMS system to convey messages on different national, religious and cultural occasions. Sometimes, a "Greetings from the President," SMS, or a "The government is here to protect your rights" can serve as a more hope-generating message than a one hour speech through TV or Radio.
9. The local governance structures should be meaningfully created and used to communicate transition-related messages to the public at the local level. The local governance structures are good tools for conveying the messages to the people. They also help mobilize the localities to act as civil defense structures against the insurgent groups and undermine the insurgent propaganda and the local level.

10. In addition to choosing a right tool for communication, it is also important that messages needs to be positive. Hence, in communicating the transition process to the public, the GIRoA and IC should make sure that the messages should be:
    (a) Flawless and skillfully tailored to the different audience categories,
    (b) Provide satisfactory answers to lingering questions and concerns in the mind of public,
    (c) Highlight the flaws of the Taliban and insurgent claims to weaken their position,
    (d) Communicate through a various mediums in local dialects, in consonance with the traditional norms and cultural practices.

## Future Scenarios

In the event of continuation of the present ill defined and inadequate communication strategy, the most likely scenario is that the Taliban will maintain their edge over the GIRoA and its allies in exploiting the use of the modern and traditional communication means of communication to their advantage. Although the ability of the Taliban to use the modern communication tools such as radios and TVs has been limited, they enjoy far greater access to local traditional means such as social networks and religious forums particularly in volatile provinces. The messages conveyed by the GIRoA and its international backers have not resonated well among the people due to their lack of understanding of the human terrain, particularly in large swathes of the south and east.

The GIRoA and its allies need to design cost effective and inclusive strategic communication and public awareness programs to reach the target audience in easily accessed forms (i.e. news bulletins, public radio announcements, leaflets, madrassas). Moreover, the strategic communication and public awareness programs need to involve and motivate the people to trust the process and support its agenda. If the government and its allies do not change the present approach and if the transition fails to yield the intended results, Afghanistan may slide into chaos and will become a haven for international terrorists. It is thus critical to have a coherent and well coordinated strategic communication strategy and information campaign to prevent the reversal of gains in the near and long term.

### Notes

1. Karl F. Inderfurth, "Afghanistan in Transition", *The New York Times*, 14 November 2011, http://www.nytimes.com/2011/11/15/opinion/afghans-in-transition.html?_r=3. Accessed on 12 December 2011.
2. "NATO not to leave Afghanistan after 2014 transition", *Xinhua English news*, http://www.infowars.com/nato-not-to-leave-afghanistan-after-2014-transition/, accessed on 1 December 2011.

3. محمود حکیمی -افغانستان ملی حاکمیت حق تعریف ؛لیزبون. . http://www.gmic.gov.af/dari/index.php/transition-analysis/258-2010-11-28-05-57-49. Accessed on 20 December 2011.
4. David Galula, *Pacification in Algeria 1956-1958*, Rand Corporation: 2006, p 143.
5. "Operations in Afghanistan—Defense Committee", July 2011, http://www.publications.parliament.uk/pa/cm201012/cmselect/cmdfence/554/55404.htm. Accessed on 20 November 2011.
6. Madrassas are Islamic seminaries that teach mostly Islamic subjects leading to graduation as a cleric (*maulvi, maulana* or *mulla*).
7. A jirga is a tribal assembly of elders, which takes decisions by consensus; these are most common in Afghanistan. It is similar to that of a town meeting in the United States or a regional assembly in England, where important regional matters are addressed among the people of the area.
8. Interview with Attaurahman Salim, Former Deputy Minister of Haj and Religious Affairs, Government of Afghanistan, Kabul, 2 December 2011.
9. Ibid.
10. Interview with Dr. Hassan Akhlaq, Member of the Afghan Science Academy, Kabul, 5 November 2011.
11. Interview with Eshraq Hussaini, Former Afghan Deputy Minister of Education and Taj Muhammad Wardak, Former Minister of Interior, Kabul in November 2011.
12. Ibid.
13. Interview with Ajmal Obaid Abidi, Director of Aria TV, Kabul in December 2011.
14. Article 38, *The Constitution of Afghanistan*, http://www.embassyofafghanistan.org/constitution.html. Accessed on 12 December 2011.
15. شئونیزم گروه در وامنیت صلح ،ملی وهویت سیاسی حاکمیت قبیله. 25 Asad 1990, Ariana Online News Service, http://www.ariananet.com/modules.php?name=Artikel&op=view&sid=12471. Accessed on 25 November 2011.
16. *The Constitution of Afghanistan*, http://www.embassyofafghanistan.org/constitution.html. Accessed on 12 December 2011.
17. *Afghanistan Looking Ahead: Challenges for Governance and Community Welfare*, Afghanistan Research and Evaluation Unit (AREU), December 2011, http://www.areu.org.af/Uploads/EditionPdfs/1130E-Afghanistan%20Looking%20Ahead%20PN%202011.pdf. Accessed on 20 December, 2011.
18. Douglas Saltmarshe & Abhilash Medhi, *Local Governance in Afghanistan, A View from the Ground*, June 2011, http://www.areu.org.af/EditionDetails.aspx?EditionId=542&ParentId=7&ContentId=7&Lang=en-US, Accessed on 20 November 2011.
19. "Afghanistan", The World Fact Book, Central Intelligence Agency, https://www.cia.gov/library/publications/the-world-factbook/geos/af.html. Accessed on 22 November 2011.
20. Interview with Ishraq Hussaini, Former Deputy Minister of Education. Kabul, 12 November 2011.
21. Nick Grono, "Rule of Law and the Justice System in Afghanistan", http://www.crisisgroup.org/en/publication-type/speeches/2011/rule-of-law-and-the-justice-system-in-afghanistan.aspx. Accessed on 28 November 28, 2011.
22. Ibid.
23. Heracleous, L. & Langham, B., "Strategic Change and Organisational Culture at Hay Management Consultants.", vol. 29, no. 4. 1996.
24. Ibid.

25. Hirschfield, Rebecca, *Strategies for Managing Change.* 1999, http://www.hunter-group.com. pp. 1 & 3-5. Accessed on 3 October 2011.
26. "Afghans Concerned Over Security Transition", http://www.bamdad.af/index.php/english/story/1458. Accessed on 15 December 2011.
27. Interview with Behzad Oghli, Secretary of the Afghan Parliament. Tolo TV, 28 October 2011.
28. Seyla Benhabib Calhoun, ed., *Models of Public Space,* (Habermas: 1992), p. 87.

# SECTION IV

# REGIONAL AND INTERNATIONAL COMMUNITY'S PERSPECTIVES ON TRANSITION

# 10

# Is Regional Consensus on Afghanistan Possible?

*Haroun Mir*

The conflict in Afghanistan is indeed multidimensional, and the regional dimension of it has always been dominant. The country due to its geographic position is an integral part of South and Central Asia and thus belongs to the security complexes of these regions. In addition, because of Iran's influence and potential long-term U.S. military presence in the country, Afghanistan has also become a factor in the security complex of the Middle East.

The ensuing civil war after the collapse of the communist regime in 1992 was a direct consequence of the failed Geneva Accords, which was signed in April 1988 between Afghanistan and Pakistan under the supervision of the former Soviet Union and the United States (U.S.). Consequently, the Red Army left the country, the U.S. disengaged from the region, and a peaceful transition of political power was thwarted by regional spoilers, thereby initiating a new Great Game. Afghanistan instead of regaining its old buffer state status, became prey to a long-lasting proxy war with dire consequences not only for the domestic and regional security but also the international security, which ultimately lead to the 9/11 terrorist attacks on the U.S. homeland.

The U.S. military intervention in Afghanistan in 2001, supported by a broad international coalition, was intended to put an end to the conflict. After the signing of the Bonn agreement in December 2001, the overwhelming majority of Afghans welcomed the International Security Assistance Forces (ISAF) mission in the country. The international financial assistance in the following years contributed enormously to the rapid political, social, security, and economic improvements in the country.

However, even after a decade of international commitment in Afghanistan, the Taliban continue to pose a serious threat. The NATO, has been unable to militarily defeat them because they have enjoyed safe havens, sanctuaries, and financial support within the region. In addition an army of radicalised religious fighters from various countries such as Pakistan, Central Asian Republics, Bangladesh, China, Arab countries, and even Muslim citizens from Western countries have joined the Taliban in their struggle against the international coalition forces.

However, the growing economic strain and decreasing public support has compelled the U.S. administration to narrow its objective in Afghanistan from defeating the Taliban and promoting a democratic regime to a limited counter-terrorism capability in order to deny a return of Al-Qaeda. The change in the U.S. strategy required formulation of new policies such as reaching out to the insurgents and engaging regional stakeholders in search of a negotiated settlement.

The objective of this paper is to evaluate the possibility of a regional consensus on Afghanistan among relevant regional players, having high stakes in the country and have been involved in the three decades of conflict, either directly or indirectly.

## Relevant Regional Players[1]

In addition to Afghanistan's immediate neighbours such as Pakistan, Iran, the Central Asian Republics and China, a number of major regional powers such as India, Russia, Saudi Arabia, and Turkey have interests in Afghanistan, for both security and economic reasons.

### *Pakistan*

Of all the countries in the region, only Pakistan has had a major and contentious territorial dispute with Afghanistan. In fact, the long border between Afghanistan and Pakistan has never been officially ratified by the two countries. This open border question is at the root of Pakistan's attempts to destabilize Afghanistan. Pakistan's military establishment also fears that their country might be squeezed between two hostile neighbours -India and Afghanistan. Therefore, Pakistan's objective is to impose its hegemony through a subservient government in Kabul.

### *India*

Afghanistan and India have always enjoyed fruitful and constructive relations. History has seen India's sustained support of the Afghan government during challenging circumstances. The only time India did not recognize the regime in Kabul was during the Taliban era, when that regime adopted a hostile policy toward New Delhi. Pakistan is not the only country that would benefit from a secure Afghanistan. India has a shared interest in a peaceful Afghanistan, as it also seeks increased access to Central Asian reserves of fossil fuel, and access to their markets.

### *Iran*

Bordering Afghanistan from the West, Iran is another neigbouring country that has historically enjoyed political and economic leverage over Afghanistan. Iran's Afghan policy over the past three decades has been based on its geo-strategic interest, and a key objective of this policy is the expansion of Iranian influence in the region through an increased Shiite role in Afghanistan. Iran is fearful of U.S. military dominance in the region and has openly expresses its opposition to the American presence in Afghanistan. The government of Iran further views Afghanistan as a viable competitor in serving as a 'land bridge' connecting Central Asia with the rest of the world.

### *Central Asian Republics*

Since the collapse of the Soviet Union, the Central Asian Republics (CAR) have a common interest in Afghanistan in preventing the rise of militancy and extremism, and the cross-border infiltrations. Stability in Afghanistan would quell the serious threat these radical groups pose. The presence of U.S. military bases in Central Asia, as well as NATO's recent decision to use the Central Asian Republics (CAR) as an alternate supply route—Northern Distribution Network (NDN), offers them important financial and economic incentives. Since the Central Asian Republics are landlocked and depend on Russia for access to world markets, a stable Afghanistan could serve as an alternative, cost-efficient point of access. Another factor is the role of Russia, which is unwilling to abandon its influence over the Central Asian states for various economic and strategic reasons. Therefore, the fulfillment of Central Asian states' objectives in Afghanistan is contingent upon Russia's desire for regional influence.

### *Saudi Arabia*

Since the end of the Cold War, Saudi policy in Afghanistan has shifted from defeating communist ideology to containing Iranian influence in South Asia and the newly liberated Central Asian Republics. Believing radical Sunni Islam to be a natural obstacle to the propagation of a revolutionary Shiite doctrine in the region, the Saudis invested heavily in radical madrassas in Pakistan, where a considerable number of Afghan and Pakistani youth sought religious education. In addition, the Saudi government funded several mujahideen parties, to promote their Wahhabi brand of Islam in Afghanistan. Due to lack of knowledge and presence in Afghanistan, the Saudis relied mainly on the Pakistani military for the delivery of aid to a select number of Afghan radical groups. The Saudis believed these groups could play an influential role in countering Iranian influence in Afghanistan, and thus had no qualms in offering financial support to extremist groups in Afghanistan and the region. It is noteworthy that Saudi Arabia was among three countries that officially recognised the Taliban regime in 1996.

*China*

Until recently, China was a passive player in Afghanistan, and exclusively supported Pakistan's Afghan policy, owing to its close alliance with the country. However, Chinese policies toward Afghanistan are shifting for two reasons. First, the Chinese have growing economic interests in Afghanistan's mineral resources. Second, they perceive Afghanistan as important for maintaining their own internal security. The past few years in China have seen the growing influence of extremist and separatist groups such as the Uighur movement, which enjoys inspirational and other support from radical groups, including Al-Qaeda and the Taliban. A number of Uighurs who received paramilitary training and were radicalised in the Pakistani training camps pose a growing threat to the stability of Xinjiang province in China.

*Russia*

Russia is again asserting itself in the region, and its objectives are closely linked to its national interests in Central Asia. Russia envisions its role as a sole protector of Central Asian Republics against foreign threats such as radical Islamist movements, including Al-Qaeda. Thus, the presence of U.S. and NATO forces in Afghanistan is of serious concern for the Russia, as it nullifies its influence in the region.

*Turkey*

Turkey's role in Afghanistan became prominent because of its military contribution to ISAF. Turkey wants to regain its earlier influence of the Ottoman Empire in the Islamic world and particularly in Central Asia, where people still have ethnic and linguistic affinity with Turkey. Therefore, Turkey's interest in Afghanistan is part of its wider pan-Turkism strategy specifically in northern Afghanistan among Turkic ethnic groups.

## The Missed Opportunity after International Intervention in 2001

The military intervention in Afghanistan by a broad international military coalition, which resulted in the collapse of the Taliban regime in 2001, created a unique opportunity to engage all relevant regional players in order to seek a consensus on Afghanistan. Either countries such as Pakistan for fear of harsh reprisal by the U.S. administration consented to cooperate in the war on terror or countries such as Russia for sympathy with the U.S. showed strong support for the U.S. military intervention in Afghanistan. However, Bush Administration's unilateralism created resentment and fear among these countries. For instance, Khatami's government in Iran had shown serious desire to start a dialogue with the U.S. administration on Afghanistan.[2] However, instead of widening the international consensus by engaging these countries, the U.S. administration further alienated them.

The U.S. military intervention in Iraq in 2003 evoked strong international condemnation even from key NATO members such as France and Turkey. The unanimous international support for the U.S., after the terrorist attack on 9/11, splintered on the eve of the Iraq war. Meanwhile, the U.S. military had to take its valuable military assets away from Afghanistan to Iraq, which left a small number of ISAF forces in Afghanistan. Iranian and Pakistani intelligence services restarted their subversive activities in the country, which led to reemergence of the Taliban in remote villages along the Afghan-Pakistan border as early as 2004. Consequently, the security situation started to deteriorate rapidly. The ISAF did not have the capacity to respond to security threats initiated by reemergence of the Taliban and their associate terrorist networks such as Al-Qaeda. For almost eight years the U.S. administration lacked a proper strategy for Afghanistan, primarily because of its focus on Iraq. It took the election of President Obama, for the U.S. administration to develop a comprehensive strategy for Afghanistan.

## The Obama Administration's Regional Approach

The new U.S. foreign policy team, which had gained ample experience in regional multilateral diplomacy during President Clinton's era particularly in the case of Balkans, moved swiftly towards a similar diplomacy in Afghanistan, which was expressed in Mrs. Clinton's speech during the international conference on Afghanistan in Hague on March 31, 2009. She said, "...just as these problems cannot be solved without the Afghan people, they cannot be solved without the help of Afghanistan's neighbours. Trafficking in narcotics, the spread of violent extremism, economic stagnation, water management, electrification, and irrigation are regional challenges that require regional solutions."[3]

Further, the nomination of Late Ambassador Holbrooke, the architect of the Dayton Accords, as the special envoy for Afghanistan and Pakistan was a testimony to the White House's desire to seriously engage regional stakeholders in seeking a regional solution to the Afghan conflict. However, because of the complexity of regional issues, which date back to the colonial era and the Great Game between the Russian and British Empires, the U.S. administration did not have a specific plan for its new regional policy. Ashely Tellis in his concluding essay for Carnegie's 2010 report "Is a Regional Strategy Viable in Afghanistan?" put forward various U.S. regional approaches for Afghanistan:

> (i) Expanding the Afghan theater to include Pakistan in order to synergize the counterinsurgency and counterterrorism campaigns now underway; (ii) Integrating Afghan and Pakistani efforts toward securing the common goal of defeating extremist Islam in the greater South Asian region; (iii) Incorporating Afghanistan's and Pakistan's major regional neigh-

bours into a cooperative effort led by the United States and aimed at defeating Al-Qaeda and the Taliban while stabilising South and Central Asia; and, finally (iv) Unifying the hitherto separate security complexes of South and Central Asia by transforming Afghanistan into a region-wide trade and transit hub.[4]

Following the release of the new U.S. strategy for Afghanistan, the Obama administration initiated serious political and diplomatic efforts to implement these different concepts. Nomination of special envoys for Afghanistan and Pakistan not only by the U.S. but also by other coalition partners in Afghanistan, extension of military interventions such as drone attacks on the Pakistani side of the Durand Line, tripartite meetings between U.S., Afghanistan, and Pakistan, and reaching out to Russia and China have been some examples of such activities.

However, after more than three years of continued diplomatic efforts both at the multilateral and bilateral levels, little progress has been achieved. The culminating diplomatic effort was an initiative lead by Turkey during the Istanbul Conference in November 2011. However, the regional stakeholders did not reach a consensus on Afghanistan. Even the New Silk Road initiative, an economic vision for the economic integration of the wider region, received little appreciation in this conference. Instead the position of Afghanistan's two main neighbours Pakistan and Iran has since been hardened. In addition, China and Russia have started questioning the U.S. intention in the region.

## Reasons for the Failed Regional Diplomacy

There are many reasons why regional stakeholders have not been able to reach a consensus over Afghanistan. However, historic failure of diplomacy in this region and security concerns over long-term U.S. military presence in Afghanistan are some of the reasons as to why regional multilateralism on Afghanistan has not borne fruit.

South and Central Asia are the least economically integrated regions because countries of the region instead of exploring common opportunities have been dwelling on their differences. For instance, despite continuous efforts and creation of regional associations and organisations such as South Asian Association for Regional Cooperation (SAARC) and Economic Cooperation Organisation (ECO), limited regional cooperation has been achieved. The bulk of trade of member countries takes place with countries outside of the region rather than within the region. Tariff and non-tariff barriers are serious obstacles to regional economic integration, which are a direct consequence of unresolved regional issues.

Similarly, Shanghai Cooperation Organisation (SCO), which was created to address common security concerns of Central Asian Countries, Russia, and China, and gained momentum after the U.S. intervention in Afghanistan, faces serious challenges because of Chinese and Russian competition for influence in Central Asia. In fact, the failure of the U.S. administration to translate the new Silk Road initiative into a grand regional economic vision is related to deficit of trust among key regional countries. Other reasons are directly related to long-term U.S. military presence in Afghanistan, which has created fear in the region. For instance Iranian authorities believe that the U.S. military will use its bases in Afghanistan in order to attack Iran, and Pakistan's military and political elite is paranoid about a growing rumor that the U.S. has the intention to take control of its nuclear assets. In addition, a number of events have further fueled mistrust and suspicion about the U.S. intentions in the region.

The U.S.-Pakistan relationship has been in a downward spiral since the assassination of Osama bin Laden by the U.S. military forces at a military cantonment near Islamabad in May 2011, followed by the U.S. raid against the Pakistani outposts, which resulted in the killing of 24 Pakistani soldiers in November 2011. Thus, the U.S. long-term military presence in Afghanistan is considered to be a serious threat to the national security of Pakistan. Equally, terrorism, radicalisation, and nuclear weapons in Pakistan pose dangers to the security of the United States and its allies worldwide. For instance the Pakistani decision to block NATO supply route, close Shamsi air base, and the threat to block its air space to NATO airplanes puts the interest of the two countries on a collision course.

Similarly, on the western border of Afghanistan, differences between the U.S. and Iran has been growing. The December 2011 incident of a downed U.S. drone, and arrest of an alleged spy, who might have infiltrated to Iran from Afghanistan further added to the suspicions. The rumours about a military attack on Iranian's nuclear site and alleged attempts to effect a regime change are taken seriously by the Iranian authorities. Therefore, the U.S. long-term military presence in Afghanistan is considered to be a serious threat.

Beside Iran and Pakistan, Russia and China are also fearful of the American long-term military presence in Afghanistan. However, unlike Iran and Pakistan, they will not undermine the U.S. mission in Afghanistan because they share a common security concern of international terrorism and radical Islamist movements.

## Alternative Solution?

Afghanistan, a poor and land locked country, cannot afford to be in a state of permanent hostility with both of its neighbours—Iran and Pakistan, which provide it vital access to the sea. However, since 2001 the international support for the country has compensated for the lack of cooperation from these two neighbours. Meanwhile, Iran and Pakistan are in a serious competition to become an alternative gate way for Central Asian fossil fuel to the world market. For instance, Iran with the assistance of India constructed the Chabahar port in

Iranian Balochistan as an alternative to the the Gwadar port in Pakistan, which was constructed by China. In addition, India helped connect the Iranian Chabahar port to the Afghan ring road by constructing the strategic Zaranj-Delaram highway.

Similarly, Russia and China are in serious competition over influence in Central Asia, and Chinese rapid investment in energy sector in this region is worrisome for the Russians. For instance, Chinese companies are aggressively biding for most mining tenders in Afghanistan, while Russian investors are totally absent from the country. Competition among key regional stakeholders will create a new opportunity for Afghanistan. Therefore, the U.S. administration instead of searching for unanimity and consensus among regional countries through multilateralism could bridge their differences through bilateral diplomacy.

## The Shifting Balance of Power in the Region

The balance of power in South and Central Asia as well as in the Middle East has significantly shifted over the past decade due to the U.S. interventions in Afghanistan and Iraq. In the next decade, the renewed international commitment in Afghanistan announced during the second Bonn conference in December 2011 as well as the long-term U.S. military presence in the country will change the current status quo. Further, common challenges such as climate change, uncontrolled growth of population, lack of water management, and energy crisis are some of the important factors, which will deeply impact inter-regional relationships.

Following the renewed international commitment for Afghanistan during the Bonn conference in December 2011, the prospects for stabilizing Afghanistan during the transformation phase appears better than many countries of the region. Indeed, a successful security transition, and a peaceful transfer of political power in 2014 will enable the country to reduce its reliance on international community and invest on its own resource potential. The Afghan state's viability and survival will depend on its economic self reliance because the international economic assistance will not be permanent particularly in light of the current global financial and economic crises. The economic prospect for Afghanistan looks promising because of its mineral resources, the potential for agriculture development, a young work force, and its geo-strategic position at the cross road of the three regions.

Countries of the region such as China, India, Pakistan, Turkey, and Russia are keen to invest in Afghanistan. Chinese and Indian companies have already won important mining contracts. Similarly, the extensions of Iranian and Uzbek rail road as well extension of their electric grids into Afghanistan are encouraging examples of cooperation. The Turkmenistan, Afghanistan, Pakistan and India (TAPI) project, which will enable Turkmenistan to export its natural gas to

Pakistan and India via Afghanistan, is an important test for an effective multilateral framework for cooperation between Afghanistan, Pakistan, and India.

## Prospects for Regional Cooperation beyond 2014?

The balance of regional power would further shift during the next decade because of important events such as the Arab Spring, the U.S.-India strategic alignment; Pakistan's deteriorating relationship with the U.S., Iran's international isolation, and emergence of Turkey as an important regional power. In addition, Chinese and Russian competition over Central Asia could undermine their future relationship.

### *Pakistan*

Pakistan is facing serious economic, security, political, and social challenges. The level of poverty has considerably increased, and the annual rate of economic growth of around 2 to 3 percent does not match with the very fast rate of growth of population. According to the UN estimates Pakistan will be a nation of 350 million people by 2050. In addition, the country is paying back for its dangerous policies of corroborating with radicalism and terrorism. The surge of violence in Pakistan combined with series of natural disasters has further undermined its stability. The strained Pakistani-U.S. relation will increase the economic stress on an already bankrupt government. In the years to come, Pakistani authorities will have difficulties to overcome their domestic challenge and therefore can become a burden for the international community, which will further increase the risk of social and political unrest in the country.

### *Iran*

The Iranian authorities have had a unique opportunity to play a constructive role in Afghanistan, and thus improve its ties with the West and particularly with the U.S. However, the Iranian influence over the Shi'i in Afghanistan is waning and its efforts to organize Afghan Shi'i into a new Hezbollah in this region is shattered because the shi'i minority has tremendously benefited from NATO intervention in Afghanistan. They have a bigger share of political power and are not willing to jeopardize their gains because of Iranian rivalry with the U.S. The participation of shi'i in the traditional Loya Jirga, which gave Karzai a plebiscite to approve a long-term U.S.-Afghanistan strategic partnership, is a testimony to their desire to support the current democratic process.

### *India*

India's emergence as an uncontested regional power has been an important factor in shifting the traditional balance of power in South Asia. It is the biggest regional contributor to Afghanistan in terms of economic assistance. The recent Agreement of Strategic Partnership (ASP) between India and Afghanistan could possibly mean that India would partner with the U.S. after 2014, particularly in training Afghan security forces, when most of European and NATO members will be gone from Afghanistan.

### *Central Asian Republics*

These republics have all the symptoms, which triggered the Arab Spring in the Middle East. Political power and resources are controlled by one family or clan, the gap between poor and rich, and urban and rural population has been expanding. The oppressed political opposition has no alternative than to turn to extremist Islamist group. This situation will not be sustainable for long and the winds of the Arab Spring will reach Central Asia soon.

### *Russia*

Russia was able to reassert itself as an important regional power and is keen to hold its control in Central Asia. However, it faces tremendous challenges such as serious demographic deficit, obsolete technology, and an economy based on export of fossil fuel. Overtime, Russia's regional influence will recede vis-à-vis an aggressive China.

### *China*

China's thirst for energy and natural resources, in order to fuel its economic growth, makes it very aggressive in search of natural resources in the region. It has a high stakes in the stability of the entire region and as an emerging global power seeks to avoid conflict in its backyard. Moreover, at the current stage of its economic development, it cannot afford to jeopardize its ties with the U.S. Meanwhile, during the past decade, India has become a relatively bigger trade partner of China than Pakistan, and the two countries will avoid any confrontation in Afghanistan, which will endanger their interests in Central Asia.

### *Saudi Arabia*

Over the past decade, Saudi Arabia has significantly lost its influence in this region. Its heavy investment in radical groups has gotten the worst return for the Kingdom. Recent events in the Middle East such as emergence of Shiite dominance in Iraq, nuclear acquisitions of Iran, and the Arab Spring are considered as serious threats to its national security. Therefore, Saudis and the entire Gulf Countries will rely on American protection for foreseeable future and in return will cooperate with the U.S. in the region. For instance, they can play a constructive role in the reconciliation process in Afghanistan because many Afghans consider Saudi Arabia as the spiritual leader of the Muslim World and thus it could use its religious leverage over the belligerent Afghan parties.

### *Turkey*

Turkey like India and China is another emerging economic and military power. Turkey's ambition is to regain its lost leadership in the Islamic world particularly among Turkic nations in Central Asia. In addition, Turkey shares common democratic values with the U.S. and India, and therefore the three countries will constitute natural security alliance in the region.

Consequently, the developments in the political, social, and economic sphere in the decade to come will deeply impact the balance of power in South and Central Asia as well as in the Middle East. The NATO members will disengage from the region, while the U.S. strategic interest in the Indian Ocean, Persian Gulf, and Central Asia will continue. Moreover, Islamist radicalism, drug trafficking, international terrorism, and proliferation of fissile material will continue to be considered high risks within and beyond the region. Therefore, the U.S. will keep a significant number of Special Forces in Afghanistan in order to prevent Al-Qaeda and its associates to reconstitute their old bases.

## Policy Recommendations

From 2012 to 2014, President Karzai might not be able to fix a corrupt and dysfunctional government, which is considered the source of many problems in the country. Meanwhile, the U.S. and its other NATO allies will try to contain the political situation from deteriorating further by showing strong commitment through bilateral strategic partnerships with the Afghan government that will serve as a strong warning to the belligerent neighbouring countries. Meanwhile, in light of domestic challenges and nervous behaviour of Afghanistan's main neighbours—Iran and Pakistan, the potential for regional diplomatic engagement in the years to come seems unrealistic.

However in 2014, a successful military transition from ISAF to Afghan forces, and a peaceful constitutional transfer of political power, will create favorable conditions for the next Afghan government. The presence of the U.S. military and continued international support after 2014 and until 2024 will have a tremendous impact both on the insurgents and the neighbouring countries, which during this period will face serious political, social, and economic challenges. The Taliban leadership will not have the will to continue their struggle for another decade and their fighters will lose motivation when they will have to fight their own countrymen instead of foreign forces.

This period of transformation will provide a unique opportunity for the next Afghan government to improve governance, fight corruption, provide justice, and deliver basic services to the Afghan people, which will create a new momentum. Subsequently, the gap between the people and the government will be reduced, and better security will speed exploitation of Afghanistan's natural resources and attract foreign investment. Ultimately, confidence in the Afghan government and prospect for a better life will reduce the leverage of the neighbouring countries on Afghans, who have fallen prey to their manipulation. If these improvements could materialize in the country, then the Afghan security forces will be able to contain limited insurgency in areas close to the Pakistani border and a degree of cross-border violence will be tolerated by the people.

Meanwhile, the Afghan and U.S. administration could join efforts with the other regional allies such as India and Turkey to conduct a concerted regional diplomacy. In fact regional stakeholders have competing interests in Afghanistan. Building a consensus among them will not be possible before drastic political changes occur in Iran and Pakistan. However, working with China, Russia, Saudi Arabia, and Central Asian Republics is possible.

Eventually, the Afghan government should distinguish regional stakeholders in two categories. First those countries such as China, Russia, and Central Asian Republics with which it is possible to work on common interest and have high stakes in the stability of Afghanistan. Second, the two spoilers—Iran and Pakistan, which are committed to undermine and derail the current stabilisation process in Afghanistan. Both countries consider the U.S. military presence in Afghanistan as an existential threat, and no amount of incentive, compromise, and concession will induce flexibility in their decision making, as long as such policy decisions are made by the top military brass and religious leaders. However, the domestic pressure for political improvement in these two countries will certainly lead to positive changes in a foreseeable future. Finally, only an economically viable Afghan state capable of protecting its territory and preventing regional interferences will be able to regain its pre-1979 position and become a connector of regions.

## NOTES

1. For a description of the relevant regional players in the context of Afghanistan, see Haroun Mir, "Afghanistan" in Ashley J Tellis & Arop Mukharji, eds. *Is a Regional Strategy Viable in Afghanistan?*, Carnegie Endowment for International Peace, 2010, http://carnegieendowment.org/files/regional_approach.pdf . Accessed on 20 May 2012.
2. For example, in January 2002, James Dobbins, U.S. envoy to Afghan talks, and then Treasury secretary Paul O'Neill are approached by Iranian diplomats at an Afghan donor conference in Tokyo and told that Iran would like to open a broad dialogue with the United States. Both men relayed the message to Washington to no apparent effect. A week later, President Bush includes Iran on an "axis of Evil" with Iraq and North Korea." See Barbara Slavin, "U.S.-Iran Relations after the Revolution: A Catalog of Missed Opportunities", American Foreign Policy Project, 12 June 2008, http://americanforeignpolicy.org/overview-how-to-deal-with-iran/a-short-history-of-us-iran-relations-post-revolution#footnote_anchor_6. Accessed on 20 May 2012.
3. Glenn Kessler, "At Summit on Afghanistan, U.S. Extends a Hand to Iran", *Washington Post,* 1 April 2009, http://www.washingtonpost.com/wp-dyn/content/article/2009/03/31/AR2009033100809.html. Accessed on 20 May 2012.
4. Ashley J Tellis & Arop Mukharji, eds. "Is a Regional Strategy Viable in Afghanistan?", op. cit.

# 11

# Pakistan's Perspective on the Afghan Transition

*Rasul Bakhsh Rais*

## Introduction

No other country has been affected by developments in Afghanistan and in turn been affected by the cycles of war in that country as Pakistan. As history is evident, it can and will play a key role. But then it is just one of the key players. Over the past decade, major powers, the U.S.A., its NATO allies, and India have taken much of the initiatives. Pakistan's relations with the U.S. and Afghanistan have got mired in deep mistrust that leaves Pakistan on the margins even after making massive sacrifices in the war on terror.

Over the years, it has silently advocated negotiations with the Taliban at home and within Afghanistan, a view that seems to be gaining traction. As U.S. and other powers are in the process of transferring much of the responsibility to the Afghan government, by 2014, Pakistan finds itself on the sidelines, as its relations with the U.S. have nosedived.[1] The paper will explore what role Pakistan can play toward the 'endgame', what are the interests that drive its Afghan policy, and what are its fears about other major powers in the region?

The main argument of this paper is that transitioning Afghanistan toward a stable, peaceful and normal country will have to be collaborative and multilateral effort in which Pakistan can play a major role. Pakistan needs a proactive diplomacy to be heard, understood and accommodated in the future solution on Afghanistan.

Keeping in view the three long cycles of wars in Afghanistan (1978-2011) and the direct impact of these wars on security and social order of Pakistan and the wider region, issues of war and peace in this country cannot and should not be seen in either isolation or in a unilateral way.[2] For good or bad, no other country has been affected by developments in Afghanistan and has inversely been affected by its social and security conditions, mostly conflicts and social dislocations, than Pakistan.[3] It will be simplistic to argue that the modern Afghan wars are entirely an Afghan affair—on account of its conflictive social groups, weak character of the state, religion and political contestations. The foreign interests, great power ambitions, rivalries among external powers and regional players have enmeshed with the conflicts of rival Afghan social and political groups.[4]

Consequently, the Afghans have lost autonomy in making choices for war and peace, and even with the best intentions and efforts, have not been able to insulate themselves from foreign interference. Many of these foreign players, militant groups, countries from within the neighbourhood, and the two superpowers of the Cold War—Soviet Union and the United States have intervened on the pretext of helping, supporting, stabilising and normalising Afghanistan. The foreign quest for reforming Afghanistan ignored the historical and cultural peculiarities that resulted in the resistance in one form or another.[5] Thus, foreign ideologies, security and political interests of external powers have shaped the conflicts within Afghanistan more than its own historical fault-lines, ethnic divide, religious extremism and warlordism.[6] However, Afghanistan's own internal troubles, mainly conflict and power contestation exploited by the foreign actors—non-state and state—have continuously served as a factor, causing vertical links between Afghan groups and their foreign patrons.[7]

It is much of the same brew with different colours, flags, formations, and fresh alignments that has defined the third long cycle of war in Afghanistan since September 11, 2001, making this cycle the longest one compared to the Afghan-Soviet war (1980-88) and inter-Mujahideen, Northern Front, Taliban civil war (1992-2001). It is out of the purview of this chapter to analyse in depth the third cycle of war, its objectives, costs, successes or failure in any great length. But a brief review will be necessary to analyse the endgame.

It may sound heretical but the objectives of 2001 invasion of Afghanistan to liberate it from the Taliban rule and defeat, destroy Al-Qaeda were more or less identical with the Soviet war—establishing and defending a friendly regime with a specific template of nation and state building. The two great powers intervened with different ideological and political prescriptions for this purpose. All other aspects of intervention were alike—the choice of favourite groups, use of force and war of attrition against the resistance. Yet, another remarkable similarity is the Islamic character of the resistance, with the difference that the Taliban are not a national resistance movement but an ethnic group based in the Pashtun areas of the country. It is, in fact, the major actors involved in the conflict that changes the meanings of every term. What constitutes these terms like unity, peace, nation, state, stable and normal in Afghanistan are the ideologies, power interests and preferred security orders of external actors, of varied stripes, involved in the Afghan wars.

The third cycle of war between the ISAF and the Taliban insurgents has gone on for more than a decade. More or less, it is a stalemate; a war without winners, like the Afghan-Soviet war. It is matter of interpretation, and the choice of variables one may choose to use for assessing who suffered greater cost than the other party. Opinions of experts and analysts may vary whether the Taliban have paid greater price or the America-led ISAF forces. But the fact remains that victory against the Taliban is neither possible nor a pursuable goal anymore. As speculated from the beginning, the time factor has gone in favour of the local insurgents. And they have fully exploited the nation and state building failures—shift of attention to the Iraq war, poor investment of resources in reconstruction, political inefficiency of the Afghan government and courting of warlords by the United States.[8] There is however one remarkable success in this war, the destruction or eviction of Al-Qaeda from Afghanistan, including killing of Osama bin Ladin. This may help the Taliban leadership break the transnational linkages with the Arabs, which may, in turn, provide an impetus for negotiations.

## Towards the Endgame?

If history of Afghanistan is a guide, each war has to end—in victory, defeat or in chaos, in the later situation, producing more points of conflict and engaging new or old actors in some other form in lower or higher level of violence. It is still early to predict if the third cycle of war is coming to end or whether Afghanistan will be locked into yet another cycle of war. This time around, signs of positive developments in Afghanistan are not dim, weak or hopeless. Before envisioning the endgame, there is a need to flag these optimistic signs.

First, the international community at no time in modern history has paid so much attention to Afghanistan, as it has done during the past decade. The United States alone has spent three hundred billion dollars in security operations.[9] The foreign aid commitments for reconstruction from states and international organisations are much lower but nonetheless they are not insignificant compared to other periods of Afghan history.[10] International assistance in rebuilding the Afghan state, including its security forces, infrastructure and economic life has created a basis for further development. There also appears to be genuine efforts by the international community to support Afghanistan's revival, security and stability, as evidenced from the Second Bonn Conference in December 2011.[11] The western powers, even in the face of setbacks are not likely to walk away from Afghanistan, leaving it in a condition of civil strife.[12] This resolve may have begin to have positive effects on the confidence of the Afghan government and send a strong message to the Taliban that the international community will not allow them to reconquer Afghanistan.

Second, there is an emerging regional and international consensus on peaceful, unified and normal Afghanistan.[13] Though it is informal, a bit ambiguous but nonetheless is a very strong sentiment. Wars in Afghanistan resulting into statelessness and power vacuum have created hubs for militants with regional and international consequences. This lesson is not lost to any rational player within the region. All major states, including Pakistan, India, China and western powers would like to ensure that Afghanistan does not slide into anarchy that led to the civil war and emergence of the Taliban and Al-Qaeda in the 1990's. But much of this consensus, may hold, if only the endgame is negotiated in a way that produces peace, stability and order and the concerns and interests of the major powers within the region are accommodated.

Third, the overall political and infrastructural capacities of the Afghan state, though still in evolutionary and developing stage are better than during the time of the Mujahideen or Najibullah.[14] It's own growing defence capacity and the residual attack forces of the United States in and around the country may prevent a sudden collapse of the Afghan state, the manner in which it crumbled under the Taliban attack in 1994-96. But still, it will be too optimistic to bet on the Afghan state to fight and survive against a determined, motivated and ethnically rooted militia like the Taliban in a long-drawn scenario. Had that been the case, there was no need for negotiating the endgame, but to leave Afghanistan with its government to deal with its internal contestants is too shallow and shaky.[15]

Finally, the United States and its allies for more than one reason want to end the war—cost, time, the economic and national outlooks have changed to seek better alternatives to war, without sacrificing the central objectives about a unified and peaceful Afghanistan. After reviewing and changing the strategies of the Afghan war during the two Administrations, Washington seems to settle on negotiating with the Taliban with three pre-conditions, that have not changed as yet—the Taliban will accept the Afghan constitution, renounce their connections with Al-Qaeda and integrate peacefully into the Afghan political system. The indications of change in American policy that surprised many observers began the day the U.S. President announced to the Afghans, Americans and the world that his country would start the drawdown of its troops in Afghanistan in the summer of 2011 and will complete this process by the end of 2014. This change of policy removed many ambiguities about the American intentions, and sent a clear message to the Afghan government to prepare itself for a greater responsibility and to the Taliban adversaries that it will not keep Afghanistan under its 'occupation'.[16]

What then is the central piece of the endgame? It is not an unqualified optimism that the Afghan government left to itself will be able to ensure peace and stability, let alone defend itself against the Taliban. Also, it is not optimism of the American-ISAF forces that they will be able to defeat the Taliban or force them to surrender. The surge—building of American forces by adding thirty thousand more—to break the power of the Taliban forces in the south of the country has produced mixed results. Night raids that are detested by the Afghans and the Afghan government have disrupted Taliban communications, and according to some reports, has eliminated second tier of the Taliban commanders on the ground. The troop surge and the inclination to negotiate with the Taliban insurgent are two sides of the same strategy-to ensure the Afghan regime survives after the withdrawal of the American forces.

The objective of this paper is to examine the 'endgame' in Afghanistan with reference to Pakistan's interests, concerns, and policy outlook. The central argument is that Pakistan has been and will remain a key player in stabilising Afghanistan.[17] Being a key player, its own stability, security, social order, specifically in the border regions and economic progress has become intertwined with the fate of Afghan state and society. It has points of strength because of its long engagement with the Afghan resistant forces, but it is also vulnerable, as similar extremist elements have targeted its security forces and civil society. To explore this argument, few fundamental questions need to addressed. What are the contours of the endgame and what are the wider implications for the region? What are Pakistan's fears and interests in shaping the endgame? And, what are the probable policy paths that Pakistan is likely to pursue to protects its interest?

The underlying hypothesis of this paper is that no one power, local, regional or global can settle the Afghan war alone or on its own terms. The complexity of multiple actors—state and non-state—involved in the war will require a broader consensus among them which will depend on their legitimate interests and concerns being taken into account.

The driving forces behind the endgame are two realisations. One that an open-ended war has consumed huge resources and entailed sacrifices but is nowhere close to a definite positive outcome for the forces that invaded Afghanistan to end the Taliban regime. Second, the Taliban are now a force to reckon with and need to be brought on board, if the Afghan regime and its allies would like to bring in peace and stability in Afghanistan. In other words reconciliation between the Afghan regime and the Taliban will be the cornerstone of the endgame. But it will greatly depend on whether or not the regional players like India, Iran and Pakistan will lend their support to this vision of the endgame.

Since this paper is about the role Pakistan will or can play in the endgame, it is important to address its concerns, interests and the likely policy options it may exercise. Pakistan has played a major role, if not decisive, in the Mujahideen resistance against the Soviet occupation of Afghanistan. Both for the history of Pakistan's involvement in Afghanistan and its security and geopolitical interests, its leaders feel that it has important stake in the future of Afghanistan.[18] For the last thirty years, Pakistan's stakes in Afghanistan are determined by its policy options in Afghanistan. More or less its interest and concerns in Afghanistan have remained the same but its policies have shifted in the three cycles of war from an American ally organising the Mujahideen resistance to one of the independent player in the Afghan civil war, and then to a major partner of the United States to defeat the Taliban and Al-Qaeda.

Interpretation of what are Pakistan's interests in Afghanistan depends on who is talking or writing about them. Even within Pakistan, there is no single voice. Broadly speaking of Pakistan's interests, one end of the spectrum centres on aggressive intent—ambition to turn Afghanistan into a dependent, satellite state. The argument that Pakistan is locked into a historic rivalry with India wants a 'strategic depth' in Afghanistan. What would that mean in terms of practical arrangements—military bases, strategic alliances or a friendly regime? Actually this notion is used to batter Pakistan's security policy toward Afghanistan more than to logically explain its practical value.

The Taliban connection with Pakistan is presented as the best example of 'strategic depth' strategy. However, the extent of the influence Pakistan exercised with the Taliban on any issue of substance remains debatable. The Taliban refused to formally acknowledge the Durand Line, saying Muslims don't recognise territorial boundaries. They rejected Pakistan's calls to spare the historic Buddha statutes. And when Pakistan pressed them on a ceasefire, exchange of prisoners and reconciliation with the Northern Front, they went ahead with their own choices. On the most important issue on the surrender of Osama bin Laden in the wake of 9/11, their response to Pakistan request was humiliating. The story of Pakistan's influence with the Mujahideen leaders over formation of coalition government and signing of accords is no different; each of them blinded by power ambitions, fear and distrust went on their own way.

## What Pakistan wants in Afghanistan?

When some of the military leaders of Pakistan talked about 'Strategic Depth' in the eighties, they meant an Afghanistan that is neutral enough not to provide its territory as a strategic space to its adversaries—rival states like India and Iran or to insurgent ethnic groups working against the Pakistani state.[19] The 'strategic depth' idea is not offensive but defensive one; but it can be offensive, if the Afghan government or some of the power contenders—autonomous war lords, factions and ethnic groups independently attempt to harm Pakistan's national security. It may do what it has done in the past; select and support an Afghan faction, mainly from the Pashtun regions, and even beyond to counterbalance the threat.[20]

But that may not be the first or the best option, and perhaps a weapon of last resort after it has exhausted all other alternatives. Actually, the regional and global interest in Afghanistan, not just over the war and peace issue, but more essentially on the trade routes, mineral resources, gas pipelines and regional commerce is so critical and compelling that Pakistan would have to be part of a constructive coalition rather than on the side of typical proxies that it supported in the past. For all practical purposes, Pakistan will have to revisit 'strategic depth' with a broader view of actors and their interests in the stability of the region.[21]

The emerging consensus, at least among the political parties in Pakistan, is that wars through proxies in Afghanistan have hurt Pakistan badly, and even decades of investment in such adventures, the 'strategic depth' meaning denial of strategic space to the adversarial forces, powers and actors remains a distant dream. The alternative may lie in positive engagement with the Afghan government, and dealing with all bilateral issues on state-to-state basis. This is an overwhelmingly a majority view. But in imperfect democracy with history of troubled civil-military relations and national security taking the centre stage, the realist proclivities of the Pakistani state to match threat with threat cannot be entirely ruled out.[22] But revival of the old policy in the evolving geo-economic and energy resource-centric outlook of major players, including China, a strategic partner of Pakistan, looks a very remote possibility.

There is a need for a realistic assessment of Pakistan's position in the current balance of power in and around Afghanistan. Since the ouster of the Taliban, Pakistan does not appear to be in a position to resurrect its influence for the reason that the United States and its NATO allies have captured Afghanistan's geopolitical space and they continue to shape its future direction. But that is not to say that their hold over this space is uncontested, firm or certain. Had that been the case, then a major shift in American policy toward the Taliban that '—they are not enemies of the United States' and that Washington wants to open a dialogue with the insurgent leaders would not have come about.

Understanding what Pakistan wants in Afghanistan will help understand its current and future possible moves and options to shape the endgame. Its current threats and what has really troubled its national security in wider sense—social harmony, ethnic balance, extremism and militancy—have direct link with the developments in the Afghan backyard. From this point of view, the first condition for Pakistan's national security is peace and stability in Afghanistan, and not war. As it is evidently clear, wars of Afghanistan have become gradually wars of other regional states, as the undercurrents of Islamism and militancy have travelled across the borders, and continue to do so.[23]

The incalculable damage that Pakistan suffered on account of earlier cycles of conflict in Afghanistan—some can be monetised, but the real casualty is the modernist, moderate vision of the founders of Pakistan. With the slogans of *Jihad*, Islam and war against occupiers, the social and political forces opposed to modernist perspective of Pakistan have gained strength. How much strength they have gained in the country is question that remains unanswered. Fortunately, these forces have not yet got popular nor do they have any strong social base of support. But that is immaterial because they prefer bullets to ballots in pursuit of their ideology and political objectives. The terrorist networks that the militants have created across the borders and within Pakistan pose the gravest challenge to its domestic order and national security than any threat by conventional state adversaries.[24] Frankly speaking, the monster Pakistan faces in extremism and militancy is one of the unintended consequences of its policies toward Afghanistan.

The cost of Pakistan's participation in war on terror both in human as well as in material terms is costlier than any member of the foreign collation fighting inside Afghanistan. By official estimate more than 30, 000 Pakistan citizens have been killed in terrorist acts, the country has lost 3,500 security personnel and economic cost is estimated to be around U.S. dollars 68 billion. The cost of an image as a terrorist stricken country with poor security has caused drying up of domestic and international investment, has reduced foreign tourism, and the cost of security has outbalanced budgetary allocations for social development and infrastructure. With a burgeoning population, Pakistan has lost an important decade for development when its neighbours, China and India have done so well. Its own policy blunders, corruption and bad governance are some of the causes, but the poor climate of national security has left Pakistan far behind its even reasonable targets of development. The root cause of internal security troubles is extremism—the spill over effect of the Afghan wars and support of insurgent groups by the state as well as private religious groups.

## Pakistan's Afghan Challenge

The emerging political consensus, therefore in Pakistan is that peace in Afghanistan and its stability are in its own interests.[25] But the bigger question is how and under what conditions can Pakistan be part of the peace building effort in that country? There are two narratives on this count. The conservative—religious right narrative is that the wars in Afghanistan, including the rise of the Taliban against the American and ISAF forces is reactive, natural and consistent with the historical Afghan reality—i.e. resistance against the foreign forces. They also argue that Americans cannot win the war and should not try doing it as it will further damage the prospects of national reconciliation within Afghanistan and continue to trouble Pakistan's security. The right wing religious parties and analysts link Taliban terrorism in Pakistan to its support for the American policy in Afghanistan more than the generic reasons relating to religious extremism and intolerance in the society. The solution they suggest lies in ending of the war, withdrawal of foreign forces and dialogue with the Taliban.

The liberal-moderate narrative is not quite the opposite but it does diverge on some important points. From this point of view, religious violence and terrorist groups have existed longer than the American war in Afghanistan. This phenomenon is an outcome of Pakistan's earlier Afghan policies, and not just reaction to its support for the international coalition in Afghanistan or the use of military force against the militant groups, notably the Tehrik-e-Taliban Pakistan (TTP) in the tribal regions of the country. The liberals though a narrow band of intellectuals and political party activists, link emergence of religious militancy to flawed state security policies, construction of national security state, repeated derailment of democracy in the country and a view of national security policy dominated by the security establishment.

Using some ideas of classical realism and state-centric view of regional power plays and security issues, quite a few even within this stream of thought argue that Pakistan has done and would do what states under conditions of conflicting interests, rivalry, distrust and threat perceptions do. What it means is that Pakistan's proactive and reactive engagement with the Afghan conflict theatre is largely the function of the games great powers and regional rivals have played. Pakistan cannot be expected to pursue saintly polices or self-abnegate itself in the world of states that pursue national interests defined by their ruling elites. In doing so, they are hardly restrained by any normal moral standards, but go by the morality of power, interest and security.

Therefore, the role will Pakistan play in the endgame will also be the function of the same dynamics of national security that impel and drive other states. The choices that factions within Afghanistan, that have more ethnic or religious, sectarian than national political orientations, make about the future of their country and its ties with the neighbouring states and the outside world will be no less important, perhaps more than the role outside powers, including Pakistan might play. The root problem of Pakistan since the Saur revolution in April 1978 is that the country has been divided first along ideological lines between the communists and their Islamic, nationalist opposition, then on ethnic ground between the Pashtun Taliban and the non-Pashtun ethnic minorities cobbled together in the Northern Front, and now between the resurgent Taliban and the Afghan government, structured and sustained by the international community. Before exploring Pakistan's options in the endgame, there is a need to examine this fact of Afghanistan's social and political fabric that has consciously drawn outside powers in its bloody internal power struggles.

As a divided country, there have been in fact two faces of Afghanistan in the past 33 years; one official, propped up and defended directly or indirectly by the outside powers, and the other, unofficial that put up resistance to the one in power. This is true from the time of Soviet intervention, Taliban's ascendance to the present American war in Afghanistan. This makes it necessary to revise and revisit the myth that all Afghans have resisted outside powers intervening in their internal affairs. At least in the last three cycles of conflict in Afghanistan, a part of Afghan faction has invited and supported intervention of foreign powers, while the other part, generally out of power, has resisted intervention. If this interpretation of the Afghanistan's ethnic and sectarian fault lines is correct, then the endgame must begin with internal reconciliation among the Afghans.

In the present critical phase of the war, when the self-defence capacity of the Kabul government is questionable and the foreign forces have set a deadline, no matter how ambiguous and uncertain it might be, there is a need a negotiated settlement between the Kabul government and the Taliban, including the Haqqani network for the survival of the Afghan state. The scriptwriters of post-Bonn state and nation building in Afghanistan should have had better understanding of Afghanistan's history and a clear, unbiased vision about its future. They allowed the Northern Front adversaries of the Taliban to dominate the Afghan state that had a deep history of Pashtun domination and its nationalism and identity being driven by Pashtun self-image as the founders of Afghanistan, and its ultimate guarantors and defenders. Had the Taliban found a seat in the Bonn conference, perhaps the war in Afghanistan might have ended there.

But that was not a realistic option in the national climate of the two countries—the United States and the Afghanistan. The U.S. felt badly wounded politically and psychologically by the Al-Qaeda attacks on 9/11 on its soil and wanted to go after its leaders, no-holds-barred manner. It was angry, vengeful and determined to eliminate the Al-Qaeda, and the Taliban that refused to handover Al-Qaeda leaders. The Northern Front with their own terrible record of massacres, tortures and murder of opponents, including the Taliban were unforgiving to Taliban who in the 1990's had pursued them in deadly conflict to their ethnic territories and imposed a harsh religious and security order. Above all, they were strategic partners of Al-Qaeda who had killed their hero, Ahmad Shah Massoud.

What happened at the Bonn conference in 2001 makes one wonder about the quality of statesmanship and true reading of the Afghan history. It was also some amount of arrogance that comes with power and over confidence in evicting the Taliban regime that might have intervened in the Afghan and American calculations about exclusion of the Taliban from the post-Bonn state building in Afghanistan. One of the flawed perceptions, was that the Afghan Taliban and Arab Al-Qaeda were two sides of internationalist Islam, ideologically linked and political inseparable. Even an ordinary student of strategy would distinguish tactical alliance from strategic commitment. Perhaps it was the haziness of the moment or blinding storm of events that much of previous learning and insights were lost.

What is being recognised now could not be envisioned then; that Al-Qaeda is an internationalist, transnational network with Middle East focused Islamic agenda, and anti-West to the core. Not that it did not want Afghans and Pakistanis and others as local partners, but wanted to shape and enforce its agenda, much rooted in the Salafi tradition. On the other hand, the Taliban were and are children of local conflicts, Pashtun in culture and character and have local, Afghan agenda. Like other Afghan groups they had regional networks, political ties and mutual support networks. The Al-Qaeda and the Arab fighters that were introduced in Afghanistan during the U.S.-Pakistan sponsored *Jihad* against the communist regime in Afghanistan, were one of those networks that the Taliban relied on against their war with the Northern Front (NF). The NF was not alone in this war either, it had multiple supporters—Iran, India, Russia, some of the Central Asian states, and towards the end, the Central Intelligence Agency (CIA).

This realisation has come too late, but it is better late than never. As the United States thinks of the throwing off the gloves and burdens the fragile Afghan government with responsibility, it is necessary to revisit its fundamental propositions about the Taliban and their connections with the Al-Qaeda. So the statement of year, perhaps of the decade was made by the American Vice President Joe Biden "Taliban are not our enemies". On occasions, the tone of the Kabul government has been overly friendly too. President Hamid Karzai on occasions has addressed them as 'brother Taliban' asking them to stop fighting and join him in rebuilding the country. There are two factors that have forced the Bonn scriptwriters to change their tracks. First is the resilience and power of the Taliban, their unstoppable rise since 2005. They may not be in a position to stage another 1996 on Kabul, but they can deny security space to the government in the outer Pashtun fringes and keep attacking from margins to weaken the core in Kabul.

The second important factor is destruction of Al-Qaeda, its virtual eviction and even defeat in the Afghanistan-Pakistan areas. They have lost leadership, communication and command centres, and more importantly image of invincibility. Equally important is shrinking local support base that the drone strikes and continuous military operations by Pakistani security forces have caused. The fighting capacity of the Al-Qaeda has withered away. This cuts the Taliban loose from the internationalist, Islamic network, and gives the Taliban leadership autonomy to make decisions with a focus on Afghanistan.

Pakistan was clear about separating the Afghan Taliban from Al-Qaeda. It focused its energies on eliminating Al-Qaeda, killing and capturing and handing over operatives to the Americans. It was one of the major commitments of Pakistan to the U.S. under the third partnership during the past 60 years. It has been a costly commitment for Pakistan. While it took the brunt of Al-Qaeda sponsored terrorism that was unleashed through its local affiliates, it failed to earn any significant credit for its sacrifices from Washington, except routine, gingerly extended acknowledgements. Never did the U.S. stop asking Pakistan 'to do more', which irked the Pakistanis, more than making them feel encouraged, in occasions of grief as the terrorists mercilessly butchered its soldiers and suicide bombers struck in the heart of major cities. For its own reasons though, Pakistan had no mercy for Al-Qaeda and pursued it relentlessly.

What has been and what is likely to be Pakistan's approach toward the Afghan Taliban? Pakistan has been quite selective in its choice of leaders and commanders of the Taliban to arrest or court during the past ten years. It arrested and handed over Mullah Zaeef, Afghanistan's ambassador to Pakistan during the Taliban era to the U.S. against standard norms of diplomacy. The United States and Afghanistan have continued to accuse Pakistan of sheltering top Taliban leadership including Mullah Mohammad Omar and the Haqqani network against whom the U.S. has repeatedly insisted that Pakistan must operate in the North Waziristan area. Pakistan has refuted these claims and insists that the Taliban leadership is in Afghanistan, and it will choose its own time to launch a security operation in North Waziristan. These allegations have further marred relations of Pakistan with Afghanistan and the United States.

The trust level plummeted further when the U.S. operated unilaterally, without having Pakistan on board, to kill Osama bin Ladin in Abbotabad on May 2, 2011. Nothing demonstrates distrust more than this episode, which has forced Pakistan to re-examine the nature of its security cooperation with the United States. If Pakistan needed some more excuse to renegotiate security ties with the U.S., it was provided by an attack on the Salala check post by the NATO forces, actually carried out by American air force on November 24, 2011 that continued for about two hours killing 24 Pakistani soldiers including two officers. While Pakistan says it was deliberate, the investigation and report by the U.S. security establishment denies that puts the blame for the attack on poor communication between the local commanders. Accidental or willful, Pakistan reacted sharply to the attack and killing of its security personnel. First and foremost, it closed NATO supplies through its territory. Second, it called off its security forces manning the check posts. Third, it refused to participate in the second Bonn conference. No government in Pakistan could escape these hard decisions in the face of public reaction to the attacks and rising anti-Americanism.

Pakistan wants to renegotiate its engagement with the United States and is willing to accept cutting of military assistance. The country's political and security establishments think that Pakistan has suffered tremendously on account of it being on the side of the United States in the war on terror. How would this rough patch in U.S.-Pakistan relationship play out in the endgame is not hard to imagine. Perhaps the two sides will get back to business, if not usual, with more transparency, sensitivity and openness. That is necessary to end the war in Afghanistan. Equally crucial will be building better levels of trust between Afghanistan and Pakistan. By necessity, these three countries-Pakistan, U.S. and Afghanistan will have to cooperate to end the war and bring peace in Afghanistan. As yet, they are not on the same page, and when and on what terms they get back to negotiate the endgame will define the success or failure of the game itself.

## Conclusion

Pakistan has taken a position that without national reconciliation within Afghanistan, inclusive of all groups, peace will remain as illusive. The Afghan peace process must be Afghan-owned and Afghan-led. It has insisted that the

United States must negotiate with the Taliban to end the war. In principle, others countries, may not be averse to these ideas, but then real politics and power interests may compel them to pursue different goals. One of the important factor is the opposition of the Northern Front to the idea of talking to the Taliban, let alone accepting their role in the governance of the country. Those external powers that view the Taliban merely as an extremist religious movement, may not accept them being part of the peace process so easily unless they change their lenses or see a strategic necessity in the intra-Afghan dialogue.

There are good signs that it might happen. The Afghan government has been secretly negotiating with the Taliban representatives, though they turned out to be impostors, but it does show its willingness to engage the Taliban. The Americans with the nudging and support of Germany have also been talking to the Taliban representatives. That is good start, but how soon it will yield any results, of what nature, and to what effect is yet to be seen.

Pakistan will continue to make efforts at all levels to promote political settlement within Afghanistan. On its part, it will impress upon the Taliban leadership to negotiate both with the Afghan government as well as with the United States. But what exactly they negotiate, where and when and what deal emerges, Pakistan may not have much say. Its interests in stabilising Afghanistan will be served if the war comes to an end, and that may not be possible if Taliban are not part of the peace process.

The other flank of Pakistan's diplomacy for the endgame is to build trust with the Afghan government and help them engage with the Taliban leaders. Pakistan may not be directly involved in the intra-Afghan dialogue but will play a critical role from behind the scene. To facilitate this dialogue the two countries have established a joint peace council that will provide a forum for bilateral discussion on how to stabilise Afghanistan and what will Pakistan require to do in this respect. Pakistan is also engaged with the Afghanistan on trilateral level.

The Islamic Republic of Iran is no less important for the stability of Afghanistan than Pakistan. Both in war and peace, it will remain a very important player. Pakistan realises importance of the region around Afghanistan. Lately, it has made some moves to regionalise its foreign policy both for trade and natural resource development as well as building a sustainable peace process in Afghanistan. It has initiated dialogue with Iran, including on the Iran-Pakistan gas pipeline and procurement of more oil from Iran even in the face threat of sanctions from Washington.

But Pakistan's regional triangle may not be complete without similar dialogue and understanding with India, a major regional power and an emerging great economy. Pakistan's relations with India have improved during the past two years, but lot that needs to be done. How India and Pakistan develop an understanding on stability, peace and political reconciliation within Afghanistan will be the key to regional peace and security. The structural issues, historical baggage and misperception may cast a heavy shadow and create inhibitions. Fortunately, there is new thinking among the liberal, moderate sectors with some influence on public opinion, emerging in both the countries about Afghanistan as a region of common opportunity for trade, investment and exploitation of mineral resources. How soon this idea is translated into a common vision will depend on how soon the leaders of the two countries can come out of the old confrontational mode to newer avenues of cooperation. Prospects of working together are not all dim today.

The United States and NATO are the most critical players in Afghanistan and will remain so for many years to come. Pakistan's relationship with the U.S. at the time of writing, is stalemated, as Islamabad wants to redefine its terms of engagement. Pakistan wants better clarity, transparency and realistic expectations in its relationship with the U.S.[26] Pakistan will press upon the United States on three counts. First, it must continue to engage with Taliban to find a peaceful settlement. Second, it will like to see an orderly withdrawal and gradual military disengagement to prevent collapse of the Afghan government. Third, it will ask the United States to remain committed to rebuilding Afghanistan for longer time and assist Pakistan to deal with the social and economic cost of its participation in the war on terror.

Dealing with United States may not be easy for Pakistan as it may face tremendous difficulties as a result of pressures from Washington for taking steps that may not be possible politically, like going after the organisations declared as terrorists. It also faces pressures from the conservative religious groups and even from some of the mainstream parties in the opposition to end or considerably scale down cooperation with the United States. Pakistan's relationship with the United States will remain one of the most important relationship for the next decade bilaterally and in relation to peace and stability in Afghanistan. Despite perceptual differences between the two countries, Pakistan will remain one of the focal countries for the United States in the region for realisation of its interests in Afghanistan and in the wider South Asian region.

For the endgame to be peaceful, orderly and painless for all the parties, the following recommendations can be considered. First, national reconciliation and peace building among the ethnic groups of Afghanistan needs to be the bedrock of internal politics as well as diplomacy of external powers. Only a negotiated and workable peace settlement among Afghans will bring peace and stabilise the country.

Second, a regional understanding among the neighbours of Afghanistan, particularly between India and Pakistan must be part of the efforts toward stabilising Afghanistan. The future should be unlike the past when these two, Iran and some Central Asian states played a destructive mini 'great game'. Much will depend on the Afghan government as well; how it extricates itself from the rivalry and competition of the neighbours.

Finally, a long-term, effective and result-oriented reconstruction of the Afghan state and security institution must remain a long-term objective of the United States, European Union and NATO. Afghanistan may need sustained support for many years to come before it can stand on its own feet. Afghanistan will have to be a global concern, a collective venture of the international community to secure peace and order in this volatile region.

## Notes

1. C. Christine Fair, "Obama's New "Af-Pak" Strategy: Can "Clear, Hold, Build, Transfer" Work?," The Afghanistan Papers, *The Centre for International Governance Research*, no. 6, July 2010, pp. 1-23.
2. Angelo Rasanayagam, *Afghanistan A modern History: Monarchy, Despotism or Democracy?*(London: I. B. Tauris, 2003) pp. 162-76.
3. Barnett R. Rubin, "Saving Afghanistan," *Foreign Affairs*, January/February 2007, vol. 86, no. 1, pp. 57-78.
4. Edgar O' Balance, *Afghan Wars Battles in a Hostile Land 1839 to the Present* (Oxford: University Press, 2003) pp. 89-196.
5. Andrew Hartman, "'The Red Template': U.S. Policy in Soviet-Occupied Afghanistan," *Third World Quarterly*, vol. 23, no. 3, June, 2002, pp. 467-489.
6. Barnett R. Rubin & Ahmed Rashid, "From Great Game to Grand Bargain: Ending Chaos in Afghanistan and Pakistan," *Foreign Affairs*, vol. 87, no. 6, November/December 2008, pp. 30-44.
7. Nazif M. Shahrani, "War, Factionalism, and the State in Afghanistan," *American Anthropologist*, New Series, vol. 104, no. 3, September, 2002, pp.715-22.
8. Ali A. Jalali, "Afghanistan in 2002: The Struggle to Win the Peace," *Asian Survey*, vol. 43, no. 1, January/February, 2003, pp. 174-85.
9. Joe Stork and Jim Paul, Arms Sales and the Militarisation of the Middle East, *MERIP Reports*, No. 112, The Arms Race in the Middle East, February, 1983, pp. 5-15.
10. Christian Parenti, "Afghan Wonderland," Dispatches from the War Zones: Iraq and Afghanistan, *Middle East Report*, no. 239, 2006, pp. 12-17.
11. Hamish Nixon and Richard Ponzio, "Building Democracy in Afghanistan: The Statebuilding Agenda and International Engagement," *International Peacekeeping*, vol. 14, no. 1, 2007, pp. 26-40.
12. Amin Saikal, "Afghanistan's Transition: ISAF's Stabilisation Role?," *Third World Quarterly*, vol. 27, no. 3, 2006, pp. 525-534.
13. Barack Obama, Remarks by the President in Address to the Nation On the way Forward in Afghanistan and Pakistan, Speech At Eisenhower Hall Theatre, United States Military Academy At West Point, West Point, New York, December 2009, http://www.kas.de/wf/doc/kas_18291-544-2-30.pdf. Accessed on 12 May 2012.
14. Peter Marsden, "Afghanistan: The Reconstruction Process," *International Affairs (Royal Institute of International Affairs 1944)*, vol. 79, no. 1, January, 2003, pp. 91-105.
15. Nasreen Ghufran, "Afghanistan in 2007: A Bleeding Wound," *Asian Survey*, vol. 48, no. 1, January/February, 2008, pp. 154-63.
16. Kenneth Katzman, "Afghanistan: Post-War Governance, Security, and U.S. Policy," *Library Of Congress Washington Dc Congressional Research Service*, November, 2008.
17. Barack Obama, "Remarks by the President on a new strategy for Afghanistan and Pakistan," 27 March 2009, http://www.gees.org/documentos/Documen-03380.pdf. Accessed on 12 May 2012.

18. Namahashri Tavana, Patrick Cronin, and Jon Alterman, "The Taliban and Afghanistan: Implications for Regional Security and Options for International Action," *United States Institute of Peace,* Special Report No. 39, November, 1988, pp.1-10.
19. Marvin G. Weinbaum, "Pakistan and Afghanistan: The Strategic Relationship," *Asian Survey*, vol. 31, no. 6, June 1991, pp. 496-511.
20. Adeel Khan, "Pakistan in 2006: Safe Center, Dangerous Peripheries," *Asian Survey*, vol. 47, no. 1, January/February 2007, pp. 125-32.
21. Moeed Yusuf, Huma Yusuf, Salman Zaidi, "Pakistan, the United States and the End Game in Afghanistan: Perceptions of Pakistan's Foreign Policy Elite," *United States Institute of Peace*, July 2005, pp.1-5.
22. M. Ehsan Ahrari, "China, Pakistan, and the "Taliban Syndrome"," *Asian Survey*, vol. 40, no. 4, July/August, 2000, pp. 658-71.
23. Gilles Dorronsoro, "Pakistan and the Taliban: State Policy, Religious Networks and Political Connections," in Pakistan: Nationalism without a nation? Christophe Jafferlot, (New Delhi: Manohar, 2002), pp. 161-78.
24. Bruce Riedel, "Pakistan and Terror: The Eye of the Storm'" *Annals of the American Academy of Political and Social Science*, vol. 618, July 2008, pp. 31-45.
25. "Policy towards Afghanistan: Support dialogue, not dictation, politicians tell Pakistan", *The Express Tribune*, February 2012, http://tribune.com.pk/story/330187/policy-towards-afghanistan-support-dialogue-not-dictation-politicians-tell-pakistan/. Accessed on 21 May 2012.
26. "Parliament sets out to reorder ties with the United States", *Dawn*, 21 March 2012.

# 12

# India's Engagement with Afghanistan: Developing a Durable Policy Architecture

*Daniel Norfolk*

## Introduction

There is a widely shared perception that India has reached a 'strategic stalemate' in Afghanistan, and the expected brinkmanship between other, more immediate, players leading up to 2014 is largely out of New Delhi's control.[1] Nevertheless, while India's involvement in Afghanistan may be hostage to evolving regional and geopolitical dynamics, Indian efforts to shore-up the strategic influence it has gained in Afghanistan will, in turn, be consequential to the broader calculus of transition. India is, and will remain, a pivotal force in the region. Its deep historical ties to Afghanistan, and the dimensions into which the contemporary bilateral relationship has diffused, will not be easily undone. Given the uncertainty surrounding Afghanistan's transition process, it is unlikely that India will significantly alter its current policy trajectory, providing a reasonably reliable variable for the strategic considerations of observers and policy-makers.

The present chapter seeks to map the contours of Afghanistan's geopolitical landscape in anticipation of the U.S.-NATO withdrawal, scheduled for 2014. Speculation, including as to the very premise of this paper—whether, and in what capacity, international forces will persevere in Afghanistan until the end of 2014—can be tempered by concrete analyses of the motivations and strategies of the actors involved. Occupying a unique position as Afghanistan's leading regional development partner, India is poised to play an instrumental role; a role that is not immune to controversy. Without postulating Indian reactions to the myriad contingencies that may arise, this chapter will concentrate on India's strategic objectives, constraints, and the evolution of New Delhi's Afghan policy framework. It will examine the ways in which India has sought to position itself so that it might be indispensable to whatever circumstances emerge in Afghanistan throughout the inevitably turbulent transition period and beyond.

New Delhi's strategic framework underwent an important shift in Afghanistan following the U.S. invasion in 2001. India sought to take advantage of the U.S.-NATO presence and adopt a geopolitically active posture, more in tune with its perceived political and economic means. Departing from the guarded principles that had anchored its Afghan policy from independence in 1947, the Indian government initiated an ambitious new phase of diplomatic engagement and development assistance, intended to create an outcome conducive to Indian interests. Over nearly a decade, however, India's approach to Afghanistan repeatedly failed to secure lasting strategic objectives. Imminent U.S.-NATO withdrawal, officially acknowledged by U.S. President Barack Obama in 2009, further jeopardised India's position.

Responding to these circumstances, the Indian government began to revise and retrench its engagement with Afghanistan. The development partnership that emerged between the two countries in the wake of the U.S. invasion has, since 2009, been recalibrated according to a sober reassessment of India's own geopolitical limitations. The shift marks a return to India's traditionally restrained approach, retaining flexibility and a broad set of policy options without abandoning its core objectives. However, in an effort to spread the risks inherent in its engagement with Afghanistan, New Delhi has embarked on a trajectory that requires apprehending its region as an opportunity rather than a constraint. Indeed, India's Afghan policy today demands that it engage constructively with regional actors if it is to secure its investments and accrue strategic dividends. From this perspective, New Delhi is staking the regional geopolitical landscape with familiar policy markers while asserting itself in such a way that requires wider, innovative engagement.

The following section will briefly introduce India's historical engagement with Afghanistan, and propose that an observable shift in India's Afghan policy is underway. Discussion will then turn to an interpretation and contextualisation of the contemporary India-Afghanistan bilateral relationship, demonstrating that Indian engagement with Afghanistan following the U.S. invasion of 2001 marked a significant break from its traditional posture. Subsequently, the specific nature and implications of India's evolving strategy in Afghanistan will be analysed and motivating factors proposed. Finally, the chapter will look to the horizon, focusing on future options and outcomes.

## Setting the Stage: Early Encounters to Contemporary Constraints

India has strategic and economic interests in Afghanistan that are bound up in its complex relationship with Pakistan. Primarily concerned with security, Indian objectives are easily reconciled with those of the international community: the creation of a stable Afghanistan that will no longer export terrorism. Adding a distinctly Indian layer to internationally shared concerns, New Delhi perceives its own influence in Afghanistan as a useful countermeasure to a volatile Pakistan. Consequently, New Delhi has initiated a programme of development assistance throughout Afghanistan with a view to cultivating a stable and friendly government in Kabul and goodwill amongst the population. In this sense, greater influence and increased stability are intertwined objectives and thus do not allow easy distinctions, adding to Pakistani suspicions.

Secondly, as a rapidly growing, energy-deficient country, India is keen to access Central Asian reserves of oil and natural gas. Afghanistan, which is also endowed with a wealth of extractable resources, can provide a convenient transit-way for these commodities. Similarly, a relatively stable Afghanistan has the potential to be the over-ground nexus between regional markets, a convenience of significant benefit to the Indian economy.[2] Here, too, India's troubled relationship with Pakistan is a major impediment. Finally, aspiring to great power status, India envisages its efforts to stabilise Afghanistan as a means to harness international recognition as a global force for peace and progress, seeking external validation for its role as purveyor of regional security.[3]

India has historically enjoyed good relations with Afghanistan. From ancient civilisational ties to the contemporary influence of Hindi cinema, the two countries nurture cultural affinities.[4] Geography has freed the relationship from the complications of disputed borders that plague relations between Kabul and Islamabad on one side, and Islamabad and New Delhi on the other. However, lacking a contiguous border, India's physical detachment from Afghanistan presents a geopolitical dilemma: despite inclinations toward a closer relationship, India cannot realistically sustain its interests in Afghanistan without projecting a physical presence there, and any attempt to do so is anathema to Pakistan's political-military establishment.[5] In fact, the contemporary history of India's engagement with Afghanistan can be understood in precisely these terms, as the process by which a major regional power adapts to an auxiliary role in its own geographical neighbourhood.

The contours of India's relationship with Afghanistan have been shaped over time by geopolitical misadventure, with each contemporary episode reifying the constraints to mutual engagement. The geopolitical entity that is now Afghanistan is the manifestation of competition between the British and Russian empires, which delineated its territory to buffer between their expanding realms. When the British relinquished a partitioned Indian subcontinent in 1947, the buffer between India and Central Asia effectively shifted east, to what became the newly independent Islamic Republic of Pakistan. Although Afghanistan remained inextricably linked to South Asia in the collective psyche, Pakistan drove a geographical and political wedge between India and the states of the northwest.

As is true elsewhere, the borders drawn by colonial administrators to demarcate political-territorial entities had the paradoxical effect of undermining the sovereignty of the South Asian post-colonial states. With Pashtun and Kashmiri populations divided by Pakistan's *de facto* western and eastern borders respectively, competing irredentist and secessionist claims ensued, which have, to a large extent, shaped relations between the three countries to this day. Independent India's early interactions with Afghanistan and the demands of its Pashtun population were captured by Jawaharlal Nehru in 1950: 'The Government of India,' said the country's first Prime Minister,'is intimately interested, but it is a matter for abiding regret to us that we can only be interested from a distance without being able to help in any way.'[6] Nehru's sympathetic but detached Afghanistan policy—characterised by diplomatic cordiality (albeit at a high level), limited efforts at expanding trade, and cooperation in development and capacity building[7]—survived his death in 1964 and persisted, virtually unchanged, throughout much of the Cold War period, while both New Delhi and Kabul remained normatively non-aligned and nominally pro-Soviet.[8]

The Indian government found its policy options further constrained when the USSR seized Kabul in 1979, introducing Cold War proxy conflict into India's immediate neighbourhood. New Delhi's failure to condemn the Soviet invasion outright cost it valuable political capital, both in Afghanistan and in the capitalist West.[9] Channelled primarily through Pakistan, American and Saudi Arabian support to anti-Soviet forces in the region ultimately succeeded in expelling the Soviet Army, and radically altering the geostrategic landscape as viewed from India.

Afghanistan's communist government retained a tenuous hold on power in Kabul, but faced encirclement by various *Mujahideen* factions. Exhibiting the 'strategic restraint' that would become a hallmark of its foreign policy throughout the ensuing two decades, India developed an open and tolerant approach to accommodate the volatile circumstances. Then Prime Minister Narasimha Rao understood India's place in the quickly evolving regional security complex, and accepted Pakistan's growing influence in Afghanistan. Following the fall of the communist government in Kabul, Rao attempted to mitigate the most deleterious effects by engaging with the *Mujahideen* and moderating the differences between New Delhi and less-sympathetic Afghan power-brokers.[10] Comparisons have been drawn between India's approach to post-Soviet Afghanistan and the current trajectory of Indian policy, prompting one former Indian diplomat to describe the ongoing changes in terms of a policy 'reset' in New Delhi.[11]

In the event, Rao's policy formulations were rendered redundant by the Taliban's conquest of Kabul in 1996 and complicity in the hijacking of an Air India flight in 1999, removing the possibility for compromise.[12] Indian diplomatic and development initiatives in Afghanistan experienced a hiatus while the Taliban ruled Kabul, during which time New Delhi extended support to the non-Pashtun Northern Alliance as a strategic imperative.[13] The Northern Alliance provided the only credible counter-balance to a regime in Afghanistan directly threatening India's national security interests. Adhering to a cautious foreign policy framework designed to guide outcomes but not to create them, New Delhi continued to provide 'quiet and limited support' for the groups fighting the Taliban, but did not use force or overtly support attempts to depose the regime.[14]

## Think Global, Act Local: Experiments in Projecting Power

The objectives listed above—security, stability, influence, and status—comprise the basic incentives, the necessary conditions, for Indian engagement in Afghanistan. The sufficient condition, the perceived capacity to achieve these objectives, arose simultaneously with, and as a function of, the U.S.-NATO invasion of Afghanistan in 2001.International military deployments in Central Asia distorted regional dynamics, appearing to offer India an avenue by which to circumvent its geopolitical dilemma and establish a greater presence on the ground.

Following the swift eviction of the Taliban from power in Kabul, New Delhi enthusiastically resumed diplomatic relations with Hamid Karzai's new government, reopening its embassy in Kabul, its consulates in Jalalabad and Kandahar, and establishing two additional consulates in Herat and Mazar-e-Sharif. Though reluctant to engage militarily, India committed very substantial resources to its ambitious, multi-sectoral reconstruction effort. With U.S.$2 billion pledged, India has become Afghanistan's leading regional development partner and its fifth largest bilateral donor.[15]

India invested resources and expertise in large-scale infrastructure projects throughout the country. These include the Zaranj-Delaram highway (connecting interior Afghanistan to the Iranian border), the installation of a transmission line bringing power to Kabul from the northern grid, the construction of a large hydro-electric dam in Herat province, and, symbolically, the erection of a new Afghan parliament building.[16] Beyond this, India initiated an impressive panoply of development projects covering a range of sectors, many of which remain operational today. These have been comprised of capacity building initiatives (particularly in the agricultural sector), small and community-based development projects that concentrate on vulnerable areas and emphasise local ownership, and the general provision of humanitarian assistance.[17] Included under the 'capacity building' umbrella have been modest but politically significant efforts to train police and senior military officials.[18]

Similarly ambitious commercial ventures have been initiated. A Gas Pipeline Framework Agreement was signed by Turkmenistan, Afghanistan, Pakistan, and India in 2008. The TAPI pipeline (so-named after the initials of the four countries involved) has been under discussion since the 1990s, and envisages over a thousand miles of pipe connecting Turkmenistan's natural gas fields with energy-deficient South Asia.[19] Simultaneous plans for an Iran-Pakistan-India

(IPI) pipeline are in the offing, but New Delhi, wary of Washington's reservations and disruptive sanctions, has been reluctant to move forward.[20] A Preferential Trade Agreement (PTA) was signed between India and Afghanistan in 2003, reducing customs duty on a range of goods. Bilateral trade has increased considerably as a result, worth over U.S.$600 million in 2011, with Indian markets absorbing the largest share of Afghan exports.[21]

New Delhi's energetic re-engagement with post-Taliban Afghanistan represents a marked break from historically limited Indo-Afghan bilateral relations. More significantly, it signalled a temporary departure from what Pratap Bhanu Mehta has described as India's politics of cautious prudence—a conscious effort to behave in such a way that removes the need for force, allies, and any commitment to inducing change abroad.[22] According to this foreign policy formulation, India appreciates its limited capacity to affect change outside its borders (without recourse to force, the application of which remains only a very remote option) and will avoid enduring alliances unless driven to them by necessity.[23] Cautious prudence offers a more nuanced framework to the doctrine of 'strategic restraint', which is often cited as a guiding rationale behind Indian foreign policy, in that strategic restraint refers directly to India's reluctance to resort to force as an instrument of policy.[24]

The distinction is important, as it is clear that India has remained disinclined to engage militarily in Afghanistan, exhibiting considerable strategic restraint. However, New Delhi's bold and uncharacteristically proactive engagement with post-Taliban Afghanistan does betray an exaggerated notion of its own capacity. Drifting away from its cautiously prudent moorings, the Indian government seized an opportunity, created by the Americans, to advance its regional agenda. New Delhi envisioned an Afghanistan dependent, to some degree, on its markets and through which it might access the markets and resources of Central Asia, while containing Pakistan and cultivating India's status as a global force for stability.[25] In so doing, India amplified tensions between itself and Pakistan (significantly raising the odds of aggressive retaliation), entered voluntarily into the U.S.-led alliance (by making its level of engagement dependent on the U.S.-NATO 'security umbrella'[26]), formalised a 'strategic partnership' with Afghanistan[27], and committed to fostering a friendly government in Kabul.[28]

There are several justifiable reasons why New Delhi may have picked this moment for a modest departure from the tenets of its cautious foreign policy. The threat of militant Islam had become intolerable, perceived Pakistani belligerence might be better contained, and energy scarcity necessitated access to Central Asian oil and natural gas reserves. But all of these justifications predated the U.S. invasion of Afghanistan. What defined this particular moment was the concomitant convergence of certain Indian and U.S. objectives in South-Central Asia with the ascendance of India's economic and political power in the region. Put simply, Washington sought stability for a region in which New Delhi sought influence consistent with its rising profile.

One scholar has described this episode as 'a test case for a rising power', and it should be understood as exactly that.[29] The prism through which rising powers, and India in particular, have come to be perceived is one that juxtaposes global ambitions with regional constraints. Andrew Hurrell observed that Brazil, Russia, India, and China all illustrate the complexity of the 'regional-global nexus':

> In all four cases foreign policy is heavily shaped by the regional context—by evolving regional balances of power...by changing patterns of regional security (especially in the form of new categories of threat); and by increasingly dense patterns of social and economic regionalisation. Regions are also central to historic self-understandings. Both Russia and India see themselves as the natural leader of a closed region in which outside interference is deeply resented. And yet, on balance, it is the image of the region as constraint rather than as opportunity that emerges most strongly.[30]

Similar conceptualisations of the apparent inability to turn resources into outcomes have been articulated. David Baldwin's paradox of unrealised power describes 'the mistaken belief that power resources useful in one policy-contingency framework will be useful in a different one.'[31] Moreover, Nitin Pai has asked how India will transcend its 'paradox of proximity', the predicament wherein 'India cannot escape its neighbourhood and that its great power ambitions will be constrained by instability in that neighbourhood.'[32]

Thus, in 2001, Afghanistan presented a multi-faceted challenge to India's foreign policy. As an internationalised arena of political conflict, Afghanistan epitomised the regional-global nexus: in the immediate neighbourhood, it remained inextricably linked to Pakistan, India's traditional regional stumbling block; from the extended neighbourhood it drew various players, in one way or another, notably China, Iran, and Russia; on the global stage, Afghanistan became central to the consciousness of the international community; and permeating all three levels, the U.S. projected its influence as reluctant Pakistani ally and eminent global power.

Buoyed by successful economic liberalisation reforms (initiated in the 1990s), India saw the Afghanistan war as an opportunity to flex its economic muscles in an environment safeguarded by international security forces, and to establish a place for itself in determining Afghanistan's future while undermining Pakistan's influence there.[33] Involvement in Afghanistan also looked to provide a means of harnessing goodwill and raising India's profile as a peace-building global citizen. Its revived foray into the reconstruction of Afghanistan was adorned in signature Nehruvian rhetoric—emphasising inalienable sovereignty, a partnership of equals, the unity of cause and politics[34]—but now backed, it would seem, with the economic and political tools befitting a regional power.

However, deterred by the international community, by Pakistan's nuclear arsenal and proxy militias, by the fear of triggering an unconventional *jihad* closer to home, and by the dictates of domestic political pragmatism, New Delhi could not join the coalition of nations engaged militarily in Afghanistan. In absentia, the Indian government found itself relegated to the periphery of the international debate surrounding Afghanistan, and, thus sidelined, spent the better part of a decade as a marginalised player (despite being the country's fifth largest bilateral donor). Few doubt the prudence of the decision to hold back troops. But the reality is that New Delhi's choices were limited by its inability to project power commensurate with its relative strength in the region. India has been labelled a 'premature power' for its incapacity to neutralise vulnerabilities inherent in the political divisions of the Indian subcontinent.[35] Its economic and political preponderance does not translate easily into leverage in the regional context, regardless of the security guarantees underwritten by international forces.

Following the U.S. invasion of Afghanistan, India was presented with a challenge and an opportunity, a test, to which India responded by departing from its characteristically cautious foreign policy framework, exposing certain vulnerabilities, and ultimately failing to secure its interests. The following section will look at how India failed, how it has responded, and why it may now succeed in reversing its fortunes in Afghanistan.

## Engineering a 'Durable Policy Architecture'[36]

The development partnership that emerged between India in Afghanistan after 2001 was not the product of grand strategy. Nor was it simply a kneejerk reaction. To adapt the Clausewitzian aphorism, development assistance is, to varying degrees, the continuation of politics by other means.[37] India's development programming was intended to achieve certain political objectives, which, in turn, relied on the assumption that that the U.S. would impose upon Afghanistan and Pakistan a degree of stability adequate to allowIndia greater influence in regional affairs. Despite some impressive achievements in the development sphere (improving the lives of Afghans and garnering popular goodwill[38]) Indian engagement did not achieve durable strategic results.

New Delhi's calculations fell short on several fronts. The Afghan war has exacerbated instability in Pakistan and failed to pacify the Taliban. Attacks on Indian projects, facilities, and personnel increased in size and frequency between 2002 and early 2010.[39] Not only were attacks on its projects and resources on the ground becoming routine, but India's efforts were never genuinely and actively encouraged by the U.S. or coalition governments, which remained highly sensitive to Pakistan's real and imagined grievances.[40] Indian protestations surrounding the prospects of reconciling with the Taliban (maintaining that moderate Taliban did not exist) were roundly ignored.[41] Although the successes of India's development programme were widely-acknowledged, no effort was made at the international level to consult the Indian government on Afghanistan or bring it into any meaningful decision-making processes.

Furthermore, Indian initiatives were not securing access to markets or significant resources. On the contrary, increased visibility contributed to making India's corporate ventures and development projects more vulnerable.[42] The TAPI pipeline, heralded for its potential to improve energy security and economic interdependence on the subcontinent, came to a virtual standstill. The India-Afghanistan Preferential Trade Agreement (IAPTA) has been under-utilised, trade between the two nations having to circumvent an obstructive Pakistan.[43] India did succeed in ushering Afghanistan into the South Asian Association for Regional Cooperation (SAARC) by 2007, and this may yet prove to be one of the more important steps toward regional cooperation (the SAARC mechanisms could be instrumental in forging future frameworks for energy cooperation, for example[44]) but there have been few tangible yields from Afghanistan's incorporation by the regional body.

Finally, in April 2011, Pakistan's army chief, General Ashfaq Parvez Kayani, and Prime Minister Yusuf Raza Gilani, met with President Karzai in Kabul to formalise an agreement that would allow the Pakistani army a role in negotiations between Kabul and the Taliban (Washington has since backed up this commitment, confirming that any reconciliation process will involve Pakistan[45]). The Pakistani media hailed the agreement as a 'historic breakthrough' that could align the 'shared destinies' of Kabul and Islamabad.'[46] The most fundamental of India's objectives—diluting Pakistani influence over Kabul—appeared increasingly unsalvageable.

Delhi could not justifiably maintain an approach that manifestly failed to yield the political results initially envisioned by its policy makers. The Indian government began to internalise the barriers to its expanding physical presence in Afghanistan following the 2008 bombing of its embassy in Kabul and the murder of nine Indian civilians in an attack on a Kabul guesthouse in 2010.[47] The culmination of several of India's largest infrastructure projects in Afghanistan from 2009 onwards has provided India with an opportunity to scale-down its physical presence there without conceding defeat. New Delhi insists this is not a direct response to the security vacuum anticipated when the U.S. ends its combat role in 2014. Instead, Indian policy makers frame the shift in terms of seizing an opportune moment to redefine the country's Afghan strategy.[48] It is likely that a combination of factors, including the conditions of the rapprochement between Islamabad and Kabul, began to circumscribe India's position to the point that New Delhi could no longer credibly defend its mode of engagement.[49]

Inherent to New Delhi's mode of engagement, as discussed above, had been the notion that a friendly government and relative stability in Afghanistan would ultimately allow India to emerge as the purveyor of regional security. If confidence in such an outcome had diminished over the course of the decade, Karzai's overture to Islamabad confounded the notion beyond a doubt. India's strategic reformulation had to acknowledge Pakistan's centrality to the regional algebra: that Pakistan, for better or for worse, would remain a critical variable in the operations and relations between actors in the region, and the disputed porous border between Pakistan and Afghanistan would render durable peace contingent on Pakistani compliance.

Rather than withdraw from its commitments to Kabul, the Indian government reaffirmed the development partnership and deepened its financial support to Afghanistan. An exchange of high-level visits between the two countries in 2011 indicates that India is moving towards an enhanced role in developing the full spectrum of Afghan capacity, from workforce to security force. The Indian Prime Minister committed to increasing development outlays, raising total bilateral assistance to U.S.$2 billion, and emphasised India's focus on the social sector, agriculture, capacity building, access to the Indian market, and continued investment in infrastructure. The two sides signed a Strategic Partnership agreement covering security, law enforcement, and justice, and India pledged to strengthen the capabilities of the Afghan security forces. Significantly, PM Manmohan Singh expressed support for Kabul's decision to begin an Afghan-led process of negotiation and reconciliation with the Taliban.[50]

Unpacking India's commitment reveals a policy framework designed to adapt to changing circumstances. Setting aside very justifiable apprehensions, India has adjusted its posture to accommodate the flow of events. By deepening ties with the Afghan security sector and nurturing relations with Afghans on a local level (through increasingly localised development programming) New Delhi is refashioning its dual or two-pronged approach toward Afghanistan. Indian policymakers appreciate that by simultaneously providing the Afghan government with what it needs to govern and the people with what they need to live, it has a greater chance of making itself indispensable to whatever situation emerges in Afghanistan. Placating the two spheres (the public and the political elite) improves the environment within which the Indian commercial sector can operate, allowing increased private-sector investment and another layer of influence.

Often referred to as strategy-less, India's approach to Afghanistan has evolved over the years and has experienced several setbacks, but it has nevertheless developed into a flexible strategic framework. Now, by courting Afghanistan's security establishment and introducing itself into the Afghan power equation, New Delhi can afford to offer balancing concessions in the form of a nod towards an Afghan-led negotiation with the Taliban. On the surface, this shift appears counterintuitive: Indian policymakers know that reconciling with the Taliban essentially allows an indirect bargain with Pakistan, tacitly conferring to Pakistan's Inter-Services Intelligence (ISI, Pakistan's intelligence agency) a legitimate claim to space within which it can manoeuvre in a post-U.S.-NATO Afghanistan.[51] Furthermore, it is very likely that Pakistan will use this leverage to undermine India's relationship with Kabul. However, India is taking steps to avert such an eventuality.

Making India less visible in Afghanistan, without reducing its influence, has become a priority for policy makers in New Delhi.[52] While its larger infrastructure projects wind down, India has expanded its delivery of targeted small-scale aid, whereby money is channelled through the Afghan government to local communities who have applied for assistance. These Small Development Projects (SDPs) ensure greater local ownership and participation and, according to the Indian Ministry of External Affairs (MEA), none have been targeted by militants.[53] Programme oversight provided by Indian consulates enables New Delhi to cultivate direct links with the communities involved, amongst predominantly Pashtun communities to which India has historically been sympathetic.

While there is little available information surrounding the nature of these interactions, consular activities are publicly construed as acts of espionage by Pakistan, which frequently accuses India of engaging in clandestine efforts to foment insurgency within its borders.[54] While there is little evidence to support these claims, Indian SDPs are highly concentrated in areas of Afghanistan bordering Pakistan's north-west, and a recent study has alluded to intelligence confirming that 'India's involvement in Afghanistan is not entirely benign.'[55] That Indian projects and consulates rouse Pakistani suspicions is expected. That India has been able to expand its network of SDPs and enhance localised programming efforts without eliciting a violent response speaks to the success of the hands-off approach and to the acquiescence of local Taliban.[56]

India has also indicated its openness to engaging in multi-sectoral trilateral projects with international partners.[57] The U.S. has conveyed an interest in collaborating on certain projects and programmes.[58] Such projects could minimise operating costs by exploiting India's proximity to Afghanistan and utilising its relevant expertise, particularly in agriculture and communications technology, while allaying Pakistani suspicions with a third-party guarantee (however, both the U.S. and India will be careful to avoid the optics of collusion).In a move that will further discredit Pakistan's more excessive claims, the Indian government has pushed through plans to set up its own foreign aid agency, the Indian Agency for Partnership in Development (IAPD), which will assume the development-oriented functions of the MEA and possibly alleviate political pressure and divert unreasonable criticism.[59] Policymakers have welcomed the move, claiming that the agency will not only make aid delivery more efficient, but it will make way for a cohesive aid strategy that can better incorporate and manage Indian interests.[60]

On the issue of security sector cooperation, Afghan Defence Minister,

General Abdul Rahim Wardak, said in New Delhi in June 2011, 'We will welcome any cooperation in the field of training and helping our national security forces to be able to defend their country', and added that military equipment supplies were also under discussion.[61] Wardak's Indian counterpart, A.K. Antony, confirmed India's commitment to building the capabilities of the Afghan National Security Forces (ANSF, composed of the Afghan National Army and Police, ANA and ANP respectively).[62] According to leaked correspondence from the U.S. embassy in New Delhi,

> Currently, the GOI [Government of India] trains approximately 100 ANA members annually in India, and would like to step up this programme. India has offered its Advanced Light Helicopter to Afghanistan as well as pilot training to the new Afghan air force. The GOI has provided cars and trucks to the Afghan military. Officials tell us they have discussed with Afghan officials the possibility of training Afghan police women and bomb disposal specialists, but no large-scale training has yet taken place.[63]

India now has an entrenched relationship with the Afghan security forces and has bolstered its assistance to the ANP. By nurturing this relationship, New Delhi's ties extend beyond the strictly political to institutions that may outlast the present Afghan government. This may prove particularly significant if the security situation in Afghanistan deteriorates considerably and the Afghan army begins to splinter. The ANA high command is largely composed of Tajiks who fought alongside the U.S. in the Northern Alliance.[64] From this perspective, New Delhi may be aligning itself with future proxies, should circumstances demand it.

At the political level, New Delhi is bracing itself for an uncertain future. Offering unwavering support to President Karzai's regime, New Delhi has endorsed the Taliban reconciliation programme—a presidential initiative that inevitably, and paradoxically, compromises the president's power and, counter intuitively, cedes space for Pakistani influence. Yet this represents a realistic assessment. Negotiations with the Taliban will proceed, however intermittently, with or without New Delhi's approval; an obstructive posture would alienate India from the mainstream and secure no dividends. A conciliatory approach brings forth the durable policy architecture adopted by New Delhi following Soviet withdrawal from Afghanistan in 1989 (when then-Prime Minister Rao committed to dealing with whoever rose to power in Kabul) and allows India the flexibility it needs to engage Afghanistan in the future. As M.K. Bhadrakumar explains,

> This brings us to a template that is going to be very crucial. The [Indian] government has done extraordinarily well in doing all that is possible to dispel the cloud of suspicion in the Pakistani mind about India's intentions in Afghanistan—that our two countries needn't be locked in a zero-sum game...Of course, Pakistan would have lingering suspicions;

> and India's security worries, too, are profound. And it is going to be a long way down the line before India and Pakistan can actually think of cooperating in the stabilisation of Afghanistan. But the incremental removal of the 'Afghan contradiction' from the cauldron of India-Pakistan differences...will make a little bit lighter the burden of working out an enduring Afghan settlement.[65]

As its politicians craft an increasingly flexible strategy, the Indian commercial sector, too, is developing a creative approach to Afghanistan. In an unprecedented move, the Steel Authority of India Limited (SAIL) announced in July 2011 that it would bring together six Indian steel companies to form a consortium designed to acquire Afghanistan's Hajigak iron ore deposits.[66] The consortium's successful bid for three of the four Hajigak blocks was announced in November 2011.[67] The announcement came one month after Indian newspapers reported tentative government plans to construct 900km of railway track, connecting the Hajigak region of Afghanistan with the India-financed Chabahar port in Iran.[68]

Public-Private Partnerships (PPPs) have become popular in India, but the SAIL initiative is a rare instance of an Indian PPP bidding for a foreign raw material asset. The impetus behind the consortium, a first in India and impressive given the companies' traditional rivalry, was twofold: first, the disparate bids of 15 independent and state-run Indian companies could not compete with the global giants (such as the China Metallurgical Group, currently developing Afghanistan's Aynak copper mine); second, there is strength in numbers, the consortium will be better placed to defend its assets. One steel company spokesperson expressed an interest in partnering with an American or European firm to exploit the presence of U.S.-NATO forces (an idea that parallels the trilateral development proposition mentioned above[69] ). Opportunities for collaboration in security and transportation could be explored with the Canadian company that acquired the single remaining Hajigak concession.

There are evidently geopolitical considerations behind the Indian government's decision to back the bid, which will allow India a greater role in Afghanistan's transformation. The 1.8 billion tonne Hajigak iron ore mines lie in central Afghanistan's Bamiyan province, once a nodal point along the ancient Silk Route. Today, plans are emerging for an international effort to develop Bamiyan province into an industrial centre, reintegrating Afghanistan into the global market.[70] This is part of a larger effort to re-establish Afghanistan's traditional role as a trade and transport hub, linking Europe and the Middle East with the Indian sub-continent and South-east Asia.[71] A future thus envisioned largely depends on the actions and interactions of Afghanistan's neighbours. In this respect, Afghanistan should be understood as a test case for regional cooperation. As India refashions its Afghan strategy and international influence in the region begins to diminish, the emerging test will involve incremental movements towards a hitherto elusive regional consensus.

## The Way Forward

### *Think Regional, Act Regional: The longue durée*

As described above, India's engagement with Afghanistan in 2001 was driven by the convergence of its enhanced capacity and the opportunity to circumvent Pakistan by way of the American security umbrella. Other regional players were undoubtedly a consideration, but Pakistan and the U.S. were essential to rising-India's keen agenda in Afghanistan—these were the crucial variables at the core of the Afghan 'test case'. Over time it became clear that the U.S. did not have the appetite or the means for stabilising 'Af-Pak', and Pakistan remained an obdurate central feature in Afghanistan, requiring New Delhi to develop an accommodative posture.

U.S.-NATO withdrawal from volatile Afghanistan, leaving Pakistan and its desperately aid-dependent military vulnerable, recalls the attendant circumstances of the Soviet retreat in 1989. Now, as New Delhi reflects on its position, it has recourse to policy markers established fleetingly during that chaotic period two decades earlier. While it appears that New Delhi is incorporating these flexible parameters into a strategic framework, there is an important distinction between India's position then and now. In the intervening years, India acquired an enormous amount of economic, political, and social capital. These were the assets that encouraged India's active involvement in Afghanistan after 2001, and these are the assets that will bolster its engagement today. With receding U.S. influence and a near-stalemate with Pakistan, New Delhi needs to redeploy these resources to leverage its neighbours and work towards building a regional consensus.

Discussing Indian foreign policy, Raja Mohan has evoked the image of three concentric circles encompassing, respectively, the immediate neighbourhood, in which India seeks primacy; the extended neighbourhood (reaching across Asia and the Indian Ocean littoral), in which India seeks to balance; and the international arena, in which India seeks status.[72] Regarding Afghanistan at the present juncture, the flexibility and strategic potential of New Delhi's policy options are arguably greatest at the intermediate level, where relations with regional players are uncertain but the need to constructively engage is plain.

Relations are uncertain to the extent that the political will necessary to craft a regional approach to Afghanistan is lacking. It is understood that a critical step towards creating an environment conducive to Afghanistan's reconstruction involves the reduction of divergence and competition in regional strategies.[73] Yet, most believe that the 'wider forms of regional cooperation that are in principle desirable to foster stability and development in Afghanistan...will in practice be unattainable.'[74] Although competing national interests cannot be easily reconciled, it is certainly possible for incremental efforts to consolidate those interests that do overlap. India is well-placed to encourage such a process. Despite the deviating interests of other key players in the region (China, Russia,

Iran, the Central Asian Republics, and Saudi Arabia) and the U.S., India's interests and policies broadly converge with most involved (with the obvious exception of Pakistan).[75]

Given the divergent strategies of other relevant actors and the limited resources available to the MEA, New Delhi cannot facilitate a grand bargain. However, India has already taken a lead by actively promoting the economic integration of Afghanistan and South Asia, and similar efforts should build on this approach. There is a relatively broad consensus amongst development scholars and practitioners that the only viable long-term path to rebuilding and reintegrating Afghanistan is by reviving its historic function as a continental cross-road.[76] India, which has been actively building transit routes and communications infrastructure within Afghanistan, can be at the forefront of international and regional efforts to this end.

India's unique position has been summed up by Afghanistan's Minister for Mines, Wahidullah Shahrani, in an interview with *Business Standard*:

> India is in a very advantageous position. Besides the traditional and historical linkages between the two countries and their strategic relationship, India has become the fourth largest economy in the world and, by 2030, India will become the world's largest consumer of commodities. After Hajigak, in July this year, I will put five major projects on tender: Three copper and two gold deposits in different parts of the country and, in February 2012, I will put a huge oil basin in the northern city of Mazar-e-Sharif on tender. In addition, we are having good negotiations with Indian companies for developing chromite deposits. The economic advantage of most of Afghanistan's deposits is that they are open-pit deposits, and commercially very viable. Plus the potential of cement. We are a post-conflict country, which is expecting to consume about 6.5 million tonnes of cement annually. India is the world's third largest producer of cement and we have been negotiating with a number of Indian companies for investment in this very important sector.[77]

India's domestic demand for raw materials has the potential to drive growth in Afghanistan, but its industrial investments will also need outlets outside India, requiring cooperative regional partners. India has indicated its support for a suitable forum to bring together the major regional stakeholders in Afghanistan.[78] However, periodic attempts to structure a formal regional approach, through such avenues as the Regional Economic Cooperation Conference and the Istanbul Conference, have not yielded concrete results.[79] Beyond the scope of ad hoc initiatives, a move toward increasingly institutionalised mechanisms for regional cooperation might prove successful.

High on the agenda at the 10th summit of the Shanghai Cooperation Organisation (SCO) in June 2011 was the issue of expanding the six-nation regional body, which has been dominated by China and Russia for a decade. India and Pakistan currently hold observer status at the SCO, and both are being considered for full admission. There are also plans to upgrade Afghanistan's status from SCO invitee to observer.[80] The traumatic experience of the Soviet war in Afghanistan makes Russia and the Central Asian states reluctant to engage in security-related activities there.[81] Nevertheless, the SCO is in a position to play an important role in the stabilisation, reconstruction, and reintegration of Afghanistan after 2014. According to Kazakhstan President Nursultan Nazarbayev, whose country held the rotating chairmanship until July 2011, 'We cannot rule out that the SCO may have to bear the brunt of resolving many problems that Afghanistan will face after the withdrawal of the international coalition forces in 2014.'[82]

India's reservations concerning U.S. withdrawal from Afghanistan have been rendered irrelevant by events on the ground—the incremental drawdown of American and coalition troops has commenced. The SCO offers a promising avenue by which India can offset some of its anxiety surrounding the possibility of a security vacuum, and can work to achieve several of the objectives that remained elusive throughout its engagement with Afghanistan since 2001. By entering into an association led by China, India will be addressing a wider and more acute strategic priority—managing relations with its larger, more powerful neighbour—but it may also enable New Delhi to indirectly pressure Pakistan into cooperating in Afghanistan, particularly given that China's own 'jihadist challenge' is on the rise and increasingly linked to Pakistan.[83] Although Chinese behaviour in and over Afghanistan is designed to avoid aggravating Islamabad, Beijing's leverage over the Pakistani establishment is not negligible, and may prove useful if afforded space by incremental improvements in India-Pakistan relations. Increased cooperation with the SCO will also improve India's access to Central Asian energy reserves and markets. Here, again, the members and mechanisms of the SCO can discourage Pakistani recalcitrance.

Uniquely, New Delhi acknowledges the centrality of Iran to the regional security equation, and openly encourages greater engagement with Iran on issues pertaining to Afghanistan. Indian Foreign Secretary, Ranjan Mathai, recently called on the international community to 'add Iran to the list of countries needing to be discussed' when looking at 'the prospects for stability in Asia in connection with Afghanistan.'[84] Despite their troubled trade relations (and Washington's opposition), India has extended an overture to Iran concerning Afghanistan, and New Delhi and Tehran are now engaged in structured consultations on the issue.[85] The widening gulf between Tehran and Washington will prevent New Delhi from acting as an effective bridge between the two (particularly as Tehran refuses to countenance a sustained U.S. presence in the region).[86] However, India realises the need to incorporate actors that share its anxiety over a resurgent Taliban. In so doing, New Delhi is demonstrating its commitment to regional cooperation on Afghanistan (to the potential detriment of its relations with the U.S.), and endorsing a regional project that involves all stakeholders.

The trajectory of India's current Afghan strategy requires that it engage with its regional counterparts. It is unlikely that India will, in the near future, have the capacity or leverage to persuade neighbouring states to rally around a broad political agenda.[87] However, regional actors agree that alignment over Afghanistan is necessary. Subsumed within slowly evolving regional political-economic structures, India's historical linkages and progressively dynamic engagement with Afghanistan can be integral to coordinating a regional approach.

***But who has the time?***

Of Western forces in Afghanistan, the oft-quoted Taliban assertion holds that "they have the watches, but we have the time." The same cannot be said of Afghanistan's regional neighbours, most of whom glance furtively at their watches as 2014 approaches, uncomfortable with the knowledge that time is on their side, too, and Afghanistan's uncertain future is theirs to inherit. India's long-term strategic considerations in Afghanistan have been discussed above, couched in the broader regional context. The final section of this analysis will briefly examine the state of affairs closer to New Delhi.

While remaining vigilant as NATO prepares to unveil a post-2014 blueprint, the Indian government intends to press ahead with all its commitments to Afghanistan.[88] Nevertheless, India is under no illusion that much could yet go wrong. Circumstances may deteriorate considerably, and New Delhi's policy options may be dramatically reduced. In the event of a security vacuum, many observers suspect that the Indian government will put its development and commercial operations on hold, withdraw, and seek to bolster support for some formulation of the erstwhile Northern Alliance (mirroring its policy trajectory from the period of post-Soviet *Mujahideen* conflict in 1989 to the Taliban take-over of Kabul).[89] According to this formulation, New Delhi would provide aid and clandestine logistical support to anti-Taliban forces in northern Afghanistan, possibly in concert with Russia and Iran, and pursue a deal for basing rights at the Ayni airbase in Tajikistan.[90] As mentioned above, India's ties to the Tajik-dominated high command of the ANA may be an indication that New Delhi is hedging for such an outcome.

However, should a friendly (or India-neutral) government retain power in most urban centres and in the north of Afghanistan, with security forces remaining sufficiently consolidated as to prevent low-level conflict from escalating into civil war, then India's greatest challenge will be to maintain its chosen mode of engagement in Afghanistan without over-stepping its bounds and exacerbating underlying grievances. This has been one of the major impediments to smooth relations with India's more immediate South Asian neighbours; by failing to convince smaller neighbours that its growth and influence are genuinely benign, India has forfeited valuable political capital in its region.[91] Pakistani obstructiveness and non-state spoilers can only succeed insofar as there are real sentiments to leverage in Afghanistan. So far, India's recalibrated engagement with Afghanistan (its move from high-profile, personnel-heavy projects to less-visible capacity building and commercially-driven investment) has not elicited a backlash of any magnitude.

Nevertheless, if India perceives its vital interests to be at stake in Afghanistan, New Delhi must be careful not to appear overtly self-serving or to favour exclusively the political-military establishment. From this perspective, India's geostrategic interests are likely best served by maintaining robust, local-level development programming throughout the country. Opinion polls consistently reveal that Afghans rate India as the most favourable foreign presence in their country. The same polls show that Afghans reject a role for Pakistan in determining the country's future.[92] This alone is a major strategic asset.

India is acutely aware of the political capital to be won through the optics of good intentions in Afghanistan. Despite a 'soft power' advantage, however, policy makers in New Delhi are aware that the fierce allegiances of the Pashtun people are also fickle.[93] New Delhi remembers how quickly it fell out of favour when it failed to formally oppose the Soviet occupation of Afghanistan in 1979. Its soft power currency could easily be reversed if India were to be seen capitalising on Afghan resources without giving back (by providing jobs, infrastructure, education, etc.)By this logic, India is servicing its own vital interests by servicing the day-to-day needs of regular Afghans. And this has potentially significant implications for future engagement.

## Conclusions

But sound foreign policy, as the history of 20$^{th}$-century politics demonstrates, is as much a matter of sound historical judgment and a subtle negotiation with the realities of power as it is a question of raw capabilities. It may turn out that India's caution will serve it better than the recklessness that comes with illusions of power.[94]

The contemporary history of India's engagement with Afghanistan substantiates Pratap Bhanu Mehta's prognosis. Although India's approach to Afghanistan has never been reckless, the preceding discussion has demonstrated that a departure from traditionally restrained policies occurred in New Delhi following the American invasion of Afghanistan in 2001. This policy shift came at the apogee of sustained economic growth and reflected, in part, a misconceived interpretation of Indian geopolitical capacity. India's illusion was not of power itself, but of the ability to translate power resources from one context to another.

Delhi is now developing a flexible policy framework in Afghanistan that accords with its strategic regional interests and reflects a reassessment of its geopolitical limitations. Politically, India is preparing to engage with any formulation of government in Afghanistan. New Delhi has entrenched relations with the Afghan security forces, and indicated a willingness to enhance cooperation in this sector. On the development front, India is substituting its high visibility projects for a hands-off approach, while maintaining a widespread network of localised assistance and capacity-building initiatives. By deepening its ties with both the population and the political elite, India will increasingly make itself indispensable to whatever situation emerges in Afghanistan. Furthermore, nurturing these relations allows India to better pursue its commercial and energy interests in Afghanistan and Central Asia.

Looking forward, India's strategy in Afghanistan increasingly relies on a conciliatory regional environment. As international forces withdraw from Afghanistan, India is positioned to be at the forefront of a regional approach to the reconstruction and stabilisation of Afghanistan. Moreover, the broad convergence of Indian interests in Afghanistan with those of other key regional actors provides occasion for India to apprehend its region as opportunity, rather than constraint.

## NOTES

1. Conversation with Brigadier Gurmeet Kanwal (retired), Director of Centre for Land Warfare Studies (CLAWS), New Delhi, 23 September 2011; Conversations with C. Raja Mohan, Centre for Policy Research, New Delhi, September 2011.
2. Harsh V. Pant, 'India in Afghanistan: A Test Case for a Rising Power,' *Contemporary South Asia*, 18:2, June 2010, p.145.
3. Conversation with Harsh V. Pant, King's College, London, 19 March 2011. On India's quest for status, see, for example: Pratap Bhanu Mehta, 'Still Under Nehru's Shadow? The Absence of Foreign Policy Frameworks in India,' *India Review* 8:3 (July-September 2009) p. 217.
4. Daniel Norfolk, 'Why India Matters in Afghanistan: Development Assistance at a Decisive Moment,' *Pragati: The Indian National Interest Review* No.51 (June 2011), p.13.
5. Conversation with C. Raja Mohan, Centre for Policy Research, New Delhi, 7 April 2011.
6. I.P. Khosla, 'India and Afghanistan,' in Atish Sinha and Madhup Mohta eds., *Indian Foreign Policy: Challenges and Opportunities* (New Delhi: Academic Foundation, 2007), p.549.
7. Shanthie Mariet D'Souza, 'India, Afghanistan, and the "End Game"?' *ISAS Working Paper* No.124 (Singapore: ISAS, National University of Singapore, March 2011), pp. 4-5; Khosla, 'India in Afghanistan,' p.549.
8. See Harish Kapur, *Foreign Policies of India's Prime Ministers* (New Delhi: Lancer Publishers, 2009).
9. Surjit Mansingh, *India's Search for Power: Indira Gandhi's Foreign Policy 1966-1982* (New Delhi: Sage Publications, 1984), p.158.
10. M.K. Bhadrakumar, 'Manmohan Singh Resets Afghan Policy,' *The Hindu*, 16 May 2011.
11. Ibid.
12. David Malone, *Does the Elephant Dance? Contemporary Indian Foreign Policy* (New Delhi: Oxford University Press, 2011), p.290.

13. See VikeshYadav and Conrad Barwa, 'Relational Control: India's Grand Strategy in India and Pakistan,'*India Review* 10:2 (April-June 2011), p.108.
14. Nitin Pai, *The Paradox of Proximity: India's Approach to Fragility in the Neighbourhood* (New York: Center on International Cooperation, New York University, 2011), p.7.
15. 'Charity Begins Abroad: Big Developing Countries are Shaking up the World of Aid,' *The Economist* (13 August 2011), http://www.economist.com/node/21525836. Accessed on 12 May 2012.
16. See Indian Ministry of External Affairs, 'India and Afghanistan: A Development Partnership,' Public Diplomacy Division, Ministry of External Affairs, Government of India, http://meaindia.nic.in or http://meakabul.nic.in. Accessed on 12 May 2012.
17. Ibid.
18. Correspondence with AjaiShukla, 1 July 2011;
19. John Foster, 'Afghanistan, the TAPI Pipeline, and Energy Geopolitics,' *The IAGS Journal of Energy Security* (23 March, 2010), see: http://www.ensec.org/index.php?option=com_content&view=article&id=233:afghanistan-the-tapi-pipeline-and-energy-geopolitics&catid=103:energysecurityissuecontent&Itemid=358. Accessed on 12 May 2012.
20. Sandeep Dikshit, 'U.S. Backs TAPI but Avoids Mention of IPI,' *The Hindu*, 21 July 2011.
21. See: Press Trust of India, 'Afghanistan Seeks Indian Investment to Boost its Agri Sector,' *Business Standard*, 3 December 2010; See Asian Development Bank, 'Key Indicators for Asia and the Pacific 2011,' p.4, http://www2.adb.org/Documents/Books/Key_Indicators/2011/pdf/AFG.pdf. Accessed on 12 May 2012.
22. Pratap Bhanu Mehta, 'Still Under Nehru's Shadow? The Absence of Foreign Policy Frameworks in India,' *India Review* 8.3 (2009), p. 230.
23. Ibid., pp. 230-231.
24. Sunil Dasgupta and Stephen P. Cohen, 'Is India Ending its Strategic Restraint Doctrine?' *The Washington Quarterly* (Spring 2011), 163; See also, C. Raja Mohan, 'India and the Balance of Power,' *Foreign Affairs* 85.4 (July/August 2006).
25. Harsh V. Pant, 'The Afghanistan Conflict: India's Changing Role,' *Middle East Quarterly* (Spring 2011), 31.
26. C. Christine Fair, 'Under the Shrinking U.S. Security Umbrella: India's End Game in Afghanistan?'*The Washington Quarterly* (Spring 2011), p.180.
27. Indian Ministry of External Affairs, 'Address by Prime Minister to the Joint Session of the Parliament of Afghanistan,' MEA Speeches and Statements, 13 May 2011, see: http://meaindia.nic.in/mystart.php?id=530117626. Accessed on 12 May 2012.
28. Pant, 'India's Changing Role,' p.32.
29. Harsh V. Pant, 'India in Afghanistan: A Test Case for a Rising Power,' *Contemporary South Asia* 18.2 (2010), pp.133-153.
30. Andrew Hurrell, 'Hegemony, Liberalism, and Global Order: What Space for Would-be Great Powers?' *International Affairs* 82.1 (2006), 8.
31. David Baldwin, 'Power Analysis and World Politics: New Trends versus Old Tendencies,' *World Politics* 31.2 (1979), 164.
32. Pai, 'The Paradox of Proximity,' p.18.
33. Conversation with Harsh V. Pant, King's College, London, 19 March 2011.
34. See Indian Ministry of External Affairs, 'India and Afghanistan: A Development Partnership,' Public Diplomacy Division, Ministry of External Affairs, Government of India, http://meaindia.nic.in or http://meakabul.nic.in. Accessed on 23 May 2012.
35. Shyam Saran, 'Premature Power: India has to Leverage its Swing Status, Engage with all and Align with None,' *Business Standard*,17 March 2010.

36. The term, 'durable policy architecture,' refers to M.K. Bhadrakumar's description of New Delhi's search for a policy framework following the Soviet withdrawal from Afghanistan. See M.K. Bhadrakumar, 'Manmohan Singh Resets Afghan Policy,' *The Hindu*, 16 May 2011.
37. Variously translated, Carl von Clausewitz's famous aphorism holds that 'War is the continuation of politics by other means.' See: Carl Von Clausewitz, in Michael Howard and Peter Paret eds., *On War* (New Jersey: Princeton University Press, 1976), Book 1, Chapter 1, Section 24.
38. Public opinion surveys have consistently found that India is viewed favourably by Afghans. See: Shubhajit Roy, 'With Thumbs Up from Afghans, India Explores more Areas of Aid,' *Indian Express*, 5 January 2010.
39. Jorge Heine and Partha Ghosh, 'The Elephant in the War: India and the Afghan-Pakistan Link,'*Canadian Foreign Policy Journal* 17:1 (June 2011), p.51.
40. Malone, *Does the Elephant Dance? p.*291.
41. Arvind Gupta, 'The London Conference: It is Time for India to Reassess its Afghan Policy,' IDSA Comment, *Institute for Defense Studies and Analyses* (1 February 2010).
42. Confidential conversation with Indian Ministry of External Affairs official, 8 April 2011.
43. Frederic, Grare, "Pakistan," in Ashley Tellis and Aroop Mukherjee (eds.) "Is a Regional Strategy Viable in Afghanistan?" *Carnegie Endowment for International Peace* (Washington: Carnegie Endowment, 2010), 21.
44. Shanthie Mariet D'Souza, "India, Afghanistan, and the 'End Game'?"*ISAS Working Paper No.124* (Singapore: ISAS at National University of Singapore, March 2011), 7.
45. Anita Joshua, "Bid to Placate Pakistan on Afghanistan," *The Hindu*, 4 August 2011.
46. C. Raja Mohan, "Two Sides of the Durand Line," *Indian Express*, 19 April 2011.
47. Alissa J. Rubin, "Guesthouses Used by Foreigners in Kabul Hit in Deadly Attacks," *New York Times*, 26 February 2010; See also: Subhash Agrawal, "India's Role in Post-2011 Afghanistan: Can Canada and India Collaborate?" *Asia Pacific Foundation of Canada*, Canada-Asia Agenda, Issue 8 (28 April 2010), 4.
48. Confidential conversation with Indian Ministry of External Affairs official, 8 April 2011.
49. In January 2011, Afghanistan designated Pakistan a formal facilitator in the process of reconciling with moderate Taliban. The two sides agreed on creating a joint commission for reaching out to Afghan Taliban. This represented an about-face in their bilateral ties. See: 'Pak gets "Facilitator" Role in Afghan Peace Talks with Taliban: Report,' *Indian Express*,28 January 2011.
50. See MEA Statements, 'Address by Prime Minister to the Joint Session of the Parliament of Afghanistan,' Ministry of External Affairs Website, 13 May 2011; and Teresita and Howard Schaffer, 'India and the U.S. Moving Closer on Afghanistan,' *The Hindu*, 1 June 2011.
51. Teresit and Howard Schaffer, 'India and the U.S. Moving Closer on Afghanistan?' *The Hindu*, 31 May 2011.
52. Confidential conversation with Indian Ministry of External Affairs official, 8 April 2011.
53. Confidential conversation with Indian Ministry of External Affairs official, 8 April 2011.
54. See Jayshree Bajoria, 'RAW: India's External Intelligence Agency,' *Backgrounder* (Washington: Council on Foreign Relations, 7 November 2008); 'RAW is Training 600 Baluchis in Afghanistan: Mushahid Hussein,' Boloji.com, 14 May 2006, http://www.boloji.com/index.cfm?md=Content&sd=Articles&ArticleID=2503. Accessed on 1 June 2012.
55. C. Christine Fair, 'Under the Shrinking U.S. Security Umbrella,' p.184.

56. Taliban spokesman,Zabihullah Mujahid, claimed the organisation did not want India out of Afghanistan. See: 'Taliban Say they can : "Reconcile" with India,' *The Times of India*, 26 March 2010.
57. Norfolk, 'Why India Matters in Afghanistan,' *Pragati*, June 2011, p.14; Confidential conversation with Indian Ministry of External Affairs official, 8 April 2011
58. See: White House document, 'The U.S.-India Partnership: The Fact Sheets,' White House website, November 2010, http://www.whitehouse.gov/the-press-office/2010/11/08/us-india-partnership-fact-sheets. Accessed on 3 JUne 2012.
59. Jayanth Jacob, 'India Setting up Foreign Aid Agency,' *The Hindustan Times*, 17 July 2011.
60. Nishika Patel, 'India to Create Central Foreign Aid Agency,' *The Guardian*, 28 July 2011.
61. See Article: 'India to Help Strengthen Afghan Security Forces,' *Defence News*, 3 June 2011, http://www.defencenews.in/defence-news-internal.asp?get=new&id=510. Accessed on 12 May 2012; or 'India to Help Strengthen Afghan Security Forces,' *Daily Outlook Afghanistan*, 2 June 2011.
62. See: Special Correspondent, 'India Committed to Building the Capabilities of Afghan Security Forces,' *The Hindu*, 2 June 2011.
63. Leaked document quoted in article, see: '2010: The Growing U.S.-India Defence Ties,' *The Dawn*, 24 May 2011, http://www.dawn.com/2011/05/24/2010-the-growing-us-india-defence-ties.html. Accessed on 1 May 2012
64. AnatolLieven, 'Afghanistan: The Best Way to Peace,' *The New York Review of Books*, 9 February 2012.
65. M.K. Bhadrakumar, 'Manmohan Singh Resets Afghan Policy,' *The Hindu*, 16 May 2011.
66. Rajesh Roy and R Jai Krishna, 'Indian Consortium to Bid for Afghanistan Deposits,' *Wall Street Journal*, 26 July 2011.
67. Dion Nissenbaum, 'India Wins Bid for "Jewel" of Afghan Ore Deposits,' *Wall Street Journal*, 30 November 2011.
68. Jayanth Jacob and Saubhadra Chatterji, 'India's Track 3: Afghan-Iran Rail Link,' *Hindustan Times*, 1 November 2011.
69. Sambit Saha, 'Steel Alliance for Afghan Mine,' *The Telegraph (Calcutta)*, 6 June 2011.
70. Prince Matthews Thomas and Cuckoo Paul, 'India's Iron Ore Play in Afghanistan,' *Forbes India*, May 2011 (see: http://www.forbes.com/2011/05/10/forbes-india-ore-play-in-afghanistan.html).
71. Andrew C. Kuchins, 'A Truly Regional Economic Strategy for Afghanistan,' *The Washington Quarterly*, Spring 2011, p.77.
72. See C. Raja Mohan, 'India and the Balance of Powers,' *Foreign Affairs* 85.4 (July/August 2006).
73. Ashley J. Tellis, 'Creating New Facts on the Ground: Why the Diplomatic Surge Cannot Yet Produce a Regional Solution in Afghanistan,' *Carnegie Endowment for International Peace* (Policy Brief #91), May 2011.
74. Jessica T. Matthews, 'Introduction,' *Through Their Eyes: Possibilities for a Regional Approach to Afghanistan* (Washington: Carnegie Endowment for International Peace, 2010), p.4.
75. Gautam Mukhopadhaya, 'India,' *Through Their Eyes: Possibilities for a Regional Approach to Afghanistan* (Washington: Carnegie Endowment for International Peace, 2010), p.33.
76. See: Kuchins, 'A Truly Regional Economic Strategy for Afghanistan.'
77. Ajai Shukla, 'Q&A with Wahidulla Shahrani, Minister for Mines, Afghanistan,' *Business Standard*, 12 June 2011.
78. Gautam Mukhopadhaya, 'India,' p.31.

79. Arvind Gupta and Smruti Patnaik, 'Istanbul Conference on Afghanistan: A Feeble Attempt at a Regional Solution,' *IDSA Comment* (New Delhi: Institute for Defence and Security Analyses), 4 November 2011.
80. Sandeep Dikshit, 'Plan to Upgrade Afghanistan in SCO of Interest to India,' *The Hindu*, 14 June 2011.
81. Vladimir Radyuhin, 'SCO: 10 Years of Evolution and Impact,' *The Hindu*, 14 June 2011.
82. Ibid.
83. Praveen Swami, 'Beijing's Increasing Jihadist Challenge,' *The Hindu*, 4 August, 2011.
84. Ranjan Mathai, 'Forging Stability in Asia: Keynote Address at MEA-IISS-IDSA Dialogue' (New Delhi: Institute for Defence and Security Analyses), 21 November 2011.
85. Harsh V. Pant, 'India's Relations with Iran: Much Ado About Nothing,' *The Washington Quarterly* (Winter 2011), p.65.
86. Correspondence with Harsh V. Pant, 2 April 2012.
87. On cooperative hegemony, see: Thomas Pedersen, 'Cooperative Hegemony: Power, Ideas, and Institutions in Regional Integration,' *Review of International Studies* 28 (2002), p.689.
88. Sandeep Dikshit, 'India Keen on Larger Economic Footprint in Afghanistan,'*The Hindu*, 14 March 2012.
89. Rahul Roy-Chaudhury, 'Chapter 11: India,' *IISS Adelphi Series—Afghanistan: to 2015 and Beyond* (London: International Institute for Security Studies) 23 December 2011.
90. M.K. Bhadrakumar, 'India Promises to Prop Up Karzai,' *Asia Times*, 6 October 2011.
91. See: Malone, *Does the Elephant Dance?* pp.104-126.
92. See Shubhajit Roy, 'With Thumbs Up from Afghans, India Explores more Areas of Aid,' *Indian Express*, 5 January 2010.
93. Conversation with C. Raja Mohan, Centre for Policy Research, New Delhi, 7 April 2011.
94. Mehta, 'Still Under Nehru's Shadow,' p.232.

# 13

# U.S. Perspectives on the Afghan Transition Process

*Marvin G. Weinbaum*

After more than a decade of involvement, the United States has begun a military disengagement in Afghanistan intended to leave behind a more self-sufficient and sovereign state. The transition process began when in announcing a military surge in December 2009, President Barack Obama also declared that American troops would begin their withdrawal by the end of 2011. The blueprint for the departure of forces gained further definition with the agreement among NATO countries in Lisbon in November 2010 that their military commitments would extend only through the end of 2014. Left open is the speed of the American troop drawdown. The Obama Administration has lacked clarity over whether the transition militarily will be governed by fixed deadlines or be condition based. But whatever the pace, a large number of civilian advisors are slated to leave along with the military's departure, and the massive spending for Afghanistan, most of it in support of military operations, is destined to trail off.

Afghans in large numbers have grown resentful of the conduct of foreign troops and welcome a transfer of powers that will allow their own leaders to assume greater responsibility. The international presence and the accompanying influx of money are commonly believed to have enriched national and local power brokers and distorted the country's economy. But many Afghans are also left uneasy and uncertain about their country's near and longer-term prospects. There are serious doubts over whether Afghan institutions are prepared to step up to the tasks they will inherit. Of particular concern is the readiness of Afghan security forces. Fears are also strong that with declining foreign influence, ethnic divisions will flare and domestic politics will become even more combustible. The anticipated significant economic impact on the Afghan government's budget and national economy has many worried that the country's stability and chances for recovery will be threatened. Many Afghans are apprehensive about the possible erosion of social gains realised during the last ten years

This chapter first examines the goals that have mainly guided U.S. involvement in Afghanistan and the shifting strategies employed to pursue them. It gives particular attention to reconciliation and regionally focused approaches intended to ease the departure of U.S. forces and leave behind a peaceful and stable Afghanistan. The chapter then examines the inevitable financial hurdles Afghanistan faces with declining foreign assistance and how U.S. aid policy is setting priorities that it hopes can minimize the impact. Drawing from these discussions four distinctive scenarios are suggested for how Afghanistan may fare in the transition process. They carry varying degrees of probability, but all have a reasonable degree of plausibility. Taking into account U.S. strategic objectives, the chapter concludes with a set of policy recommendations that might improve chances for a smooth and effective transition.

## Goals and Strategies

U.S. plans for a transition aim to leave behind in Afghanistan at least a minimally effective state. It should have a stable and legitimate national government, capable of delivering basic goods and services and be able to defend itself. To succeed the transition must address urgent issues of economic management, governance, capacity building and strategic investment. Above all for the U.S., Afghanistan should not again serve as breeding ground for international terrorists, be they from Al-Qaeda or any other terrorist organisation with a regional or global agenda. The transition that will complete the transfer of most responsibilities to Afghan institutions by 2014 also assumes that it will remain a dependent state, in need of assistance to its economy and development for at least another decade.

American policy looks to preserve and extend areas of progress. It aims to sustain successes since 2010 in arresting and partially reversing the insurgency's momentum and pins its hopes mainly on the ability of an expanded national army (ANA) and police (ANP) to operate independently and with greater effectiveness.[1] Progress is also likely to be measured by sustaining the impressive gains in educational opportunities, especially schooling for girls, and a health care delivery that has seen impressive advances in survival rates for children and women in childbirth. A successful transition is seen as contingent on the continued, albeit slow, growth in the administrative capacity of government ministries, and on improvements in local governance and development activities at the district level. While Afghanistan's economic growth is certain to suffer over the next several years, American policies seek to buffer a decline in aid with investments designed to build institutional capabilities.

The transition comes with military and civilian surges winding down and a diplomatic surge still in full swing. The first marks the decline of about 15,000 American troops from the nearly 100,000 that were available through 2019 and the now scheduled drop to 68,000 by the end of 2012. The remaining troops are expected to defend the military gains made in the south and the north and extend them in the east where there has been relatively little progress against the insurgents, particularly in blocking infiltration routes from Pakistan. Increasingly, responsibilities are being handed over to units of the Afghan army. By mid-2012, the ANA was in control of more than half the districts in the country, though most were in the country's less contentious provinces. The transition continues to call for U.S. and NATO forces to mentor Afghan troops and partner in joint military operations. A May 2012 NATO conference in Chicago made clear, however, the alliance's intention to have all combat operations Afghan-led by the summer of 2013. Although the NATO meeting did not announce a retreat from the principles of a comprehensive counterinsurgency, it left little doubt that the coalition's emphasis on security had shifted its strategy back toward counterterrorism.

A companion piece to American transition plans is the strategic agreement signed in advance of the Chicago meeting. It is meant to assure the Kabul government that the U.S. would not be abandoning the country, especially its security forces, after 2014. The agreement was intended also to send a message to the neighbouring countries that the transition will not leave a power vacuum in Afghanistan that they can exploit. Although the accord is lacking in details, the assumption is that the U.S. will retain in the country somewhere between 15,000 to 30,000 troops, mostly assigned to training the Afghan army and police, but with the ability to defend themselves. Mostly to assuage the suspicions of Afghanistan's neighbours, Washington insists that there are no plans for permanent military bases on Afghan soil.

President Hamid Karzai was anxious to have a long-term agreement that would lock in an American commitment to Afghan security and financial wellbeing beyond 2014. In November 2011, he convened a Loya Jirga of mostly trusted representatives from around the country and won approval both for the principle of an agreement and the acceptable terms. Yet it took many months of difficult negotiations to reach a deal with Washington. To win over skeptical Afghan lawmakers and a suspicious public, and also help burnish his nationalist credentials, Karzai bargained hard and won on two major sticking points in the negotiations: gaining concessions on the transfer of control over detained insurgents and the command of night raids against insurgents.

As it were, the strategic agreement is devoid of critical details and leaves some issues unresolved. American and Afghan negotiators have not settled on the types of equipment to be transferred to the Afghan military. Karzai has requested high performance aircraft and more technically advanced tactical weapons. Although conceived as a temporary measure, the future role of an

American-supported Afghan Local Police (ALP) program remains unclear. These locally based paramilitary units that are scheduled to grow from a current strength of nearly 10,000 to 30,000 are often described as corrupt and rapacious. Left for later negotiations and likely to be contentious is a status of forces agreement that would spell out the legal status of remaining American military personnel.

The second surge begun in 2010 saw the arrival of civilian advisors assigned to military related programs as well as government offices in Kabul and the provinces. The surge was designed to use the period of transition to accelerate improvements principally in governance, law enforcement and rural development. At least 1,000 new positions were created, most filled by U.S. government employees from the State Department and several other federal departments. The surge has also included large numbers of well-compensated civilian contract workers including lawyers, accountants, engineers and agronomists agreeing to serve for at least a year. As the transition progresses, civilian participants are expected to be drawn-down together with the military units. Those serving with Provincial Reconstruction Teams (PRTs), long a target of derision by President Karzai, can anticipate an early phasing out.

The third surge has been the U.S.'s commitment to an invigorated diplomacy aimed at improving chances of reconciliation with the insurgents and mustering regional cooperation. Both promise a political solution designed to accelerate an end to the conflict and better ensure post-2014 Afghan economic growth and stability. The U.S. has been persistent in trying to start up peace talks involving high-level Taliban leaders while also endorsing efforts to reconcile middle and lower level insurgent leaders and their foot soldiers. The diplomatic surge was initially also focused on pressing the Karzai government to strengthen governance and improve delivery of services, and adopt strong anti-corruption measures. The rising security agenda seems, however, to have de-prioritised reform. While sensitive to charges of interference, American officials and more broadly the international community have sought to encourage reconciliation among Afghanistan's political factions. A Kabul government distracted by domestic political turmoil is seen as an unreliable partner for the transition process.

The Afghan presidential election scheduled in 2014 is expected to have a serious impact on the transition. In light of the bitterly criticized 2009 election, it is a matter of concern to Washington and other western capitals that the coming contest be perceived as legitimate in the eyes of the Afghan people. All elections to date were made possible with external funding, mainly by the U.S. The combined domestic revenues available to the Afghan government can barely cover the cost of a single national election. International actors, in their commitment to Afghanistan's retaining its democratic character, are unlikely to deny financial support well into the future. But the U.S. and others, the UN political mission above all, will need to continue to promote the independence of electoral monitoring and appeal bodies.

Yet outsiders can have only marginal influence in inducing Afghan domestic reforms. However much U.S policies may affect the transition, its chances of success hinge most heavily on the Afghans themselves. Failings of governance and the absence of more inclusive politics are certain to complicate the transition. Minimal progress has occurred in instituting anti-corruption measures, and the rule of law remains poorly served. Despite repeated attempts, American advisors have been unable to convince Karzai to permit political parties to assume a more direct role in the election process. This along with a peculiar voting system has contributed to the country's fragmented politics and often immobilised legislative process. American leverage with Afghan leaders in pressing for reforms is almost certain to decline as its presence in the country diminishes.

## The Reconciliation Track

The U.S. is faced with rising domestic doubts about involvement in Afghanistan and like most of its NATO partners is prepared to explore routes toward an early conclusion to the conflict. The idea of negotiations with the insurgent leadership leading to a ceasefire and permanent settlement had seldom been broached until 2010. There had been few if any peace feelers from the Taliban, and with the insurgency making steady gains in recent years, there seemed little reason to expect any overtures. But the decision in Washington to bring closure to U.S. military involvement combined with notable if fragile gains on the battlefield heightened receptivity to the idea that the time had come to find a political solution. A weariness in the U.S. with what was to become the U.S.'s longest war assured considerable public support. Public attitudes in Europe had already turned against prolonging the conflict and the Afghan people understandably welcomed the possibility of a cessation of fighting. A peace campaign also fit President Karzai's attempts to deflect continuing criticism over his controversial election and desire to burnish his nationalist credentials. Karzai's initiative helped to change the agenda of the U.S. and others from incessant demands on him to address corruption to joining him in exploring the possibilities for reconciliation. His creation of a High Peace Council to establish ties and negotiate with the Taliban won popular approval. Political pundits in the U.S. and abroad began to portray the Taliban as pragmatic Afghan nationalists with no Islamist regional or global agenda and the U.S. and NATO presence as prolonging the war. The British and German governments became strong advocates for a striking a deal.

Initially, many U.S. officials were cautious if not cynical about the possibilities of a negotiated end to the conflict. They largely refrained, however, from discouraging the Afghans and others from exploring the possibilities out of concern that any observed reluctance to endorse peace talks could leave Americans accused of being responsible should there be no progress. But during

2011, U.S. diplomats took the initiative in exploring the possibilities of holding talks. When Ambassador Marc Grossman assumed the position of U.S. Special Representative for Afghanistan and Pakistan (SRAP) in February 2011 following the death of Richard Holbrooke, the diplomatic focus that had been on a strategic dialogue to improve Afghan governance become instead a dedicated pursuit of reconciliation. Extensive diplomatic efforts were undertaken to ignite peace talks with Mullah Omar's Quetta Shura and the Haqqani Network.

The prevailing view among a team of advisors to the SRAP was that the war could not be resolved by military means alone; therefore, a political solution had to exist and would be found with sufficient will and persistence. The short time frame for military withdrawal was thought to add some urgency to the search for interlocutors. It was concluded that a hurting stalemate existed and the insurgent leadership could be enticed to the negotiating table. Bringing high-level insurgents into talks was also thought likely to have a demoralising effect on Taliban combatants. State Department officials counted as well on defections among hard-pressed insurgents. Secretary Hillary Clinton summed up U.S. policy during congressional testimony in October 2011 as "fight, talk and build."[2]

The diplomatic push to open lines of communication to insurgents revealed clear differences in emphasis between the State Department and the Department of Defense. The Pentagon did not question that both military and peace tracks could be pursued simultaneously. But the generals doubted the time was ripe for negotiations. They argued that an acceptable outcome could only come from negotiating from a position of strength achieved through progress militarily. A willingness to come to the table and compromise could only be achieved once the counter-insurgency had brought about a deeply exhausted insurgency. The military's view was that there was a far greater probability of arriving at a political outcome through a gradual process of reintegration of Taliban middle-level commanders and their fighters than through a grand bargain with the Taliban leadership.

Notwithstanding the American, European, and Arab efforts to get talks going, Washington has long insisted that a peace process should be Afghan-led. The U.S. has regularly endorsed the Karzai government's stated demands that the insurgents disarm, accept basic principles of the Constitution, and agree to join the country's political process. Washington also expressed the hope that key political and social forces in Afghanistan would be allowed to have a voice in any negotiations with the insurgents. The U.S. and the Western countries gave assurances that they would resist trading away those social and human rights realised over the last decade, either to satisfy the Taliban or to accommodate Afghanistan's traditional conservatives. It was also acknowledged by Washington that Pakistan's legitimate interests had to be given consideration in any settlement.

And yet the January 2012 decision by the Taliban leadership—reached after considerable American prodding—to establish an office in Doha, Qatar, has raised questions about what the U.S. might be willing to concede to get talks underway. There was an apparent understanding that several high-ranking Taliban would be released from Guantanamo and transferred to Qatar. The discussions that led to the opening of an office were American rather than Afghan-led, and the Taliban indicated their intention to hold negotiations with the U.S. and not the Kabul government.[3] They also left no doubt that they would not abandon their determination to impose their version of a *Sharia* state. Only reluctantly did Karzai, under pressure from the U.S. and Europeans, agree to recognize a Taliban office, and most of the Afghan political opposition rejected negotiations from which they would be excluded. Pakistan appears to have been bypassed in the decision to locate a Taliban office in Qatar. Yet its failure to vigorously criticize the Taliban's agreement with the U.S. could suggest that Pakistan may nevertheless be coordinating its plans with the insurgents that it hosts.

For their part, aside from the willingness to open an office in Qatar, the Taliban have by their words and deeds shown little interest in compromising with the Karzai government or its international allies. The carefully planned killing of Peace Council president Burhanuddin Rabbani in September 2011 was by most accounts their clearest message. None of the discussions to date has ever explored the actual terms of a possible compromise. The probability that an agreement could be realised anytime during the course of the transition is difficult to conceive. Nearly all grand bargains that have ended lengthy conflicts have seen negotiations stretch on for years. Even were serious peace talks now to begin, it might be difficult to know whether the interlocutors were in fact negotiating on behalf of all the groups outside and inside Afghanistan that constitute the insurgency.[4]

The idea that Mullah Omar's Quetta Shura or the Haqqani leadership would bid for cabinet positions or provincial appointments does not fit what we know about the Taliban. It assumes that they can be induced to accept a democratically inclined, coalition government that could also constitutionally incorporate their Islamic doctrinal aims—this with a movement whose leadership has never shown much tolerance for those who did not share their particular worldview. The elemental Taliban precondition reaching an accord has always been that foreign troops must first leave. In other words, that the Kabul government should effectively leave its fate to a Taliban force that has no intention of disarming.

At present there is, then, little that drives the Afghan Taliban leadership toward seeking a political settlement and a great deal that motivates them to sustain their fight. Despite setbacks during the military surge in 2010 and 2011, the Taliban are not, as some contend, a dispirited fighting force, willing to take best deal they can get. That the Karzai regime, the Americans, and many of their NATO partners have refused to relinquish hopes in a peace deal very likely demonstrates to the insurgents their adversaries' desperation and not their confidence. While others may have concluded that only a political solution can end the fighting, it seems that the Taliban alone continue to believe in a military outcome. The insurgents at both the higher and middle levels are for the time being convinced that they are holding their own militarily, indeed winning. Why even consider compromise when you have only to wait a few years while international troops transition out of Afghanistan? From the time that they first emerged in Afghanistan, the Taliban have always been convinced that they have time and God on their side.

## The Regional Track

For most of the decade following the Bonn conference of December 2001, creating the framework for a post-Taliban Afghanistan, the U.S. and its NATO partners largely ignored the possibility that the region could as a whole contribute to Afghanistan's economic growth and political stability. But U.S. strategy for the transition to a post-2014 Afghanistan has sought to revive the cooperation that existed at Bonn among all the regional powers. The approach that begin under Ambassador Holbrooke was meant to complement the on-going search for reconciliation by getting Afghanistan's neighbours and near neighbours to commit to greater responsibility for the country's security and economic progress. The U.S. sought to promote the vision of an economically more integrated region in which the neighbours would recognize their collective stake in a peaceful and prospering Afghanistan. Given the name the New Silk Road, Afghanistan would serve as an indispensable land bridge connecting intersecting parts of Asia. It would provide economic growth and trade across the region that at present has remarkably little internal trade. A New Silk Road was conceived as improving the chances of the Kabul regime's survival following the U.S. military's departure. A regional buy into Afghanistan's economic and political viability could ensure a softer post-2014 landing for the country.[5]

With a greater sense of responsibility for Afghanistan's future, it was also hoped that the neighbours and other interested countries would become more involved in contributing to the country's governance and development. Ideally, declining U.S. funding during the transition and after would be compensated for by offers to help through bilateral programs that could include the training of government personnel at the national and subnational levels and investment in infrastructural programs. Washington was even willing to encourage countries in the region, excepting Iran, to assist with training the Afghan army and police.

A regional engagement strategy has also been seen in Washington as potentially furthering the cause of Afghan reconciliation. It was thought that collective action could increase pressures on the insurgents to come to terms on an agreement. Pakistan might be more inclined to put pressure on the insurgent groups to accept compromise. In the event of reconciliation with the Taliban, collective actions might contribute to maintaining the peace. Because of the mutual suspicions among Afghanistan's regional stakeholders, a broad agreement on Afghanistan was thought likely to provide confidence-building measures that could minimize the likelihood that any nation would play spoiler. Regional cooperation among countries would be expected to include pledges of non-interference in Afghanistan in exchange for an understanding that Afghan territory would not be used against any of them.

A November 2011 regional conference on Afghanistan's future stability and development in Istanbul was seen by U.S. officials as offering an opportunity to create a multilateral forum that would provide a continuing focus on long-term security safeguards and support for economic stability and investment opportunities. As conceived in Washington, a periodically held multilateral forum would not only exchange views and identify common goals but could develop rules of engagement for Afghanistan that might produce a mechanism to monitor members' compliance. It was envisioned that this informal body would tacitly acknowledge that the U.S. still had a pivotal role in charting Afghanistan's future.

The Istanbul conference was to be a prelude to a larger international conference to be held in Bonn the following month on the 10th anniversary of the first Bonn conference. Participating in Istanbul were China, India, Iran, Pakistan, Saudi Arabia, Kazakhstan, Kyrgyzstan, Russia, Tajikistan, and Turkmenistan. Besides the U.S., also in attendance were delegates from NATO, the EU, and the UN. The Americans had not expected to assume a highly visible role in Istanbul. Rather, they hoped to guide the meeting from behind the scenes. Tellingly, however, while Western delegations had sought observer status, they were instead designated as "supportive countries." The self-described "core Asian countries" were clearly determined to distance the West from the regional dialogue.

The Istanbul conference endorsed a long list of principles and projects for Afghanistan. The participants agreed on the need to respect Afghan sovereignty and territorial integrity, and the importance of cooperating in the fight against terrorism and drug trafficking. They approved future discussions on joint projects in the areas of reconstruction and health. Despite their display of cooperation, however, the regional powers at Istanbul seemed equally engaged in positioning themselves for the withdrawal of U.S. and NATO forces. The core Asian delegations balked at adopting a more structured approach in addressing Afghanistan's future. There were no binding commitments or enforcement mechanisms that could implement the conference's lofty principles. The Kabul government was particularly disappointed by the meeting's failure to directly address the issue of terrorist sanctuaries in Pakistan and its use of radical groups as proxies.

The U.S.'s efforts to secure cooperation on stabilising Afghanistan was interpreted by many delegates at Istanbul as an attempt by Washington to retain its geo-strategic influence in the region well after 2014. Russia criticised American proposals for creation of a regional forum as outside interference. The Chinese also balked at the idea, arguing that the framework for regional cooperation aimed at creating a broad regional transport infrastructure and connectivity of energy projects already exists within the six-member Shanghai Cooperation Organisation (SCO) that has Afghanistan, Pakistan, Iran and India in observer roles. Pakistan similarly showed no interest in the American initiative thought unnecessary with the existence of the Economic Cooperation Organisation (ECO), whose members include Pakistan, Iran, Turkey, and Afghanistan and all of the former Soviet Central Asian Republics.

American officials came away from Istanbul refusing to acknowledge that the U.S. had fallen far short of its objectives, instead choosing to put the best face on the outcome by characterising it as a good first step. Attention was particularly drawn to what was seen as the willingness of the core regional states to remain committed to Afghanistan after 2014 and having succeeded in defining common goals. Little was made of the fact that most of the principles and goals agreed to carry no means for holding countries to their commitments at Istanbul. Nor was there a sense of urgency. A meeting of foreign ministers of participating countries was approved but not scheduled to occur until June 2012.

The results of the Istanbul conference did not augur well for the December conference in Bonn that drew 85 nations and nearly two-dozen international organisations. The one-day meeting was intended to provide an opportunity for an international community supportive of Afghanistan's security and development to address a future of declining U.S. and NATO countries military and economic assistance. Although not a donors meeting, it was hoped that countries would recommit financially and signal their willingness to contribute to improving Afghan governance and continuing reconstruction. The possibility that it would also deal with the issues of terrorism and reconciliation were first dimmed by refusal of the Taliban to send representatives and then Islamabad's announcement that Pakistan would not participate. Pleas by the U.S., Germany, and others for Pakistan to attend could not overcome domestic anger over the deaths of Pakistani troops in a border confrontation with U.S. and Afghan forces. As in Istanbul, the principle of non-interference won wide backing but without any mechanism created to ensure its observance. The best that could be said of the Bonn conference is that it gave recognition that the mission to rebuild and secure Afghanistan was still a work in progress.

## The Financial Implications

It is generally conceded that with the military drawdown there will be a corresponding decline in assistance to the Afghan economy and that the adjustment will be difficult and probably painful. The country will have to compensate for the certain shrinkage of external support, most of all from the U.S., aid that in 2010-11 totaled $15.7 billion. At 90 percent of total public spending, this is virtually the size of Afghanistan's entire GDP. The greatest concern is that U.S. and other sources will make abrupt funding cuts over the next three years rather than gradual, predictable reductions in nonmilitary assistance. In any case, the full impact on Afghanistan's economic growth, fiscal sustainability and service delivery will probably not be felt until after 2014. According to a recent World Bank study, unless the international community steps in, aid-reliant Afghanistan will face a yearly budget deficit of $7 billion from 2014 through 2021. The growth rate is expected to decline to 5 to 6 percent from current pace of 9 to 10 percent, and if the mineral deposits are not exploited, the growth rate will decline to 4 percent.[6]

Actually, only a minor portion of external funding finds its way to central government coffers or is actually spent in Afghanistan. Most of it goes to enrich donor country industries or is captured by payments to foreign contractors and individuals. Moreover, the Afghan government's lack of absorptive capacity means that some of what is received cannot be spent. Even so, the expected decline in overall outside financial support could have deep budgetary consequences, especially so if the U.S. and others fail to pay the bill for the Afghan army and police. Without foreign funding, it is difficult to see how a post-2014 projected security force of anything like the projected 352,000 members can be sustained. The price of training and maintaining the army and police after foreign troops leave could run from $6-8 billion for a country whose total domestically raised revenues are presently between $1.5 and $2 billion.[7] Likely operating expenses of both the security and non-security sectors will be almost twice the expected size of collected revenues over the next ten years—assuming that there is a 4.5 to 6 percent average annual growth in the economy. Most of what will be available will be needed just to address current domestic requirements and cannot address the need to enhance public services. The transport, power and rural development sectors are already seriously underfunded.

U.S. aid strategy to deal with this inevitable drawdown of financial assistance is to readjust the areas in which it chooses to invest in Afghan development. Rather than putting development funds into short term, hand-out projects, there has been a shift to what the United States Agency for International Development (USAID) calls "foundational investment," spending that aims at creating an enabling environment that will fortify the country after the transition has run its course.[8] This form of investment directs funds to governance, institutional capacity, human resources and economic growth. It moves away from the current heavy security driven approach to development in favour of building infrastructure, expanding education, and agricultural development and food security. The approach aims as well at weaning the country off foreign assistance and a donor dependent economy in ways that lay the basis for sustainable private sector growth to complement increased public sector capacity. This more entrepreneurial approach puts great stock on the future proceeds from mineral and energy extraction.

The principles of inclusivity, equitability and sustainability supposedly also guide a transition-oriented U.S. aid program. Until now, American support has mostly enriched only a small proportion of the society, slighting rural agriculture districts and those provinces with less conflict. More funds are slated be moved through the central government, presumably using the Reconstruction Trust Fund (RTF) set up under World Bank auspices. But there are also plans to channel greater assistance to the provinces, the purpose of which is to get Afghans to accept local ownership of programs. Successes already achieved under the government's National Solidarity Program (NSP) through its Community Development Councils (CDCs) suggest the possibility of achieving accountability. It remains to be seen whether the trust required in a greater bottom-up approach to development by the U.S. aid givers can be established without increased Afghan institutional capacity. Overcoming a heavily criminalised economy is another major obstacle.

The level and direction of American development aid is deeply dependent on the course of events in Afghanistan over the next several years. Assistance geared to the transition is plainly contingent on a security environment hospitable to externally funded aid programs and sufficient domestic political stability. National elections in 2014 and 2015 could affect whether the U.S. has an interested and capable partner in development. A country embroiled in inter-ethnic conflict could be too distracted to cope with its financial challenges. Reconciliation that includes a power sharing arrangement with Taliban insurgents would probably significantly alter the American aid role. It is doubtful that Washington or any other Western capitals will be as keen to lend a hand to the Afghan economy or that an Islamist-oriented regime would welcome many of their programs.

## Alternative Scenarios

Afghanistan in transition faces many uncertainties. Will the insurgency's momentum be arrested and reversed? How will the country's politics affect the transition? Will the military withdrawal motivate the Kabul regime to take tough decisions? How deeply will the U.S.'s shrinking aid budget impact Afghanistan? Will the U.S. and its allies have the patience through 2014 and can they stay committed beyond? Out of these uncertainties and many others, it is possible to draw at least four plausible possible scenarios of varying probability occurring over the next three years.

### 1. *The transition exceeds expectations; the U.S. maintains a strong engagement*

- Strong progress made against the insurgency. The Afghan security forces are able to operate with considerable independence. The reintegration process shows steady progress.

- A strategic partnership with the U.S. is reached. Even with a contraction in overall American military spending, there is a full U.S. commitment to support the Afghan security forces. U.S. development funding drops but not drastically, and other donors make up much of the shortfall in critical sectors of the economy.
- President Karzai observes the Constitution, does not seek reelection, and the 2014 election goes relatively smoothly. A more inclusive government emerges.
- Governance reforms are undertaken that show strong signs of winning public confidence. Gains are made against corruption and the quality of justice improves.
- The neighbours respond to Afghanistan's improved stability by increasing economic cooperation through bilateral agreements and collectively through regional organisations. Pakistan yields to U.S. pressure by adopting a more aggressive posture against Afghan insurgents.
- Agricultural sector growth advances. Gains are made in reducing opium poppy cultivation as substitute crops and progress is made in creating alternate forms of employment in the rural areas.

2. ***The transition is good enough; the U.S. makes a gradual phased withdrawal***

- The insurgency is kept from making major gains as foreign forces depart. Security improves but continues to be fragile and reversible. The U.S. and NATO countries hold to the timetable for concluding operations by the end of 2014. A strategic agreement is signed with the U.S. leaving at least 15,000 troops. The residual military contingent in the country after 2014 props up an improving ANA that is still not a self-reliant force.
- Political and economic reforms are few. Most of the security sector reforms, including the dismantlement of illegal armed groups and appointments on merit in the police and army are not realised. The patronage based, aid-enhanced power structures remain intact.
- The international community finances the 2014 and 2015 elections. Both are again highly contentious but differences are eventually resolved and the new president and parliament manage to acquire sufficient legitimacy.
- Afghanistan's neighbours and near neighbours continue their hedging strategies and retain their capacity to meddle. But none makes a concerted effort to destabilize the country. Pakistan retains its protective mantle over the Haqqani network and Quetta Shura.
- Drug cultivation is not a high government or international priority and levels of production remain largely unchanged.

### *3. The transition breaks down; the U.S. accelerates disengagement*

- American and NATO combat and support troops are pulled out of Afghanistan before the end of 2014. No strategic agreement is reached between Afghan and American negotiators. Political and economic pressures in the U.S force economic assistance to be slashed, and programs focusing on security sector support, development activities, and improve governance are sharply reduced or terminated.
- Afghan security forces fall far short of their goals, and the insurgency regains its earlier momentum. The U.S. adopts an over-the-horizon counter-terrorism strategy that increasingly relies on drone and air attacks.
- Drug production spreads to nearly all provinces and levels rise.
- Lacking adequate financing, it becomes impossible to hold nationwide elections and the government's legitimacy is placed in doubt. There begins a struggle to revise the Constitution to create a parliamentary system.
- Ethnic and sectarian rivalries strengthen and the army begins to fracture. Regional power brokers forge links with different patron regimes in the region. Afghan-Pakistani relations become tenser and military coordination in the border regions largely ceases.

### *4. The transition is overtaken by various events; the U.S. loses its options*

- The assassination of President Karzai and/or growing domestic political discord among factions derails the transition process.
- Major setbacks in fighting the insurgency upset most of the transition plans as the focus turns mainly to security issues. Emergency rule is instituted.
- Relations between the U.S. and Pakistan and/or between Afghanistan and Pakistan rupture and American lawmakers force a rapid disengagement from the region.
- A negotiated political settlement with the insurgents is reached that allows for power sharing and constitutional changes. A new coalition government sets terms for foreign participation in the security and reconstruction that are unacceptable to the U.S. and Western countries and the transition process is effectively terminated.
- Ethnic groups in the north reject a reconciliation agreement and the country progresses toward civil war. A de facto division of the country occurs. Millions of Afghans flee into Pakistan and Iran. Foreigner aid workers depart.

## Recommendations for the U.S.

The following recommendations are offered as means by which the U.S. can increase the likelihood of a successful transition over the next three years. Many of them may necessitate changes in current perceptions and plans for Afghanistan.

1. Be prepared to revisit timelines in the transition and adjust them to reflect evolving military, political and social developments. Devote those U.S. and allied troops remaining through the drawdown increasingly toward facilitating the transition, whether in training Afghan security forces, enhancing governance, or protecting development.
2. Count on providing economic and development assistance for at least another decade. Accept the fact that Afghanistan will be for some time a minimally effective, dependent country.
3. Consider scaling back in the transition the projected size of the Afghan army from the projected 350,000 so the future burden on the Afghan government will not be so onerous and it is able to meet other critical responsibilities.
4. Assume that Afghanistan will remain a politically unsettled country for the foreseeable future. Do not set unachievable goals for political or social change but demand adherence to basic civil liberties and human rights.
5. Conceive of a political strategy for Afghanistan as more than striking a deal with the Taliban. Have it focus on strengthening institutions and processes that can contribute to the legitimacy of central and provincial authority. Encourage a more inclusive political system by threatening to withhold funding without reforms to the country's electoral system.
6. Signal to the region the U.S.'s long-term commitment to Afghanistan. Be sensitive to Pakistan's legitimate security needs yet also prepared to push back against attempts by Pakistan to dictate Afghanistan's future. Find ways to include Iran in regional discussions involving Afghanistan. Promote cooperation among regional powers but do not have high expectations for early progress on a Silk Road. However, worthwhile the vision of a Silk Road, bilateral agreements are likely to prove more realistic for the foreseeable future.
7. Endorse Afghanistan's becoming effectively a non-aligned state. A strategic agreement should be crafted that as much as possible allays the suspicions of neighbours and near neighbours of American intentions. Disavow intentions to create permanent military bases.
8. Do a better job of explaining why U.S. strategic interests require that it remain engaged with Afghanistan and the region. Indicate that while the possible revival of Al-Qaeda is of deep concern, the impact of a radicalized Afghanistan on nuclear-armed Pakistan and the consequences of major conflict on the Indian subcontinent are critical to American interests.

9. Find mechanisms for political intervention that rely less on military means, and muster the political will domestically to match the U.S.'s military capabilities internationally.

## NOTES

1. By the end 2002, the projected size of the Afghan national security force is 352,000, of which 195,000 would be from the army. *Report on Progress Toward Security and Stability in Afghanistan*, U.S. Department of Defense, p. 22.
2. Testimony before the U.S. House Foreign Affairs Committee, 27 October 2011.
3. *The New York Times*, 20 January 2012, p. A 10.
4. For a contrary view suggesting possible steps toward a peace agreement see Lisa Schrich, "Designing a Comprehensive Peace Process for Afghanistan," U.S. Institute of Peace, 2011.
5. For a critique of the Silk Road initiative see Joshua Kucera, "Clinton's Dubious Plan to Save Afghanistan with a New Silk Road," *The Atlantic*, 2 November 2011.
6. Alissa J. Rubin, "World Bank issues alert on Afghanistan Economy", *The New York Times*, November 23, 2011. Also see *Transition in Afghanistan: Looking Beyond 2014*—Executive Summary, The World Bank, 18 November 2011.
7. The U.S. contribution which in fiscal year 2012 totaled $11 billion could drop to as low as $3 to $4 billion with the NATO countries providing and additional $1 billion. Reuters Online U.S. edition, 16 January 2012. www.reuters.com/article/2012/01/16/us-usa-afghanistan-troops-idUSTRE80F19Z20120116. Accessed on 12 May 2012.
8. USAID report, "Foundational Investments for Afghanistan's Future," 11 July 2011, p. 3.

# Index